THE CRITICAL REPUTATION OF ROBINSON JEFFERS
A Bibliographical Study

The Critical Reputation of
ROBINSON JEFFERS

A BIBLIOGRAPHICAL STUDY

Alex A. Vardamis

ARCHON BOOKS

1972

Library of Congress Cataloging in Publication Data

Vardamis, Alex A   1934–
    The critical reputation of Robinson Jeffers.

    1. Jeffers, Robinson, 1887-1962–Bibliography. I. Title.
Z8451.5.V37   016.811'5'2   74-38715
ISBN 0-208-01252-4

© 1972 by The Shoe String Press, Inc.
Hamden, Connecticut 06514
Published as an Archon Book 1972
All rights reserved

Printed in the United States of America

To my wife, Fran, for
her devotion, encouragement
and assistance. Without her,
this book would not have
been possible.

CONTENTS

PREFACE

This bibliography consists of three sections. Section A includes reviews of Jeffers' books and critiques of major productions of his plays. Section B contains periodical articles, more extensive critical studies, and reviews of minor productions of the plays. Excluded are newspaper and magazine articles of a trivial and purely biographical nature. Section C lists books and portions of books about Jeffers. With a few exceptions, encyclopedias, biographical dictionaries, and introductory notes in anthologies have been omitted. When applicable, articles and books are cross-referenced by number of entry. All entries are intended to summarize the main critical opinions contained in the article or book. Editorial comments on the content or the validity of the reviewer's opinions have been provided in an attempt to clarify what might otherwise be a confusing mass of material. Care has been taken to avoid distortion of the writer's viewpoint, and when possible his own words are used to summarize the content. The introduction contains a brief biography, a discussion of Jeffers' critical reputation, and a literary analysis and evaluation of his poetry.

An attempt has been made to include all available material of significance. This includes all secondary Jeffers material in various university libraries and especially in the Occidental College Library (Pasadena, California), which has the largest Jeffers collection in the country. All the secondary material in Random House's Jeffers files is also included. Unfortunately, Random House has no files on the volumes it published before 1945; therefore the reviews from the thirties must be considered representative and not complete. Almost all the secondary material listed in Alberts' 1933 bibliography [C40] is annotated. Where, in a few instances, the material Alberts listed was of extreme brevity, it has been omitted. No attempt has been made to make a complete listing of foreign critical material, although some foreign books and articles of interest are included. No attempt has been made to list all editions of book entries Graduate theses and unpublished dissertations have not been included. An annotated bibliography of the thirteen doctoral dissertations written on Jeffers before 1968 can be found in the September 1969 issue of the *Robinson Jeffers Newsletter* [B405].

The appendix contains a chronology of important dates in Jeffers' career and a checklist of his major publications.

I wish to give special thanks to Professors John Unterecker and Joseph V. Ridgely of Columbia for their encouragement and assistance in the first stages of this bibliography; to Professor Oliver L. Lilley of the Columbia University Library for his technical advice; to Mrs. Cheryl Sanford of the Occidental College Library and to Miss Charlotte Snyder of the United States Military Academy Library for their untiring aid in locating Jeffers material.

THE CRITICAL REPUTATION OF ROBINSON JEFFERS
A Bibliographical Study

INTRODUCTION

In the late twenties, at the crest of his popularity, Robinson Jeffers was both difficult and fascinating copy for journalists. Here was an artist whose life style conformed with popular romantic conceptions of a poet. High on a rocky headland above the wild Pacific, he dwelt in a lonely tower that he had hewn out of living rock with his own hands. Beyond this highly romantic external evidence, little was known of Jeffers' private life, and descriptions of the poet often were limited by the infrequent audiences newspaper men received from the melancholy semi-recluse. In fact, Jeffers was neither completely a wild romantic nor a dour hermit.

He was born, on January 10, 1887, in Pittsburgh, Pennsylvania, the eldest son of Annie Robinson Tuttle and Dr. William Hamilton Jeffers, professor of Old Testament and Exegesis at Western Theological Seminary. In childhood and youth he traveled extensively in Europe and for some time attended a Swiss boarding school. The family returned to the United States in 1902, and for one year, before moving to Southern California, Jeffers studied at the University of Pittsburgh. He graduated from Occidental College in 1905. Continuing his education, he took courses at the University of Southern California, where, in a class on Goethe's *Faust*, he met and fell in love with Una Call Kuster, the young wife of a lawyer. In 1906, Jeffers' parents returned to Europe and took their son with them, hoping to break this budding romance. Jeffers studied for a while at the University of Zurich before returning to Los Angeles to study medicine, again at Southern California. He had no particular interest in becoming a physician, however, and in 1912, he left to enroll at the School of Forestry at the University of Washington.

Meanwhile, he was writing poetry, and in 1912 his first volume of verse, *Flagons and Apples*, was published. On August second of the following year, Una Kuster, having obtained an amicable divorce from her husband, married the young poet. The receipt of a small legacy permitted Jeffers to devote all his time to writing, and the couple planned to settle in Europe. The outbreak of World War I prevented that, and in 1914 they moved to Carmel, California.

Their decision to live in Carmel had a profound influence on his writing; with the exception of some few short poems on Ireland and Taos, all of Jeffers' mature work bears direct relationship to the harsh landscape of that part of California. In the early years at Carmel he divided his time between the construction of his home and the writing of poetry. *Californians* was published by Macmillan in 1916, the same year that Jeffers' twin sons, Garth and Donnan, were born.

After the United States entered the war, Jeffers volunteered for the balloon corps, but the fighting ended before he could be inducted. His horror at the senseless violence of the conflict and also, perhaps, other more personal events cryptically mentioned in his letters, effected a radical change in his poetry. Eight years after *Californians*, his next work, *Tamar and Other Poems*, appeared, and the difference, both in style and content, was enormous.

Already before the publication of *Tamar*, Jeffers had established a style of living that would not radically change for the rest of his life. The periods of both fame and critical silence seemed never to affect Jeffers, the man. He considered passing fashions of little value and claimed to write for a thousand years hence. A tenet of Jeffers' doctrine was that man should always be in contact with the immutable physical world. Thus, the poet not only built his home and his studio-tower with some skill, but also, over the years, planted on his property a small forest.

He delighted in camping in the more inaccessible reaches of the Coast Range Mountains, but he did not particularly enjoy the townlife of Carmel. His undeniable lack of civic spirit is partially the basis for his reputation as a recluse. The heyday of Carmel's life as a center of important west-coast Bohemia was largely over by the time Una and Robinson Jeffers first arrived there. They came, as Jeffers said in *Visits to Ireland, Travel Diaries of Una Jeffers* [C95], "loving the sea-beauty of the place but knowing at first no person there." They later became friends with some of that earlier group, including Edgar Lee Masters and George Sterling, but still Una Jeffers was the family's main contact with the town, and her husband visited it as little as possible. With the somewhat pseudo-artistic townsfolk he seemed to have little sympathy, though, throughout the years, he shared with them an anxiety over the vulgar encroachment of the outside world on the attractive little village. The town early boasted of him as one of its resident writers, but Jeffers did not respond with Carmel's favorite divertissements: poetry readings and semi-amateur theatricals. The greatest extent of his community participation was in the early forties when, in a Del Monte Summer Theater production of his *Tower Beyond Tragedy*, he contributed his son as an extra and attended some performances.

Jeffers, however, while avoiding the mob, seldom was without friends. In 1926, when he had become famous, and therefore appropriate copy for the society column of the local newspaper, frequent note is made of weekend house parties at the Jeffers home. The guests included Benjamin DeCasseres, Edgar Lee Masters and, most frequently, George Sterling. The relationship between Jeffers and Sterling deserves additional biographical investigation. It is here sufficient to note that the suicide of Mr. Sterling, shortly after the appearance of his *Robinson Jeffers: The Man and the Artist* [C5], greatly saddened Jeffers and perhaps led him further into misanthropy and isolation.

Nevertheless, Jeffers failed to fit the popular conception of him as hermit. In 1929, after completing three more long poems, *The Women at Point Sur, Cawdor* and *Dear Judas*, he visited Ireland and Great Britain with his family. Again in 1937 and 1948 he and his wife visited the British Isles. In 1930 they also spent time in Taos, New Mexico, as guests of Mabel Dodge Luhan, the high-priestess of the Taos artist colony. The Luhans and the Jeffers were for a while good friends and exchanged frequent visits in Taos and Carmel.

Jeffers was strongly opposed to the United States' intervention in World War II. The violence of yet another worldwide conflagration horrified him and seemed to confirm his opinion that mankind was bent on self-destruction. With the exception of a poetry reading tour in 1941, he spent the war years in Carmel.

The 1947 opening of his play, *Medea*, was the occasion for another visit to New York. Large cities, however, held no pleasure for the poet of the California wilderness. His last extended trip was the journey to Ireland in 1948, which was supposed to include the opening of *Medea* in London. Jeffers became ill, however, and, confined to an Irish hospital, could not make the opening. This final journey confirmed, for him, that the world seemed to have moved still farther away from the pristine purity he had celebrated. In notes in *Visits to Ireland*, Jeffers wrote of Yeats' tower:

> We climbed the winding stair of the old Norman tower; every window had been broken, every corner was full of filth and broken bottles. Una notes in her diary, "I shall never come here again. It is too sad." It was the end of an epoch. [C95]

Una Jeffers' death on September 1, 1950 deprived the poet of a companion, a goad, a source of inspiration and a wife.

The loss was reflected in all that Jeffers wrote thereafter. In his youth he had built his home on a lonely headland and planted around it a forest. In his old age taxes forced him to sell much of his land. In his final years, the poet of individualism lived in the midst of a modern subdivision, and if tourists came by, they did, more likely, not to catch a glimpse of the old bard, but to see Carmel's architectural wonder, the "Butterfly House," that clings to the tip of the headland where once the hurt hawk had wandered, returning "in the evening asking for death." Robinson Jeffers died on January 21, 1962, his dour predictions of the future apparently and unhappily realized.

Few poets have generated more disagreement on the merits of their work than Robinson Jeffers. Restraint was rarely a quality of either his supporters or detractors. When he was praised, it was with extravagance, and when he was disparaged, it was with vehemence. Until recently there seemed to be little possibility of a balanced appraisal of this poet's work. Further, few poets have experienced such a drastic change in their critical reputations during their own lifetimes as did Jeffers. Within a period of less than two decades, his literary stature rose very high and fell very low. In the twenties, his work received a wildly enthusiastic reception, but critical opinion reversed itself in the thirties; as if to counter the unreasoned intensity of Jeffers' earliest admirers, the later reviewers, not content merely to point to Jeffers' poetic failures, often heaped scorn upon the poet who had been rated the greatest American genius since Whitman. Occasionally criticism extended to *ad hominem* attacks; Yvor Winters, for example, suggested that, rather than write any more poetry, Jeffers should consider suicide. The violent condemnation of the thirties quieted to neglect in the forties. The Broadway production of *Medea* in 1946 caused a flurry of new interest in Jeffers, but he now was considered a dramatist rather than a poet. Other than the interest accorded *Medea*, Jeffers, during the last thirty years, has been largely ignored. His poems rarely appear in new anthologies, and few English departments teach him other than as a quaint figure of historical interest. This is not to suggest that supporters of his poetic talents have totally vanished, for a small band of devotees resolutely attempt to keep his voice alive. For example, the *Robinson Jeffers Newsletter* is dutifully printed and distributed on a quarterly basis by members of an enthusiastic Jeffers cult. But most important critics have paid him little attention; at Jeffers' death in 1962, one reviewer expressed surprise that he had not expired long before. Yet, time may be on Jeffers' side. Recently there have been indications of a renewed interest in his works. Several scholarly articles and books, to include his *Selected Letters*, have appeared in the last few years. Random House reports increased sales of Jeffers' *Selected Poems*. New Directions has recently published a paperback edition of *Cawdor/Medea*. The latest *Norton Anthology of Poetry* (1970), a popular choice with many English departments, devotes seven pages to Jeffers' poems. His ideas, his prophecies, are gradually being recognized for their relevance to our present time. This cycle of interest suggests that factors other than the quality of Jeffers' poetry contributed to his displacement from the ranks of major American poets. These factors not only pertain to American literary trends, but they also reflect extra-literary historical considerations. To examine the curve of Jeffers' critical reputation is to measure the literary and historical pulse of America in the last forty-five years.

The history of Jeffers' critical reputation had a mild beginning in 1916, the year Macmillan published *Californians*. *Californians* hardly received wide recognition and must remain critically insignificant; but already, in this atypical Jeffers collection, critics noted his devotion to nature and his masculine boldness. Jeffers himself held a low opinion of the poetry in this apprentice volume and excluded it from his *Selected Poetry*, published by Random House in 1938.

Jeffers chose to consider the beginning of his mature work the appearance in 1924 of *Tamar and Other Poems*, published by Peter Boyle. He had been obliged to pay for its publication himself. *Tamar* went unnoticed until Jeffers sent a copy to his friend, George Sterling. Sterling was planning an anthology of California authors, to be entitled *Continent's End*, and he had invited Jeffers to contribute some verse; along with his poems, Jeffers mailed a number of copies of *Tamar*. Sterling read it, was deeply impressed, and enthusiastically sent a copy to James Rorty, a professional journalist, who in turn introduced it to Mark Van Doren and Babette Deutsch. Rorty, Van Doren, and Deutsch expressed their praise in influential reviews appearing in the *New York Herald Tribune, Nation,* and *New Republic.* Their highly favorable remarks sparked rapid sales and many now agreed that a poetic genius had arrived on the American scene. Jeffers was on his way. Sterling called the title piece, "Tamar," the "strongest and most dreadful poem" he had ever read [A16]; Rorty said it was as good as anything of its kind written in America [A14]; Van Doren labeled Jeffers a major poet [A17]; and Deutsch, with double arrogance, compared reading Jeffers' poetry to Keats looking into Chapman's Homer [A10]. Already, however, some of the patterns of adverse criticism were beginning to appear. His weak characterization, his "lapses into prose" [A9], and especially the "loathsome" [A15] aspects of his work were noted and condemned by several critics. But apparently few cared to contradict Rorty, Deutsch, and Van Doren. Significantly, one of the most adverse reviews, which found "scarce a redeeming line" in the book [A13], appeared months prior to the initial estimation of these three influential critics.

Because of the overwhelmingly laudatory nature of these early reviews, Jeffers was able to find a publisher, Boni and Liveright, for a new edition of "Tamar" and two additional long narratives, "Roan Stallion" and "Tower Beyond Tragedy," and several short poems. The new volume, a best seller, created a sensation, and Jeffers, from this single book of poetry, achieved fame and financial reward. His work was widely discussed; reviews appeared in many prestigious literary publications such as *New Republic, Dial, New York Times Book Review, Poetry, Saturday Review of Literature,* and *Nation.* The local *Carmelite* fondly devoted an entire issue to him which included tributes from Lincoln Steffens, Carl Sandburg, Edgar Lee Masters, and others. Jeffers began to contribute poems to many important periodicals, to include *Nation, New Republic, Overland Monthly, American Mercury, San Francisco Review, Poetry, New Masses* and *Literary Digest.* During the years 1925-1928 his poems appeared in eight different anthologies, including, among others, Louis Untermeyer's *Modern American and British Poetry* and Mark Van Doren's *Anthology of World Poetry.* The extraordinary reception accorded the book can be attributed in part to the subject matter. "Tamar" deals with incest and "Roan Stallion" with sodomy, both placed within an atmosphere of violence. Some critics praised the victory over censorship barriers that this represented. Others, of a more conservative nature, depicted the volume as vulgar, obscene, and pagan. Certainly it seemed that initial exposure, especially to "Roan Stallion," produced a profound emotional effect upon the reader. Whatever defects critics found in it, most agreed that Jeffers had successfully created a consistent mood and atmosphere, solemn and severe, but powerful. His admirers compared him to Whitman in his verse style and to the Greeks in his violent subject matter. One of his most fervent supporters, Benjamin DeCasseres, accorded Jeffers probably the most extravagant praise any poet has ever received. In *The Superman in America* (1929), DeCasseres compared Jeffers favorably to Aeschylus, Shakespeare, Chopin, Blake, Coleridge, DeQuincy, Baudelaire, Dostoievsky, D'Annunzio, Dante, Wagner, Nietzsche's Antichrist, and Nietzsche's Superman [C16]. Such unrestrained adulation was not only embarrassing, but it also aroused the suspicion that no one could be that good. As one critic stated, "The admirers of Mr. Jeffers, indeed, bid fair to damn him with excessive praises" [B35]. But meanwhile, Jeffers' reputation soared. His original discoverers (Sterling, Deutsch, Van Doren) continued to accord him heavy praise. Sterling, shortly before he committed suicide in 1926, wrote *Robinson Jeffers: The Man and the Artist* [C5] in which he placed Jeffers at the summit of poetic achievement. And even though Sterling, the earliest discoverer, was now dead, many other important critics had joined ranks to praise. Percy A. Hutchison of the *New York Times* wrote that some portions of *Roan Stallion* were "equalled only by the very great" [A41]; Mencken felt it a solid achievement [A45]; Edwin Seaver admired Jeffers' poetic imagination [A49]. A few did disparage the book. Harriet Monroe, writing in *Poetry*, found "Roan Stallion" revolting [A46]. Along with others, she pointed out that shock was no substitute for quality. But adverse criticism was unusual. When the English edition of *Roan Stallion* was published in 1928, Jeffers' fame became international. F. S. Flint, in *Criterion*, called Jeffers a superior tragic poet [A60], Robert Hillyer in *New Adelphi* found the poetry glorious but the sex and violence revolting [A61], and A. E. (George Russell) predicted that Europeans would read the poems with wonder [A62]. In all the reviews, little mention was made of the short poems.

Jeffers' next book, *The Women at Point Sur* (1927), published by Liveright, baffled and angered the critics, and certainly failed to fulfill the expectations aroused by *Roan Stallion*. Whereas many had expected change and development Jeffers was offering more of the same, only more intensely and shrilly. This long poem was condemned for its unevenness and its excessive violence and despondency. Even his earliest admirers were forced to apologize, to defend. Deutsch found it contained "irrelevant sordidness" [A82], Rorty felt that Jeffers was on an "unfortunate and dangerous" track [A100], Hutchison judged it inferior to his earlier works [A92], and Howard Mumford Jones found in it an "excess of sex, insanity, and perversity" [A93]. *The Women at Point Sur* was almost a critical disaster. It led Jeffers to explain, to apologize. Even as late as 1938, in his preface to his *Selected Poetry*, he wrote that *The Women at Point Sur* was "the least understood and least liked" of his poems. There was, however, consistent praise for the strength of particular passages and for Jeffers' treatment of nature. Yet most critics began wishing for a change, for development, in what was now often labeled a poet of great, but unfulfilled, promise. As Van Doren wrote, "He seems to be knocking his head to pieces against the night" [A103].

Cawdor and Other Poems (1928) received somewhat better, if fewer, reviews, and helped dispel the serious doubts caused by the preceding book. Deutsch declared that Jeffers had "lost none of his immense power" [A117] and Van Doren was prompted to compare him to Euripides, Sophocles, and Shakespeare [A123]. Although several of his admirers pleaded for a change, most agreed that Jeffers' poetry contained power, a quality that even hostile critics would rarely deny. His detractors condemned his violence, his philosophy of despair, and his verbosity. Some detected that Jeffers' poetry was often prosy; Peter Quennell, for example, admitted "flashes of real beauty," but "beauties which should belong to prose" [A127]. Generally, however, *Cawdor* contributed substantially to Jeffers' reputation.

A definite change appeared in the next volume, *Dear Judas and Other Poems* (1929). The title poem was generally judged on the basis of the reviewer's tolerance of Jeffers' highly unorthodox treatment of Christ and Mary; it understandably provoked Christians, and frequently, after the publication of *Dear Judas and Other Poems*, Jeffers was accused of atheism. The second long poem in this volume, "The Loving Shepherdess" was, on the other hand, well received by most of the critics as a tender, beautiful allegory of sacrificial love. Perhaps, most significant, however, in the history of Jeffers' critical reputation, was Yvor Winters' condemnation of this volume; Winters' comments appeared in *Poetry* in February 1930. In the years to follow, Winters would conduct what amounted to an almost personal vendetta against his fellow Californian, which was, as was all criticism, both favorable and adverse, apparently ignored by Jeffers. Winters, in any case, found the work in this volume "revolting," "maudlin," "anecdotal," and lacking in structure [A157]. In a review of *Thurso's Landing* in 1932, Winters, in *Hound and Horn*, would state his case more succinctly: "The book is composed almost wholly of trash" [A211]. Winters' reviews had a deleterious effect upon Jeffers' reputation; his dogmatic utterances were rarely challenged, not even by Deutsch and Van Doren. As for Rorty, he had quietly removed himself from the camp of fervent followers. It is not surprising that Winters detested Jeffers, for one of the things Winters found most disagreeable in a poet was the quality he labeled "primitivism," an ambiguous term that is frequently applied to Jeffers' verse. But Winters' criticism of Jeffers, once he warmed up to his prey, ran to bitter sarcasm. He rendered his *obiter dicta* on "Dear Judas" in comic detail, finding that the poem had no quotable lines "save perhaps three," and those "heavy with dross." Coupled with a natural reaction to the excesses of such praise as that of DeCasseres, Winters' nearly manic hostility contributed to the almost complete disappearance of serious consideration of Jeffers, as a poet, in the late forties and fifties.

Jeffers' relationship with Winters suggests one aspect of the treatment Jeffers received from the New Critics. They either adopted a condescending attitude towards Jeffers, directing scornful remarks at him from an immeasurable height, or, what may be worse, considering their influence, they totally neglected him. Examples of the former attitude may be found in Allen Tate's charge in *New Republic*, April 6, 1932, that Jeffers is guilty of a "fictitious primitivism" [B171], R. P. Blackmur's remarks in 1952 concerning the "flannelmouthed inflation in the metric of Robinson Jeffers" [B282], Robert Penn Warren's discoverey in 1937 that

Jeffers is "deficient in the dramatic sense" [A231], or in Randall Jarrell's analysis in 1963 of Jeffers' style as "a matter of simple exaggeration" [B351]. Why, if Jeffers is trash, asks John Crowe Ransom in *The New Criticism*, 1941 [C70], bother with him at all? As Radcliffe Squires points out in *The Loyalties of Robinson Jeffers* [C101], Ransom, in compiling a list of the major and minor poets of the first half of this century for *Kenyon Review*, Summer, 1951, refuses even to mention Jeffers. This is perhaps the most blatant example of a neglect that helped to keep Jeffers out of many poetry anthologies in the forties and fifties, out of the influential journals that are most read in the universities, and consequently out of the main stream of instruction.

An interesting sidelight to the fate of Jeffers' general popularity is his "literary reputation" in Pittsburgh, the city of his birth. Here DeCasseres' 1927 article in the *Bookman* [B43] came to the attention of the local press. In addition, DeCasseres suggested in a letter to the editor of the *Sun-Telegraph* that that city's ultimate fame would lie with Jeffers [B58]. Jeffers was enthusiastically accalimed by the press. Then a critical article appeared in *Carnegie Magazine* in which Jeffers was declared obscene and unfit to be "read aloud in the family circle" [B57]. A review of this article thanked the author for saving the citizens of Pittsburgh the difficult task of reading the poem [B51]. From that time, mention of Jeffers, as a favorite son of Pittsburgh, waned.

In 1929 Jeffers and his family visited Ireland. The result was a volume of short elegiac poems, *Descent to the Dead* (1931). The new serenity they introduced into the body of his work was generally praised, the Marxist critic, Rolfe Humphries, in *Poetry*, being one of the few important reviewers condemning the work. He censured Jeffers' lack of "will, so great that he can neither quit crying nor fight back" [A169]. An influential admirer, Horace Gregory, who was to praise Jeffers' poetry for over three decades, penned his initial criticism of Jeffers in a review of *Descent to the Dead.*

He predicted that "it is entirely possible that his boast of immortality will be justified by future generations of readers who will not fail to recognize his name" [A168].

If one year were to be chosen as illustrative of the apex of Jeffers' literary popularity, it should be 1932, for in that year the wave of his critical reputation reached its crest. *Thurso's Landing and Other Poems* received a favorable reception; his picture appeared on the cover of *Time*; DeCasseres returned to predict that "in fifty years only two living Americans will be read, Robinson Jeffers and James Branch Cabell" [B159]; and Mabel Dodge Luhan dedicated to Jeffers her book on D. H. Lawrence's sometimes ludicrous adventures with her in New Mexico, *Lorenzo in Taos* [C35]. She was seeking a successor for the dead Lawrence, to recreate Taos in literature, and it is indicative of Jeffers' literary stature that she selected him for her prey. Her attempt to lure Jeffers was largely in vain, for although he did visit Taos, he was to write only a few short, forgettable poems about the area. Lawrence Clark Powell's doctoral dissertation, published as *An Introduction to Robinson Jeffers* [C37], also appeared in 1932. This was the core of several later editions of what still remains the definitive biography of Jeffers. Although Jeffers failed to win the Pulitzer Prize in 1932 (he was never to receive it), Henry Canby reflected general critical opinion when he declared that Jeffers should have been given the prize and that he was "among the few poets of unquestioned eminence" writing in America [B157]. Several influential critics accorded him highest praise that year. Granville Hicks wrote that "Thurso's Landing" swept "forward on the wings of an imagery even nobler than that we have known" [A198], Percy Hutchison found the new book Jeffers' "crowning achievement to date" [A200], Louis Untermeyer declared Jeffers' poetry "full-throated" and unforgettable [A209], and in an inconsistent review, Rolfe Humphries declared on the one hand that "Jeffers' shockers fail to come off," but on the other hand found Jeffers comparable to

Shakespeare in some respects [A199]. In the following year, 1933, appeared the definitive and last-attempted complete bibliography of Jeffers' work, S. S. Alberts' *Bibliography of the Works of Robinson Jeffers* [C40]. The publication of a full-length bibliography of a living poet only a few years after his first major work appeared, indicates the extent of Jeffers' fame. On the other hand, Winters' above mentioned *Hound and Horn* article appeared in 1932. Philip· Horton in the *Nassau Lit* saw Jeffers "stewing in his own muddy emotionalism and insular idleness" [B164]. And, significantly, James Rorty, the early supporter, who had cooled to Jeffers, suggested, "A new literature is emerging, the work of poets ardently partisan for human life and the conquests of human consciousness. Their ardors are just as valid as Jeffers' enthusiasm for basalt and grave maggots" [A206].

For 1932, the year that witnessed the zenith of Jeffers' critical reputation, also ushered in the historical events that were to contribute significantly to the gradual decline of Jeffers' critical reputation; before the thirties were over, few important reviewers would consider him a major poet. Critics, in that decade, caught up in the excitement of the New Deal and remembering, only too well, the great depression, demanded a socially and politically conscious literature; Jeffers did not fit the mold. First of all, his emotionalism was attacked, as was his pessimism and his lack of constructive social criticism. Unfavorable reviews of *Give Your Heart to the Hawks* (1933) reflected that the poet was swimming against the current of his time; the book was not a success. The inhuman creed of the title poem was criticized, as were the shallow, hopelessly neurotic obsessions of his characters. Two years later the merits of *Solstice and Other Poems* (1935) were questioned on the same basis. Critics found no message for the times, no solace in the work. *Solstice*, which contained numerous poems predicting the death march of contemporary events, received probably the most abusive reviews of any of his works, and retains the reputation of being the worst book he ever wrote. Ruth Lechlitner, writing in the *New Republic*, mirrored the disgust that those critics, deeply concerned with social reform, directed at the poet who now seemed content to predict doom, when everyone's efforts were needed to improve society. She chastised Jeffers for sitting "alone in his stone tower, surrounded by California scenery, while the whole disgusting business is going on," content to "dash off a last poem or two before Peace gathers him to her bosom" [A227]. A new accusation was directed at Jeffers in a review of *Solstice*, an accusation that would linger unpleasantly through the war years, and which occasionally finds voice even now. Philip Rice, in a review for the *Nation*, found that Jeffers' ideas resemble "good fascism" [A230]. This charge, which would further damage his critical reputation, stemmed from the Wagnerian subject matter of the second long narrative in *Solstice*, "At the Birth of an Age," dealing with the rise of Attila, and was additionally nourished by passages in *Be Angry at the Sun* (1941), which caused Babette Deutsch to remark, in a review of the book, that it gave "color to the suspicion that Jeffers has fascist sympathies" [A260]. Even as late as 1971, John Hughes, in an article in the *Saturday Review* accused Jeffers of describing "Hitler as a genius," and deplored his "proto-fascism" [B428].

In addition to the misgiving that Jeffers was a cryptofascist and to the scorn over his lack of social commitment, increasing application of the tenets of New Criticism were also undermining his reputation and were reflected in the now frequent notice of the looseness of his rhythms, the absence, as Robert Penn Warren noted, of "concentration of interest in detail that gives a short poem its power" [A231], and his general lack of human understanding. By the end of the thirties the New Critics had begun to ignore him completely.

Before departing with his family for a second trip to Ireland in 1937, Jeffers completed the manuscript of *Such*

Counsels You Gave Me and Other Poems. Published by Random House in 1937, it, too, received poor reviews. Louise Bogan felt the characters were not depraved, but "simple minded" [A235] and Muriel Rukeyser found Jeffers' thinking confused [A240]. Only Louis Untermeyer, an early and persistent admirer, praised these "impressive monoliths of poetry" [A241]. With the possible exception of *Solstice* this was Jeffers' most poorly-received work, and, as with *Solstice*, critics found fault mostly with Jeffers' rejection of humanity and his lack of social commitment. As one reviewer commented, "he has removed himself too far from his own age to be seriously listened to as a prophet" [A244].

The late thirties were not entirely devoid of recognition. In 1937, Jeffers was elected to the National Institute of Arts and Letters. Usually, Jeffers declined, as politely as possible, to join any literary organization. He was never of a coterie. Furthermore, he refused to review other poets' works. He did, by way of fulfilling obligations to his early admirers, review Rorty's *Children of the Sun* in 1927 and Mark Van Doren's *Now the Sky* in 1928; but with the exception of these early efforts, he remained entirely aloof from literary criticism. Consequently he excluded himself from informal membership in the society which might have sprung to his defense in the thirties. His apparent indifference extended to his steadfast refusal to commit himself to any political or economic organization. This particularly exasperated many influential Marxist critics who were either to ignore him or to treat him as an extreme example of bourgeois decadence. Thus, Horace Gregory, torn between his politics and his early admiration for Jeffers, praised him in 1934 as a member of a corrupt society who preferred death to participation. Gregory spoke of the poet in the past tense, implying that Jeffers was, in a critical sense, dead [B178]. Rolfe Humphries, on the other hand, condemned Jeffers' failure to point out the specific evils of America's degenerating capitalism and declared that Jeffers served "a very useful

purpose to the governing class" by telling men that it is futile
to protest against man's hard, inevitable lot [B185]. Alan
Swallow praised Jeffers' skill as a poet, while condemning his
ideas as "completely within the burgeois culture" [B197].
Finally, V. F. Calverton declared Jeffers' tragedies "a reflection of the violent, toppling ruins of a dying civilization"
[B138]. The Marxist critics, coupled with the New Critics,
had succeeded in extinguishing the brilliant reputation Jeffers
had earlier acquired. In 1938 his *Selected Poetry* was
published by Random House, but again Jeffers failed to
receive the Pulitzer Prize. The award went, instead, to John
Gould Fletcher. An anonymous critic in the *Saturday Review
of Literature* aptly commented: "The number of minor poets
who have won Pulitzer Prizes in years when Jeffers had books
in the field is a serious reflection on the standards of the
poetry award" [B204]. Lesser recognition arrived, however,
in 1940 when Jeffers won the Helen Levinson Award from
Poetry.

Some academic and critical interest continued. During the
thirties and early forties, several rather lengthy, thoughtful
studies of Jeffers' philosophy appeared. Among these were
Harlan Hatcher's "The Torches of Violence" [B179], Hilde-
garde Flanner's "Two Poets: Jeffers and Millay" [B194],
Hyatt Howe Waggoner's "Science and the Poetry of Robin-
son Jeffers" [B201], Louis Wann's "Robinson Jeffers—
Counterpart of Walt Whitman" [B202], Frajam Taylor's
"The Hawk and the Stone" [B211], Delmore Schwartz's
"Sources of Violence" [A254], Frederic I. Carpenter's "The
Values of Robinson Jeffers" [B216] and "Death Comes for
Robinson Jeffers" [B217], and Harold Watts' "Multivalence
in Robinson Jeffers" [B227] and "Robinson Jeffers and
Eating the Serpent" [B228]. Unfortunately for a sensible
evaluation of his work, Jeffers still continued to have his
wildly extravagant admirers. Melba Berry Bennett, in
Robinson Jeffers and the Sea (1936) [C52], admittedly
found it "impossible to be temperate" in discussing Jeffers'

poetry, and to Rudolph Gilbert in *Shine Perishing Republic* (1936) [C53], "The force of his creative imagination disrupts . . . like an electric drill boring into a rock."

World War II gravely distracted Jeffers, and the quality of his poetry was seriously affected. Whereas he had earlier ascribed to the theory that poetry suffered for being involved in contemporary affairs, in both books of poetry published in the forties, *Be Angry at the Sun and Other Poems* (1941) and *The Double Axe and Other Poems* (1948), Jeffers displayed an obsession with the war. His prefatory remarks to the 1941 volume serve warning that the themes of his poetry have changed: "I wish to lament the obsession with contemporary history that pins many of these pieces to the calender, like butterflies to cardboard. Poetry . . . in general is the worse for being timely. Yet it is right that a man's views be expressed, though the poetry should suffer for it." This social conscience, of course, is exactly what was found lacking in his poetry during the thirties. Both the 1941 and the 1948 volumes are "violently" pacifist. In *Be Angry at the Sun and Other Poems* Jeffers issues a passionate albeit vain plea for the United States to avoid what he saw as its inevitable entanglement in a European war. In one of the book's secondary poems, "The Bowl of Blood," which Stanley Kunitz called "the greatest masque since Comus" [A265], Adolph Hitler (called only "The Leader") appears as an inverted Christ figure. Surprisingly, the reviews were generally favorable, but *Be Angry at the Sun* did not win wide general recognition, for by 1941 few major critics were bothering to review Jeffers. An illuminating remark was made by Kunitz. In questioning the propriety of making Hitler a tragic figure, he commented: Jeffers must, now that he "returns to the historical sense" accept "moral obligations and human values." If he did not he would "range himself on the side of the destroyers. It is a critical moment in his career" [A265]. Perhaps it is not unfair to the critics to note that not only did they demand a social conscience from Jeffers, they also wanted him to agree with their own political alignment. Jeffers' pacificism in the forties was fully as unpopular with them as was his lack of social commitment in the thirties. In 1948 *The Double Axe and Other Poems* appeared. The political views it expressed proved so embarrassing for Random House, that they prefaced the book with a denial of responsibility for the material it contained. This preface often sparked more comment than the poetry. Violently anti-war, the title poem deals with a dead soldier who returns to engage in an incestuous affair with his mother and to find his father spouting empty "patriotic" slogans. In some of the shorter poems Churchill, Hitler, Roosevelt and Stalin are mentioned as warlords all equally guilty. Although Jeffers received some praise for his technical abilities, his philosophy was almost universally condemned. A not untypical review appearing in the St. Louis *Post-Dispatch* declared that "only the most devout followers of the right wing nationalists, the lunatic fringe, and the most ardent of Roosevelt haters could, after reading 'The Double Axe,' welcome the return of Robinson Jeffers . . . " [A285]. The most extreme reaction, perhaps, was the suggestion by Gerard Meyer, in a letter responding angrily to Selden Rodman's by no means favorable review in the *Saturday Review of Literature.* Meyer, who felt Rodman had been too lenient with the poet, stated that "Jeffers and those of his ilk," were responsible "for much of the totalitarian madness that has been loose upon the world, which had led so many human beings to death" [A298].

By 1948, however, Jeffers, the poet, had been, by far, eclipsed by Jeffers, the playwright. The theatrical quality of his poems had not escaped the notice of the critics. As early as 1932 a dramatic adaptation of "Tower Beyond Tragedy" was presented, to favorable criticism, by the University of California (Berkeley) Players. An adaptation by John Gassner of this play was produced by the Del Monte summer stock company in 1941 in Carmel's Forest Theater. Judith Anderson played Clytemnestra in this modern version of the

Oresteia, and Jeffers, the otherwise semi-recluse, attended three of the four performances. Miss Anderson also succeeded in convincing Jeffers to write an adaptation of *Medea* for her. He completed the play in 1945, and it opened in New York on October 20, 1947. But two weeks prior to its opening Jeffers' Broadway debut came with the controversial adaptation by Michael Meyerberg of the 1929 poem, "Dear Judas." This version of Jeffers' poem played for a week in Ogunquit, Maine, in August 1947, despite a storm of controversy over the poet's interpretation of Christ and Judas. Apparently what was at least tolerated in book form aroused righteous indignation when presented on stage; predictably the play was banned in Boston on moral grounds. In October the New York critics found the play neither inspirational nor offensive, but simply boring. Most of the blame for the failure fell on Meyerberg's staging and adaptation and not on the original Jeffers poem. *Dear Judas* closed the day before the poet arrived in New York to attend the premiere of *Medea*. This loose adaptation of Euripides' play had been published in 1946 and had had a mixed reception; many literary critics objected to the poetic liberties Jeffers took with the original. But after *Medea* opened, there could be no question that his streamlined version was successful theater. George Jean Nathan chose it as Best Play of the Year, and named Judith Anderson for Best Female Acting Performance. Jeffers had become, ironically enough, a theatrical personality to be reckoned with, and Broadway clamored for more.

On November 26, 1950, ANTA opened its series with a new production of *Tower Beyond Tragedy* with Judith Anderson again the star. Jeffers overcame his reluctance to appear in public and flew to New York to attend the opening. The play received generally good reviews, though not so ecstatic as those accorded *Medea*. Brooks Atkinson praised the "lines of fire" [A437] with which Jeffers formed the drama, and William Hawkins of the New York *World-*

Telegram and Sun called him "our most distinguished theater poet" [A444]. A few critics questioned the play's highly emotional tone.

The final play Jeffers wrote was *The Cretan Woman*, another classical adaptation, this time of the Phaedra legend. During a trip to Ireland in 1948 Jeffers fell ill, and rather than waste the days spent in convalescence in a Dublin hospital, he wrote *The Cretan Woman* in fulfillment of a promise he had made to Agnes Moorehead. It was produced in Washington in May 1954 and Off-Broadway in New York in the summer of the same year. *The Cretan Woman* had a lukewarm reception in both cities although Brooks Atkinson liked "the craggy verse" [A454] and Robert Coleman of the New York *Mirror* called it a "taut, compact drama" [A459].

Jeffers wrote no other plays. *Medea* was staged in several American and European cities. One of Jeffers' last public appearances was at a production of *Medea* in Monterey, California, only months before his death. During the period of his theatrical career, Jeffers, the poet, had almost disappeared from the realm of literary criticism. With one or two exceptions he had become merely a name in the footnotes. Significantly, one of the most thorough and intelligent essays on Jeffers during this period, Joseph Roddy's "View From a Granite Tower," appeared in the June 1949 *Theatre Arts* [B274].

Jeffers' wife, Una, died in 1950. Her lengthy illness and death deeply absorbed Jeffers' mental and physical energies; the keen sense of loss remained with him to the day of his own death. Much of what he wrote after 1950 reflects his bereavement. Although the fifties could hardly be termed a period of renaissance in Jeffers' critical reputation, some minor recognition was accorded him. In 1951 he won the Eunice Tietjens Memorial Award, in 1952 he received the Union League Civic Arts Foundation Award, and in 1955 he won the Borestone Mountain Poetry Award for the 1954 volume, *Hungerfield and Other Poems.* This was the last book

Jeffers completed. *Hungerfield*, curiously, received a majority of favorable reviews, although most of them originated from relatively minor sources. There is a new, mellow tone in the book particularly apparent in the tender tribute to Una which frames the title poem. Several of the few important critics who reviewed *Hungerfield* wrote adverse remarks, though generally sprinkled with grudging praise. Dudley Fitts found many of the poems marred by preaching, politics, or simple hatred, yet felt they contained the "yesness of real poetry" [A332]. Howard Nemerov condemned the title poem but praised "The Cretan Woman" [A345]. Selden Rodman detected an "unrelieved sadism of imagery," but conceded that Jeffers possessed exceptional narrative ability [A347]. On the other hand, Charles Poore [A346], Louis Untermeyer [A349] and Horace Gregory [A335] found much to praise. Gregory, in particular, had kind words. He declared Jeffers' position in American poetry "secure and singular" and especially lauded the short poems in the volume. Increasingly, critics who had first turned to the short poems for relief from the narratives, now found great beauty in many of Jeffers' lyrics.

An important event in the history of Jeffers' critical reputation was the appearance in 1956 of a book-length study of him, the first in sixteen years. James Radcliffe Squires' *The Loyalties of Robinson Jeffers* is a thorough, balanced re-evaluation of the poet. Squires deals primarily with Jeffers' philosophy, as it is developed in the long narratives, rather neglecting the short poems. In discussions of this critical work, Jeffers himself was often the object of reappraisal. Perhaps the most violent anti-Jeffers attack since Winters' essays in the early thirties was Kenneth Rexroth's review of Squires' book in the *Saturday Review*. Rexroth felt "Jeffers' verse is shoddy and pretentious and the philosophizing is nothing but posturing. His reworking of Greek tragic plots make me shudder at their vulgarity" [B299]. This attitude was, however, hardly characteristic of other criticism of that decade. In the same article, Rexroth reveals, significantly, that in talking to his young students, it was impossible to find any who had even heard of Jeffers, much less read any of his poems. A few more honors were accorded Jeffers before his death. He was elected a fellow of the Academy of American Poets in 1958 and in 1961 he received the Shelley Memorial Award from the National Poetry Society.

Jeffers died on January 20, 1962. The death of the poet who in 1925 had been proclaimed across the nation as, at the least, the greatest American poet since Whitman, received first-page notice only in the San Francisco *Chronicle*, the Baltimore *Sun*, the Washington *Post* (ten lines) and the Los Angeles *Times*. Several newspapers that had once proclaimed his extraordinary power did not deem his death worthy of notice, and in Carmel, coverage of the final day of the Pebble Beach Golf Tournament effectively obscured the passing of the poet who had helped make famous this central California coast. In no case were his volumes of poetry considered of exceptional importance. The general attitude of all the immediate obituaries may best be summarized by a portion of an editorial that appeared in the San Francisco *Chronicle* two days after his death: "The greatest thing Jeffers did for American poetry was to learn Greek . . . His version of the *Medea* . . . is a truly great work of translation" [B328].

The posthumous publication of a collection of short poems, *The Beginning and the End and Other Poems* (1963), provided opportunity for many favorable reappraisals of the poet's work. For the first time since *Descent to the Dead* (1931), a book of Jeffers' poetry was published with no long narrative poem included. The reviews were generally favorable, often enthusiastic; the rancour and the bitterness directed at him in the thirties and forties had apparently subsided, and many were ready to forgive the dead poet for his eccentricities. An important critic, the noted poet, James Dickey, offered lavish praise, declaring that, although flawed,

"Jeffers is cast in a large mold," that he filled a position in America "that would simply have been an empty gap without him: that of the poet as prophet, as large-scale philosopher, as doctrine giver" [A367]. William Turner Levy in the New York *Times* found "wonderfully unexpected poems of personal record" [A370], Winfield Townley Scott in the *Saturday Review* noted that "the neglect of Jeffers, even the scorn of Jeffers in the past three decades constitutes the major scandal of contemporary American poetry" [A375], and Stephen Spender found these last poems to have "imaginative grandeur" [A379].

Partially as a result of the re-evaluation resulting from reviews of his last book, the sixties have been a period of a gradual reawakening of interest in Jeffers' poetry. In 1962, a book-length study, *Robinson Jeffers*, by Frederic Carpenter, provided not only individual discussions of each of the narratives, but also a lengthy analysis of the short poems, biography, evaluation of Jeffers' critical reputation, and an examination of his philosophy. This latter generation's most enthusiastic Jeffers admirer, the West Coast poet, William Everson (Brother Antoninus), wrote a number of articles on Jeffers' poetry which were gathered into a book published in 1968, *Robinson Jeffers: Fragments of an Older Fury* [C136]. Everson also wrote a lengthy introduction for the New Directions edition of *Cawdor and Medea* (1970) [C142], in which he favorably compared Jeffers and Emerson. In recent years several studies of Jeffers' work have appeared. Of special note is William H. Nolte's "Robinson Jeffers as Didactic Poet" [B385], which compares Jeffers' philosophy of inhumanism with T. S. Eliot's acceptance of Christianity; and Robert Boyers' "A Sovereign Voice: The Poetry of Robinson Jeffers" [B403], which reviews Jeffers' critical reputation, citing the unfairness of writers like Winters, Jarrell, and Rexroth, and devoting special attention to the short poems. In 1965 the Sierra Club published a collection of photographs of the Big Sur Coast with Jeffers'

poetry as accompanying text. Loren Eisely, in an introduction, named Jeffers the "most powerful embodiment of the
untamed Pacific environment" [C124]. Melba Bennett's
biography of Jeffers was published in 1966 [C127], and his
selected letters appeared in a volume edited by Ann N.
Ridgeway in 1968 [C139].

There are, however, several critical studies yet to be
undertaken. First, no thorough biography of Jeffers has been
written. Melba Bennett's *Stone Mason of Tor House* (1966)
[C127] deals with Jeffers' intellectual make-up but does
little to make Jeffers, the man, come to life; her devotion to
Jeffers precluded an objective portrait. Second, a new edition
of his poems should be published. The most recent collection
is the Vintage Paperback *Robinson Jeffers, Selected Poems*,
1963. It is, however, merely a modest attempt to provide a
few samples from each of Jeffers' volumes, although it does
offer some of the work which came after the *Selected Poetry*
of 1938. Third, a primary bibliography is essential. The last
thorough effort was S. S. Alberts' *A Bibliography of the
Works of Robinson Jeffers* (1933) [C40]. Finally, detailed
explication of several of the short poems should be made.
Apparently because they appear, on the surface, at least,
easily understandable, few attempts have been made to make
a detailed analysis of them.

Since there are already many excellent and comprehensive
critiques of Jeffers' poetry, it is difficult to warrant yet
another critical commentary. My justification is that, knowing how I regard Jeffers' work, the reader can place my
abstracts of reviews, articles and books in perspective. The
following remarks are thus intended to assist the reader to
evaluate the critical evidence presented in the body of this
bibliography.

First, I believe Jeffers' poetry will endure, despite critical
trends. In attempting to label the qualities of his poetry that
will make it outlast, I think, the disfavor it has met, I am
forced into abstractions which, by their very nature, have

little to do with Jeffers' best poems. For Jeffers, above all, loved things more than ideas, and his finest efforts contain specific elements of the physical world—hawks, waves, rocks, sea gulls, trees, storm clouds. He was aware of the danger in mixing abstraction and poetry. As he proclaimed in "The Beauty of Things":

> To feel and speak the astonishing beauty of things—
>   earth, stone and water,
> Beast, man and woman, sun, moon and stars—
> . . .
>   —to feel
> Greatly, and understand greatly, and express greatly the
>   natural
> Beauty, is the sole business of poetry.

But Jeffers was also a philosophic poet and frequently he turned from the visible to the intellectual world. When he did so, however, his ideas were incarnate, rooted in physical reality; as he wrote in "Birds":

>   . . . for a poem
> Needs multitude, multitudes of thoughts, all fierce, all
>   flesh-eaters. . . .

Memorable as his philosophy may be, his greatest gift was his ability to recreate God's "divinely superfluous beauty." Whereas readers may disagree with his ideas, few cannot be moved by his passionate descriptions of the world's wild magnificence, by lines like the following from "Tor House":

> Come in the morning, you will see white gulls
> Weaving a dance over blue water, the wane of the moon
> Their dance companion. . . .

Seldom will one fail to respond to his evocation of nature's radiance, his persuasive invitation to,

> Hear the music, the thunder of the wings. Love the wild
>   swan.
>
> ["Love the Wild Swan"]

Jeffers was also a powerfully visionary poet, parochial neither in time nor space. His poems, suggesting the geological, the astronomical, consistently remind that man's

> . . . needs and nature are no more changed in fact in ten
>   thousand years than the beaks of eagles.
>
> ["The Beaks of Eagles"]

And when we are filled with our own importance, he directs our gaze to the stars:

> There is nothing like astronomy to pull the stuff out of
>   man.
> His stupid dreams and red-rooster importance.
>
> ["Star-Swirls"]

Jeffers ignored contemporary poetic fashions and he was successful in creating a unique, unmistakably different voice. In "Poetry, Gongorism, and a Thousand Years," he advised new poets to "turn away from the self-consciousness and naive learnedness, the undergraduate irony, unnatural metaphors, hiatases and labored obscurity." He felt that Eliot's "Wasteland" was the end, not the beginning of an era. Jeffers was convinced that poetry should concern itself with the permanent, not the ephemeral—he himself sought to write for an audience one-thousand years hence. Therein lies another of his poetic virtues; freed from contemporary tastes, he could be totally sincere in his poetry. By refusing to pose, by denying that man is of central importance in the cosmos, he was able to turn away from contemporary society, history, politics, and to fix his gaze on the indifferent but eternal beauty of the universe. Consequently, his poems are stern, somber, lonely; there is little hope or solace to be found in them. I doubt, in fact, if they can be read for pleasure—they move the reader, overwhelm him, cause him to wonder at nature's elemental forces, but they never flatter or amuse. For these reasons, Jeffers' poetry rarely appeals to anthropo-centric optimists; his admirers would tend, I think, to view man, history, and civilization with sobriety and stoicism, and would probably be less interested in verbal "cuteness" and clever ironies than in the range, nobility, and dignity of thought.

Jeffers' weaknesses are readily apparent: his themes are often monotonously similar; he lacks a sense of irony; he is, at times, overly pessimistic; he lacks humor. In defense of seriousness, Jeffers would answer that Pollyannas recognize only the ephemeral. He would agree with Sophocles, that man "can have no happiness/Till he pass the bound of life, nor be relieved of pain." But Jeffers, in all fairness, never luxuriated in sorrow and gloom. Rather, he attempted to supply a corrective, an antidote to empty-headed joy, to mindless fun and games. He acknowledged that man should feast and praise life, but,

> . . . the praise of life
> That forgets the pain is a pebble
> Rattled in a dry gourd.

["Praise Life"]

And, although "joy is a trick in the air . . . and pleasure is contemptible," ["Birth-Dues"] man can have peace. Man can attain a noble resignation, an awareness that although he is insignificant, he is part of a mystic whole. First, however, man must rid himself of his ignoble desires and his petty concerns about self and soul, and turn outward to the "transhuman magnificence" of the world, to the "lonely-flowing waters, the secret-/Keeping stones, the flowing sky." ["Life from the Lifeless"]

His most glaring poetic weakness is apparent only in his long narratives, where he displays certain lapses of taste that border on the ludicrous. "The Double Axe" is replete with examples of this failing. Hoult, an American soldier killed in the Pacific, decides to leave his grave and confront his parents. During his short furlough from death, Hoult, or rather his decaying, eviscerated corpse, is greeted by his mother, who understandably remarks, "You look . . . dreadful." Hoult replies, "Like something/Dug up?" Later, Hoult, weary from an argument about the war with his father, Gore, says, "I'm going up/to my room, Mother,/And groan awhile." Although the corpse is intended to shock the reader, to bring home, literally, the reality of war, it is often only comic and ridiculous. "Solstice" is another of Jeffers' narratives which contains serious aesthetic failures. Madrone Bothwell, a modern Medea, postures too much to be taken seriously. At one point in the story, she decides to "kill" her husband's car, to prevent him from leaving with her children:

> She opened the hood
>   of the engine and pried and broke
>   a bomb-shape thing from its bearings
> And flung it to the trees below. The gas-line
>   dripped stinking blood and the car died.

Jeffers was hardly the first poet to conceive an occasional farcical image, but his defects left him open to satiric attacks, and some critics, like Yvor Winters, ruthlessly exploited his vulnerability. In this respect, Jeffers resembles D. H. Lawrence who, aiming for high seriousness, occasionally becomes laughable. Perhaps the reason that Jeffers sometimes plummets to the ludicrous is that each of his long poems constitutes a major risk: he dared more than the poet who has less to say and is therefore more cautious. Jeffers, driven by an inner compulsion to tell the truth, sometimes overstepped the limits. Because his long narratives received, until recently, far more attention than his short poems, where he never lost control, these lapses of taste were frequently noted. Also, the loose structure of the narratives was censured, often by the same unfriendly critics who ignored the compact and intricate short poems. And although it must be admitted that the narratives, with the exception of the taut, intense "Roan Stallion," the concise, vigorous "Tamar," and the tender, compassionate "Loving Shepherdess," do sometimes display grave flaws and are overwrought with violence and emotionalism, these same works contain many passages that demand no apology. For example, "Cawdor" which carries much loose baggage, contains many powerful sections, two of which Jeffers justifiably included in his *Selected Poetry*: "The Old Man's Dream after He Died" and "The Caged Eagle's Death Dream." Even the worst of the narratives, perhaps *The Women at Point sur*, "The Double Axe," and "Solstice," contain many worthwhile parts. While it is certainly true that the well-wrought urn of the New Critics "becomes/The greatest ashes," the possibility cannot be excluded that "half-acre tombs" can be royal.

Like Jonathan Swift, Jeffers, too, is accused of rejecting humanity, of portraying man as a despicable creature who lacks the dignity and nobility of animals. There is ample evidence in Jeffers' poetry to support this view; most well-known is the line from "Hurt Hawks": "I'd sooner, except the penalties, kill a man than a hawk." Many critics detected his inability to depict believable, likable humans. In a work that deals primarily with the human element, as in *The Women at Point Sur*, they found Jeffers most unpleasant. I would concede that in his best work the human element is subordinated to nature. Jeffers' aloof, haughty attitude towards man, who is, after all, the only reader he has, is frequently annoying. To discover, as in "The Broken Balance," that "man's present/Lives" may be almost as valuable as the excrement of cormorants, or that, as in "Mara," men on the world are equivalent to lice on an eagle, is, at best, irritating, at least to human readers. To the charge of misanthropy, Jeffers might reply that he was trying to place man in perspective; to show that man has no right to be inflated with his own importance, or to consider himself master of the world, particularly if man uses this assumed mastery to justify his manipulation of nature. Jeffers' insults are directed at man's pomposity and arrogance; he deflates man to lead him to a new peace, a quiet sanity. A recurring symbol, in Jeffers' poetry, for man's obsessive concern with self, man's self-centered introspection and vanity, is incest. Man's conceited fixation on his own reflection, incestuous in that he turns inward, away from the inhuman beauty of the world, can only lead to lunacy. Look away from humanity, outward to the inhuman God, advised Jeffers, and become whole, healthy, and free. As he wrote in "Signpost,"

> Turn outward, love things, not men, turn right away from humanity,
> Let that doll lie. . . .
> Climb the great ladder out of the pit of yourself and man.

Particularly distasteful to Jeffers was the relentless increase in population, accompanied by the cancerous growth of a uniform, mass-produced culture. Breeding like maggots, the masses, Jeffers felt, were leveling the forests, polluting the streams, and killing his beloved hawks. In "Birth and Death" he wrote,

> Have you noticed meanwhile the population explosion
> Of man on earth, the torrents of new-born babies, the
>   bursting schools? Astonishing. It saps man's
>   dignity.
> We used to be individuals, not populations.

Jeffers found comfort in the thought that one day a storm of destruction would wash the world clean of the masses, the way the November surf covers

> . . . the cliff with white violent cleanness: then
>   suddenly
> The old granite forgets half a year's filth:
> The orange-peel, eggshells, papers, pieces of clothing,
>   the clots
> Of dung in corners of the rock, and used
> Sheaths that make light love safe in the evenings:
>   all the droppings of the summer
> Idlers washed off in a winter ecstacy.
>
> ["November Surf"]

With "people fewer and the hawks more/numerous," man will once again achieve "the dignity of room, the value of rareness." These are provocative ideas and it is suprising that more righteous indignation in defense of man and progress has not arisen to smite Jeffers.

Most damaging to Jeffers' critical reputation has probably been the charge of fascism. This is a wildly erroneous and pernicious accusation, yet it lingers, even to the present. In the *Saturday Review* (May 22, 1971), John Hughes labels Jeffers as a "proto-fascist" who describes Hitler as a "genius" [B428]. What Jeffers said of Hitler's "genius" appears in "The Day is a Poem—September 19, 1939":

> This morning Hitler spoke in Danzig, we heard his voice.
> A man of genius: that is of amazing
> Ability, courage, devotion, cored on a sick child's soul,
> Heard clearly through the dog wrath, a sick child
> Wailing in Danzig; invoking destruction and wailing
>   at it.

Hitler was, in Jeffers' terms, suffering from an insane obsession with self, from the lunacy of vanity. It is difficult to imagine anyone Jeffers could have admired less. Time and again in his poems, Jeffers, who despised war and conquest, castigated Hitler, Lenin, Stalin, and, unfortunately for his critical reputation, Churchill and Roosevelt. He felt that any ruler who pushed his nation into war, fed his "greedy/Flame on a wick dipped in the fat of millions" ["Great Men"]. One might ask why a world war couldn't serve as the destructive agent, the November surf, to clean away the faceless masses? But despite some of his poems, which express almost an indifference to the fate of humanity, Jeffers was, in fact, a gentle man who deplored senseless killing. Nature's rhythms of violence and death were never needlessly, pointlessly cruel; man at war, however, was a sick child, who killed for senseless values like patriotism or glory. Jeffers consistently rejected all and any form of war, and he particularly condemned conflicts that embroiled America. In "Shine, Empire," published shortly before the outbreak of World War II, Jeffers argued that America, "Powerful and armed, neutral in the midst of madness,/ . . . might have held the whole world's balance/ and stood/ Like a mountain in a wind. We were misled and took sides." For whatever insanity was brewing in other parts of the world, "All Europe was hardly worth the precarious freedom of/ one of our states: what will her ashes fetch?" Jeffers equally deplored America's involvement in the other two wars of his lifetime, World War I and Korea. Few American poets of this century have so consistently and so vehemently spoken out against war. Whatever cause the nation hid behind, the sword's reality was, for Jeffers, "loathsome/ disfigurements, blindness, mutilation, locked/lips of boys/Too proud to scream" ["Contemplation of the Sword"]. However, implacable pacifism in World War II was not the way to popularity. To oppose the war was to nourish the suspicion that one supported the enemy, fascism. In large part, Jeffers' pacifism in the thirties and forties contributed to the suspicion that he was a fascist. Whatever the explanations for the accusation, they cannot excuse what appears to be, at best, an unintentional distortion of his views, or, at worst, a plain case of slander.

Jeffers' obsessive concern with contemporary events during the forties seriously affected his poetry. The poems of this period are collected in *The Double Axe* (1948), probably his worst book. It is replete with examples of deplorable lapses of taste, resulting from his nearly manic preoccupation with the war. He had lost objectivity, and his poetry suffered. Even the short poems in *The Double Axe* are, for the first and only time in any of his mature works, inferior. One of the book's more striking poems, "Orca," begins with an evocative description of a peaceful ocean, loafing sea-lions, "bigger than horses," island-rocks bristling with "quiet birds, gulls, cormorants, pelicans," and in the distance, danger approaches in the form of "two black triangles, tacking and veering,/converging/Toward the rocks and the shore. . . . the dorsal fins of two killer whales." But after a promising beginning, Jeffers, again harking back to the war, can find no better metaphor for the killer-whales' attack than to compare it to the V-2 rockets that "lashed London." Jeffers apparently soon realized that he was turning his poetry into a screech of anger. Several years earlier in the forward to *Be Angry at the Sun*, Jeffers had lamented his obsession with contemporary events. In the year *The Double Axe* was published, Jeffers declared in an important essay, "Poetry, Gongorism, and a Thousand Years," (New York *Times*, January 18, 1948) that a poet should write about permanent things and not become embroiled in current events. This personal manifesto indicated, in effect, that he had relearned a lesson temporarily forgotten in the turmoil of the war.

Jeffers' finest efforts can be found, I believe, in his short poems and they may prove to be his most enduring work. In them he demonstrates a majestic power and a serene objectivity, rarely equalled. Most of his books combine a long narrative and several short poems; frequently the latter serve to redeem the former. It is interesting to note that *That Women at Point Sur* (1927), his earliest critical failure, contains no short poems. Whereas the short poems, perhaps best described as meditative lyrics, often provide relief from the intensity of the narratives, in *The Women at Point Sur* there is only the unrelieved tension of the long title poem. On the other hand, *The Beginning and the End and Other Poems* (1963), a critical success, contains no long narrative. Instead the offerings are brief lyrics of old age—tender, personal, mellow, demonstrating, once again, Jeffers' courage, eloquence, wisdom. Poems which compare favorably with his finest efforts appear in this final volume: "Storm Dance of the Sea Gulls," "Granddaughter," "Vulture," and "Birds and Fishes." It may not be an exaggeration to suggest that the critical reception any particular book received depended as much on the quantity of the short poems it contained as on the quality of its long narrative.

Were Jeffers' lyrics to be collected, they would fill an enormous volume of some of the finest poetry of the English language. Some of his best-known short poems which should be included in any collection are "Shine, Perishing Republic," "Boats in a Fog," "To the Stone-Cutters," "Night," "Hurt Hawks," and "The Purse-Seine." For the reader interested in a larger sampling of Jeffers' best, I would recommend "Summer Holiday," "Tor House," "November Surf," "Rearmament," "Love the Wild Swan," "The Beaks of Eagles," "The Soul's Desert," "For Una," "The Bloody Sire," "Ocean," "The Old Stonemason," "The Deer Lay Down Their Bones," and also the first pages of "Hungerfield," which express Jeffers' devotion to his dead wife, Una, and constitute a heart-rending and beautiful tribute to human love.

Jeffers' lyric poems are often carefully constructed, complex, and intricate, and require close reading and careful explication. The New Critics ignored Jeffers, partially because his long, loose narratives require little detailed exegesis; the surface meaning, at least, is relatively clear. The short poems are a different matter. Although they hardly contain tortuous ambiguities or verbal ironies, when subjected to close reading they often reveal new dimensions. The New Critics, indiscriminate in their rejection of Jeffers, overlooked what should have engaged their interest. William Everson (Brother Antoninus) demonstrates, in his *Fragments of an Older Fury* [C136], the suggestive imagery that can be discovered in a Jeffers poem. Using the techniques of close analysis on Jeffers' "Post Mortem," he reveals the rich significance that evades a surface reading of the poem. Since few detailed explications of Jeffers' lyrics have been made, they remain an inviting area in critical studies of the poet. When his short poems fail, it is because they contain heavy doses of didacticism, of oracular moralizing. But when the poems succeed, as they usually do, they passionately portray the physical world radiated by profound meditation.

Often overlooked are Jeffers' plays. His *Medea, Tower Beyond Tragedy*, and *The Cretan Woman* demonstrate that he was an outstanding playwright. Keenly aware that conflict of will is the heart of great drama, Jeffers was able to portray that conflict in speech that was both colloquial and passionate. Likewise, Jeffers also exhibits a fine dramatic sense in his narratives. Although they sometimes fail as poems, they always succeed as stories. Jeffers, a superb teller of tales, created a theatrical structure for his narratives, and it would be no surprise if, at some time, they were converted into stage or film productions.

There are indications that, given a change in the external conditions that helped to bury Jeffers' popularity, his literary reputation might be resurrected. It is extraordinary, in ct, how Jeffers' prophecies are again finding favor—the more foreboding aspects of American history in the sixties—the hopeless weariness after the assasinations—the loss of faith in

our leaders and in our system—the despair over the seemingly
endless war in Indochina—the rejection of the establishment—
all resemble many of Jeffers' chief concerns. To those who
scorned his lack of faith in human progress the events of the
last decade are an answer. The causes of today's youth are
remarkably similar to the issues Jeffers espoused almost half
a century earlier. It was Jeffers who, in poems like "A
Redeemer" raised his voice in the battle for conservation and
ecological balance:

> Oh, as a rich man eats a forest for profit and a
>   field for vanity, so you came west and raped
> The continent and brushed its people to death.
>   Without need, the weak skirmishing hunters, and
>   without mercy.

In poems like "Carmel Point," he expressed his distaste for
the infectious uniformity of a culture that destroyed the wild
beauty of America, "this beautiful place defaced with a crop
of suburban houses." He repeatedly scorned urban, middle-
class standards of circumscribed pleasure, manicured comfort, and bee-hive materialism and advocated a return to
nature and the simple life:

> But for my children, I would have them keep their
>   distance from the thickening center; corruption
> Never has been compulsory, when the cities lie at the
>   monster's feet there are left the mountains.
>   ["Shine, Perishing Republic"]

Rather than conquer nature, man, Jeffers felt, should labor in
harmony with it; in that way man, too, has an intrinsic
beauty and worth:

> . . . all the arts lose virtue
> Against the essential reality

> Of creatures going about their business among the
>   equally
> Earnest elements of nature.

> ["Boats in a Fog"]

It was Jeffers who, in poems like "Be Angry at the Sun,"
struck out against the establishment, at a time when such a
stance was hardly in fashion:

> That public men publish falsehoods
> Is nothing new. That America must accept
> Like the historical republics corruption and empire
> Has been known for years.

Like many of today's youth, he distrusted science, feeling
that man

> . . . taken up
> Like a maniac with self-love and inward conflicts
>   cannot manage his hybrids.

> ["Science"]

The new breed of scientist-soldiers were, for Jeffers,

> Obedient, intelligent, trained technicians like trained
>   seals, tell them to do something
> And they can do it. But never ask them their reasons,
> For they know nothing.

> ["To Kill in War is Not Murder"]

Intellect, itself, was suspect and Jeffers, again a precursor of
many of our present concerns, recommended, as a personal
cure from an overindulgence in abstractions, a return to
physical reality:

> A little too abstract, a little too wise,
> It is time for us to kiss the earth again,
>
>   . . . .
> I will touch things and things and no more thoughts.
> > ["Return"]

Finally, as has already been mentioned, Jeffers consistently expressed his repugnance for war. He saw Americans

> . . . fooled by ambitious men and a froth of sentiment,
>   waste themselves on three wars.
> None was required, all futile, all grandly victorious.
>   A fourth is forming.
> > ["The World's Wonders"]

It is uncanny how our worst fears are often expressed in a Jeffers poem. But Jeffers was far more than a prophet of disaster; he offered a possible and acceptable philosophy, as well. In an age when solutions to humanity's ailments seem increasingly less possible, his proposal to continue the futile fight but to disengage the inner soul from what ultimately remains unimportant, is a sane alternative to fanatic involvement. In discussing his philosophical attitude of Inhumanism, in the preface to *The Double Axe*, Jeffers offers "a reasonable detachment as a rule of conduct, instead of love, hate and envy. It neutralizes fanaticism and wild hopes; but it provides magnificence for the religious instinct, and satisfies our need to admire greatness and rejoice in beauty." And in an age of violence, Jeffers' serene objectivity is a beacon of peace. His answer is to know that,

> When open violence appears, to avoid it with honor or
>   choose the least ugly faction; these evils are
>   essential.

To keep one's own integrity, be merciful and
    uncorrupted and not wish for evil; and not be
    duped
By dreams of universal justice or happiness. These
    dreams will not be fulfilled.
To know this, and know that however ugly the parts
    appear the whole remains beautiful.

["The Answer"]

Jeffers will find more readers in dark times than in periods of optimism, but he will always, irrespective of the age, be regarded as a unique example of the poet-prophet. I feel, however, that the future will accord him the rank of major poet not so much for his ideas or prophecies, nor for his austere principles, but chiefly for the manner in which he combines a sensuous and passionate expression of the physical world of wild nature—hawk, canyon, stone, and sea—with profound philosophical meditation. When he uses nature merely as an excuse for moralizing, then his poems fail. But when, as in his best short poems, he strikes a balance between thing and idea, between substance and thought, between action and peace, he synthesizes, in a truly memorable fashion, the external and the internal, the transitory and the eternal. He combines, in precarious equilibrium,

. . . . bright power, dark peace;
Fierce consciousness joined with final
Disinterestedness;
Life with calm death.

["Rock and Hawk"]

A

REVIEWS OF BOOKS AND PLAYS BY
ROBINSON JEFFERS

Californians
New York: Macmillan
(1916)

A1. Anonymous. "Californians in Poetry," *Republican* (Springfield, Mass.), January 18, 1917, p. 6.

Enthusiastic early review comparing the nature poetry of California's new, vital poet with Mr. Frost's best works. "Such passionate devotion to rivers and stars and eucalyptus trees as Mr. Jeffers seems to have is certainly impressive."

A2._____. Comment on "He Has Fallen in Love with the Mountains," reprinted from *Californians, Literary Digest*, LIII (December 2, 1916), 1484.

Although not strictly a book review, this constitutes one of the few critical comments on *Californians*. Brief comment introducing reprint of poem. "Mr. Jeffers is rather severe on humanity. . . . But his misanthropy and misogeny are meant to throw into relief his love of nature. This is the most notable poem in his 'Californians.' "

A3._____. "In the Realm of Bookland," *Overland Monthly*, LXVIII (December, 1916), 570.

Enthusiastic comment from a biased California source praising one of its own. Mentions his "rare charm" as "a harbinger of the songs that count in all lands and all people. . . . His bent is toward the descriptive narrative which he handles with fine sense. His work is worth while."

A4._____ . Review of *Californians, New York City Branch Library News*, III (December, 1916), 181.

Volume listed in New Books column. Valuable only because *Californians* received scant notice.

A5. Braithwaite, William Stanley. *Anthology of Magazine Verse for 1916 and Yearbook of American Poetry*. New York: L. J. Gomme, 1916, p. xviii.

Early nationwide recognition in a list of books that "will have readers and admirers for a long time to come." *Californians* is singled out as "a volume by a new poet that has a distinctive value."

A6. Firkins, Oscar W. "Chez Nous," *Nation*, CV (October 11, 1917), 400-401.

First important review by a major critic. Comments on the masculinity and "pungency" of the verse. Notes symbolic value in Jeffers' localism. "His failings are many and grave. He rhymes with a fine boldness and a crisp bravado; his grammar is unconcerned; his construction is bushy; he envelops, smothers, his idea in language, and the lost diety to whom he could be coaxed to erect an altar is the god Terminus. Has Mr. Jeffers the patience and the humility which will loose his evident force from its no less obvious encumbrances? All turns on the answer to that question."

Tamar and Other Poems
New York: Peter G. Boyle
(1924)

A7. Anonymous. "Pacific Headlands," *Time*, V (March 30, 1925), 12.

Early popular recognition. Summarizes plots, Jeffers' biography, and the reviews of Van Doren and Rorty and compares Jeffers to Walt Whitman. " . . . he sings, as did Whitman rather by instinct than by a theory of prosody. . . . He hurls his images or bites them out; he rumbles, casts spells, croons, sooths, claps out thunder, flashes naked lightening, dreams serene or troubled beauty. . . . Jeffers is heard, unmistakably powerful, individual, a true radical poet chanting on his high Pacific headland."

A8._____ . "Praise for Carmel Poet," *Pine Cone* (Carmel, Cal.), March 28, 1925, p. 1.
The *Pine Cone* is always biased in favor of its famous local resident. Describes the praise *Tamar* has received from prominent critics. Quotes Sterling as saying that "without doubt Jeffers proves himself one of the foremost American poets." Carmel is proud to have Jeffers a resident and "is particularly pleased that the inspiration for his poems comes from the natural beauties of Carmel."

A9. Daly, James. "Roots under the Rocks," *Poetry*, XXVI (August, 1925), 278-285.
Early important criticism from a recognized critic. Notes improvement since *Californians*. Praises "genuine passion," "ruggedness of imagery," and "magnificent rhythm." Jeffers is "unsurpassed by any other poet writing in English. . . . There are flaws, of course; lapses into prose . . . occasionally bad images . . . but always he writes as one who has dared to go down into the deep pits of the mind where the imagination's ultimate eyes . . . are blinded into knowledge."

A10. Deutsch, Babette. "Brains and Lyrics," *New Republic*, XLIII (May 27, 1925), 23-24.
One of the important earliest admirers. Compares reading *Tamar* to Keats looking into Chapman's Homer. "There is thinking in these lyrics which lifts them . . . on to the plane of great writing. It is possible not to share the Oriental philosophy expressed in certain of his poems, but it is impossible to have strong poetry without the force of some equal conviction beating like a heart in its body." Admires particularly his "powerful dramatic narrative."

A11. H., D. C. Review of *Tamar and Other Poems, Pine Cone* (Carmel, Cal.), April 18, 1925, p. 7.

Extravagant, trite review from a Carmel librarian. Praises "underlying unity" and "vital truth." "Here is passion, terrible in its intensity, sweeping along out of crystal innocence into a high ecstacy of destruction, until the blackness of sin glows with the white flame of its own purity."

A12. Moore, Virginia. "Two Books," *Voices*, V (November, 1925), 70-72.

Attempt to give a balanced judgment. Mentions extravagance of other reviews. Criticizes weak characterization and lack of subtlety. However, "the smash of 'Tamar' is incontrovertible. That can never be explained away. For Robinson Jeffers has passion; he has brain; his voltage as a poet is so incredibly high that critics do well to wag their ears and marvel!"

A13. Rede, Kenneth. "Seven Books of Verse, Including Volume by May Sinclair," *Sun* (Baltimore, Md.), August 9, 1924, p. 6.

Negative brief review. "It is painfully crude throughout, with scarce a redeeming line, and is most abominably printed, so that it becomes a torture to the eye."

A14. Rorty, James. "In Major Mold," *New York Herald and Tribune Books*, March 1, 1925, pp. 1-2.

First major recognition to appear in an eastern publication. Rorty was an initial admirer. Hails a new poet, unequalled since E. A. Robinson. "The net effect of 'Tamar' is that of a magnificent tour de force. It is enough. Nothing as good of its kind has been written in America."

A15. Rorty, James and Anonymous. "Across the Editor's Desk," *Sunset Magazine*, LIII (October, 1924), 51.

Negative California review within a review. Editors print Rorty's statement that *Tamar* is "a unique accomplishment in English poetry," that though all poems in the volume are not that good, one may hope for "in future volumes a steady enrichment of his already important contribution." The editors consider this a practical joke. The work is "loathsome." They "warn our readers, that if any of them" read the book, "he must not blame us for his discomfort."

A16. Sterling, George. "Rhymes and Reactions," *Overland Monthly*, LXXXIII (November, 1925), 411.

First enthusiastic review from Jeffers' discoverer. "The strongest and most dreadful poem that I have ever read or heard of, a mingling of such terror and beauty that for a symbol of it I am reminded of great serpents coiled around high and translucent jars of poison, gleaming with a thousand hues of witch-fire. . . . its huge rhythms are those of the very ocean." Warns those who "shrink from the hidden horrors of life," to avoid this poem.

A17. Van Doren, Mark. "First Glance," *Nation*, CXX (March 11, 1925), 268.

One of the important earliest admirers. Condemns New York critics for having ignored the book, and American publishing for having made it necessary for Jeffers to publish it at his own expense. "Few volumes of any sort have struck me with such force as this one has; few are as rich with the beauty and strength which belongs to genius alone. With Mr. Jeffers, as with other major poets, humanity breaks into fire."

Roan Stallion, Tamar and Other Poems
New York: Boni and Liveright
(1925)

A18. Anonymous. "Book News," *Brith Sholom News*, II (January, 1926), 12.

Notice of Jeffers in a Yiddish-English publication indicates the extent of his fame. Brief discussion of original publication of *Tamar* and of the present edition. Jeffers' genius "is very closely akin to Walt Whitman's. The publishers feel that it is by far the most important volume of verse of the year."

A19._____. "Book Notes," *University of Chicago English Journal*, XV (January, 1926), 86.

Brief mention, complete: "Terrible imaginings conveyed in hard bright images and deliberate resistless rhythms that transfix and hold. Not for babes of any degree. It may be hoped, however, that some of the 'Other Poems' will at some time be issued in a separate edition."

A20_____. "Jeffers' Poetry Vivid and Bold, Has Great Power," *Tennessean* (Nashville), December 27, 1925, unnumbered Literary Page.

Jeffers reaches grass roots America. Although he may not be our best poet, "he is certainly the most daring and astonishing." "Roan Stallion" is "powerfully done" and Jeffers' "literary power is undoubtedly great. He should not, however, be read by people with weak stomachs or cloudy minds."

A21._____. "New Books Received," *Argonaut*, XCVIII (February 27, 1926), 9.

Brief initial reception. See A55 for complete *Argonaut* review. "The splendid, virile qualities of Jeffers, who blends Hellenic sensuousness with the homelier note of Walt Whitman, lifts him high above most of his poet contemporaries."

A22._____. "Our Thinking Work," *Chicago Schools Journal*, IX (April, 1927), 317-318.

Publication for school teachers. Mentions Jeffers' pantheism and compares him to Matthew Arnold. "His lines have the rhythm and surge of the wind and of the sea," and they have "sustained excellence."

A23._____. "Publication of Poems by Jeffers Creates Strong Demand for More," *Telegram* (Salt Lake City, Utah), November 29, 1925, magazine section, p. 1.

Brief biographical sketch by Jeffers. *Roan Stallion* is compared to the best of Whitman and the Greeks. "The emergence of Robinson Jeffers . . . is the outstanding literary event of years."

A24._____. Review of *Roan Stallion, Tamar and Other Poems, Bulletin* (San Francisco), November 28, 1925, feature section, p. 10.

Trivial, brief mention in a local newspaper. "Jeffers runs to length, but is never lacking in interest. . . . Some of the shorter numbers are pure poetry."

A25._____. Review of *Roan Stallion, Tamar and Other Poems, Transcript* (Boston), January 13, 1926.

Brief, tentative review. Jeffers' style is more prosaic than poetical. "With the exception of a few lines which achieve a grandeur of expression and a remarkable power to portray character, we may say that here is an extreme realist whose forthcoming work should be awaited with anticipation."

A26._____. Review of *Roan Stallion, Tamar and Other Poems, World-Herald* (Omaha, Neb.), January 24, 1926, magazine section, p. 6.

Favorable mid-West opinion. Portrait. Praises elemental quality, strong, moving rhythm. "The admirer of dramatic effect, who likes novels in verse, the form giving them a greater freedom than can be derived from prose, will find in them much to admire—much that cannot easily be forgotten."

A27._____. Review of *Roan Stallion, Tamar and Other Poems, Booklist*, XXII (February, 1926), 201.

Complete entry: "This is beautiful poetry, universal, often horrible, filled with passion, incest, tragedy."

A28._____ . Review of *Roan Stallion, Tamar and Other Poems, Dial,* LXXX (February, 1926), 161.

Stresses that Jeffers' is a new, primitive voice. Traces his roots to Whitman, though Jeffers "achieves a more intense objectivity."

A29._____ . "Robinson Jeffers in the Fury of His Passage," *Citizen* (Brooklyn, N. Y.), December 27, 1925, book section, p. 7.

Trivial critical comment. Extensive quotation from "Roan Stallion," preceded by: "By critical acclaim the most important contribution to American poetry of the year."

A30. Auslander, Joseph. "Dark Fire, Black Music," *Measure,* LXI (March, 1926), 14-15.

Unimpassioned discussion by a major eastern critic and anthologist. Praises vitality, but praises with qualifications. Affinity to Whitman, Greeks, California and especially himself. "While often weak and occasionally maudlin in episode and episodic strategy, his galloping lines possess momentum sufficient to sweep the reader over the shambles of the final stretch."

A31._____ . Review of *Roan Stallion, Tamar and Other Poems, World* (New York), January 3, 1926, p. 6m.

Important recognition. "Roan Stallion" has "plunging power" but Jeffers' catastrophes are "unnecessary." The "hideous wholesale destruction" in "Tamar" is pointless. Nevertheless, there is "splendor and speed here. . . . Jeffers packs a wallop . . . his yell has in it something of the centaur's huge and most irreverent flight."

A32. B[rickell], H[erschel]. "Books on Our Table," *Post* (New York), December 8, 1925, p. 14.

Recommendation of "Tamar" as an initiation to Jeffers. "Tamar" grows "more and more soul-harrowing, until its climax is like the mighty *fortissimo* passage of a great symphony." It has "something of the centaur's huge and most irreverent flight."

A33._____. "Books on Our Table," *Post* (New York), January 11, 1926, p. 14.

Continuation of December 8, 1925 review, above. Praises the beauty and narrative power of his verse, while noting the unpleasantness of his themes. "There is the germ of something big, something great. . . . "

A34. Benét, William Rose. "From Pieria to Mediocria," *Outlook*, CXLI (December 30, 1925), 674-678.

Jeffers is included among several new poets in this first review by an important admirer and critic. Finds that Jeffers tries to shock in an age when this is difficult. Notes Greek affinities. "Tamar" is "one of the most congested pieces of writing we have toiled through in moons, but we find that, in spite of all its overplus of horrors . . . its story (which requires a strong stomach) has left a powerful impression. It is the same with 'Roan Stallion.' "

A35. Brewer, William A., Jr. "Well, It's Spring Now, and So Here Come the Spring Poets," *Chronicle* (San Francisco), March 14, 1926, p. 4d.

Favorable review from a major West Coast newspaper. Not popular, tuneful poetry, "but the cognoscenti are pretty sure to call it significant." Notes Jeffers' juxtaposition of natural beauty and human sordidness in his treatment of forbidden relationships. "Only their rare handling makes them acceptable."

A36. Dell, Floyd. "Shell-Shock and the Poetry of Robinson Jeffers," *Modern Quarterly*, III (September-December, 1926), 268-273.

Lengthy early treatment of Jeffers' philosophic pessimism by one of the founders of *Masses*. Extensive summary and quotation. Notes dramatic and narrative power. However, "the current enthusiasm for these poems would seem to indicate that the spiritual wound inflicted upon the American intelligentsia by the World War has been even greater than we have been willing to recognize."

A37. Deutsch, Babette. "Bitterness and Beauty," *New Republic*, XLV (February 10, 1926), 338-339.

An original admirer and fellow poet again offers lavish praise. "Jeffers ranks with the foremost American poets not only of his generation, but of all the generations that preceded him. Of the future, no one can speak." Compares him to Whitman in form, timelessness, power, but finds him free of Whitman's "easy sentimentality."

A38. Eldridge, Paul. "Literary Shots and Snapshots," *American Monthly*, XVII (February, 1926), 373.
  Freudian criticism and comparison with Whitman. The language is "a curious mixture of prose and verse, with measured but irregular beats. . . . In spite of the freedom of this form, Jeffers is often turgid to the point of unintelligibility. Here and there, however, there are lines of terrible liveliness, sparks from the very anvil of genius."

A39. Farrar, John. "A Furious Poet from Pittsburgh," *Bookman*, LXII (January, 1926), 604.
  Important recognition. "Amazing powers of expression, . . . great strength and beauty . . . fertile if somewhat febrile imagination." Finds "Roan Stallion" unforgettable although it deals with thoroughly unpleasant subject matter.

A40. Ford, Lillian C. "New Major Poet Emerges," *Times* (Los Angeles), April 11, 1926, section 3, p. 34.
  Recognition in a leading West Coast newspaper. Reviews plots, themes. Short biography of "a major poet and one of the greatest America has yet produced. . . . In his passion and his intensity, in the daring sweep of his lines, Jeffers reminds me of Christopher Marlowe. . . . "

A41. Hutchison, Percy A. "An Elder Poet and a Young One Greet the New Year," *New York Times Book Review*, January 3, 1926, pp. 14, 24.
  First recognition by a major, consistently friendly critic. Emphasizes new freedom in Jeffers' use of material and themes. Jeffers is a mad genius comparable to the Greeks. "To us it seems that there are in this

book pages, many, many pages, which are equaled only by the very great."

A42. Lehman, B. H. Review of *Roan Stallion, Tamar and Other Poems, California Monthly*, II (September, 1926) 37.

Appreciation by a University of California English professor. Jeffers is a "poet bearing the indubitable promise of greatness." "Woodrow Wilson" is a great elegy. His poetry has rhythms and cadences "hewn out of coast range granite."

A43. Leitch, Mary Sinton. "Books and Letters," *Virginian-Pilot* (Norfolk, Va.), March 3, 1926, p. 6.

Emphatic condemnation of Jeffers' "salaciousness." "Tamar" is "utterly to be condemned," because of "a riot of lust," and "Roan Stallion" is "marred by distortions that have no place in poetry, diseased conditions. . . . " However, "when he frees himself from clogging impurities he breaks into a lyricism so beautiful, so exquisite, that the lover of pure poetry must feel his pulses leap to the enchantment of such unaccustomed music."

A44. Marone, F. B. "The Freedom of Purity," *Wasp* (San Francisco), March 27, 1926, p. 16.

Trivial. Jeffers is an encouraging light on poetry's horizon. Many readers "will abhor, shudder at this dose. It is a strong mind's potion, the head must be cool . . . instincts of truth awake and in command."

A45. Mencken, Henry Louis. "Books of Verse," *American Mercury*, VIII (June, 1926), 251-254.

Brief notice in a discussion of recent verse by an important essayist and critic. "First-hand air. . . . There is a fine and stately dignity in him, and the rare virtue of simplicity. . . . Now that success has come to him at last, it seems to be solid and promises to be enduring."

A46. Monroe, Harriet. "Pomp and Power," *Poetry*, XXVIII (June, 1926), 160-164.

Editor and founder of leading poetry journal condemns Jeffers' revolting material and lack of taste and restraint. His tales of "abnormal passion" create the danger "that such a preoccupation may make his majestic art an anachronism, without vitality enough to endure."

A47. R., L. and F. deW. P. "A Mooted California Poet," *Harvard Crimson Bookshelf*, II (February 13, 1926), 4.

Jeffers is consistently damned in Harvard publications. This is the first. He writes prose, not poetry, and his material is sensual and gross. "Mr. Jeffers has only a very tenuous claim to the name of poet."

A48. Redman, Ben Ray. "Speaking of Books," *Spur*, XXXVII (June 1, 1926), 76.

Questions frankness of work in a moderately laudatory tone. "One thing is certain: whatever he may be, Mr. Jeffers is not a 'minor' poet, his qualities and defects all have at least a hint of grandeur in them. And there is in his writing an emotional intensity that can be matched by few living poets."

A49. Seaver, Edwin. "Robinson Jeffers' Poetry," *Saturday Review of Literature*, II (January 16, 1926), 492.

Important review by founder of the Left Wing *New Masses* praising Jeffers' dramatic value and poetic imagination. "Serener than 'Tamar,' more definite in line and more economical in conception, 'Roan Stallion' is a magnificent achievement."

A50. Shipley, Joseph T. "Blending of Pity and Horror in Work of Firm-Fisted Poet," *Post* (New York), April 17, 1926, p. 4.

Extremely laudatory review comparing Jeffers to Whitman, Swinburne, Browning, and especially the Greeks. "He achieves that union of pity and horror with which the Greeks purged their souls and established the equilibrium of full, harmonious stimulation."

A51. Snow, Wilbert. "American Poetry—Vintage of 1925," *Book Notes*, VI (February-March, 1926), 91-92.

In a review of the year's poetry, Jeffers' imaginative daring is praised, although one wonders if the philosophy isn't false and the grip only stems from the horrible themes. "Even though this sober second thought dims one's enthusiasm a bit and makes one feel himself in the presence of a biased genius who does not see life as 'steadily and whole' as he should, yet, the first reading of the book is an experience of a lifetime."

A52. Swan, Addie May. "Strange Beauty in This Poetry," *Times* (Davenport, Iowa), January 23, 1926, p. 3.
A minor example of midwestern opinion. Condemns occasional unnecessary vulgarity although praise is accorded "that isolation of attitude that is wisdom without bitterness; indifference without conceit."

A53. Trembly, Clifford. "A Virile Poet," *News* (Saint Paul, Minn.), November 29, 1925, section 2, p. 4.
Minor review discussing primarily Jeffers' lack of balance. Nevertheless, "Mr. Jeffers is a poet. No mean title to bestow upon a man."

A54. V., R. L. "Poetic Pictures of California," *Post-Standard* (Syracuse, N. Y.), November 30, 1925, p. 4.
Minor review. Unusual in that Jeffers' characterization, especially in "Roan Stallion," is praised. That poem is "unusually effective in its development of the character of a woman who wanted something ... finer than the life to which she was forced by circumstances."

A55. Valentine, Uffington. "The Poetry of Robinson Jeffers," *Argonaut*, XCVIII (March 13, 1926), 8.
Mixed review in a leading California literary publication. Jeffers is representative of all perversities of modern verse. Resembles decadent English dramatists (Ford, Middleton and Webster), though "it is doubtful if Ford's worst excesses outdo 'Tamar' in sheer horror and wild lubricity. ... Yet Mr. Jeffers can be simple, and even sublimely so at times; and when one is captured, as one so easily is, by these infinite unaffectedly expressed beauties of his, it is all the harder to forgive the side of his art that desecrates the white flame."

A56. Van Doren, Mark. "First Glance," *Nation*, CXXI (November 25, 1925), 599.

Important review by an early admirer and literary editor who remained faithful. Highly favorable. This volume "not only contains those poems which given an opportunity to strike the critical world, struck them so hard; it marches forth with several important new poems, one of which I am sure is a masterpiece."

A57. Zorn, Gremin. "Books of the Moment Seen Critically by Prospectors in the Literary Mountains," *Eagle* (Brooklyn, N. Y.), January 16, 1926, p. 5.

Plot summary and quotations in a discussion of a new literary happening. "There is a terrible, daring beauty in 'Tamar' that cannot be found in any other American poet. The genius of Robinson Jeffers is evident in every image he uses."

Roan Stallion, Tamar and Other Poems
English Edition
London: Hogarth Press
(1928)

A58. Anonymous. "Hogarth Living Poets," *Times Literary Supplement*, March 21, 1929, p. 239.

Early Freudian criticism. Jeffers seems to describe the unconscious mind. "But the labour of following through a long poem this intricate symbolism" is difficult. "Mr. Jeffers is often impressive, if a little vague; and it is certainly an interesting experiment to go directly, and apparently quite consciously, to the unconscious for the material of poetry."

A59._____. "Walt Whitman Finds Hellas," *New Statesman*, XXXII (February 9, 1929), 572, 574.

Recognition of Jeffers' dramatic qualities. He is a distinguished poet when "dealing with a subject on the heroic scale." However, "his language is too often sadly unimaginative, and far below his conception. . . . 'Tamar' is too long." The best poem in the volume is "Tower Beyond Tragedy," which contains "writing as vigorous and unashamed as Whitman's, but more controlled, less vain, and full of subject."

A60. Flint, Frank Stewart. "Recent Verse," *Criterion*, VIII (December, 1928), 345-346.
Extremely important early recognition by imagist poet and critic. Praises power, language, imagination. Calls Jeffers a tragic poet. "The . . . poems gripped me from the start, and, at times, I had to read them aloud. Their imagery, their movement, their pathos gave me intense pleasure."

A61. Hillyer, Robert. "Five American Poets," *New Adelphi*, II (March-May, 1929), 280-282.
Early intelligent condemnation of the morbidity of the themes. Hillyer later became a vocal opponent of the New Critics. "His skill is professional; his subjects are revolting."

A62. O., Y. [A. E.]. Review of *Roan Stallion, Tamar and Other Poems, Irish Statesman*, XI (November 24, 1928), 234, 236.
Major Irish poet notes Jeffers' primitive, barbaric qualities. Compares vitality to Whitman's.

The Women at Point Sur
New York: Boni and Liveright
(1927)

A63. Anonymous. "Again, Jeffers," *Time*, X (August 1, 1927), 31-32.
Time popularizes Jeffers, summarizes plot using such phrases as

"white heat" and "terrific convulsions." "Homer and Sophocles have not been held too lofty comparisons for him. . . . yet he remains distinctly a product of this continent."

A64._____. "Book Notices," *University of Chicago English Journal*, XVI (November, 1927), 749.

Listing in an important journal. Complete review: "A tremendous and terrible novel in verse bitten through in every fiber with the glowing intensity of *Oedipus*. It is a fitting sequel to *Tamar*, imbedding in granite verse the madness of Preacher Barclay in his rebellion against the meaningless sanity of ordered life, of conventional religion, the family, and social order."

A65._____. "Eliot and Crane Give Poetry Grand Style," *News* (Miami, Fla.), August 7, 1927, p. 3.

Minor southern review of Jeffers included with discussions of Eliot and Hart Crane. Jeffers is compared unfavorably to both. "The man overwhelms you with feelings part ecstasy and part nausea. He is either a fool or a great poet and maybe both."

A66._____. "Jeffers in Tragic Song," *Mercury* (San Jose, Cal.), August 21, 1927, p. 8.

Minor review by local newspaper. "His latest work . . . reveals his poetic genius to a much greater degree," than *Roan Stallion and Tamar*. This "is a tremendous narrative as long as a novel and with a more powerful background than any book of prose could contain."

A67._____. "Jeffers's New Book," *Argonaut*, CII (July 23, 1927), 9.

Emphasizes tragic nature of the work. This is his "best, and as his best it must rank among the few great poems in American literature. . . . Jeffers is one of the very few American poets of the early twentieth century that the twenty-first will read."

A68._____. "A New Chant of Despair by Robinson Jeffers," *Sun* (New York), July 1, 1927, p. 10.

Quotes Edgar Lee Masters that it "is the greatest poem produced in America in many years," with "the intensity of Sophocles."

A69._____. "Our Bookshelf," *Step Ladder*, XIII (November, 1927), 273.

Brief notice. "The literature of putrescence continues to be enriched at the competent hands of Mr. Robinson Jeffers." Hardy's characters often do ignoble deeds but are human and sympathetic. Of Jeffers' "merry crew," the reader doesn't "pity them," but desires merely "to horsewhip them."

A70._____. Review of *The Women at Point Sur, Observer* (Charlotte, N. C.), August 28, 1927, p. 5.

Slight southern review. "Beneath the finely told story . . . there is that clay of genius which makes Robinson Jeffers one of the finest poets of American civilization."

A71._____. Review of *The Women at Point Sur, Express* (Easton, Pa.), September 3, 1927, p. 6.

Minor favorable review. It is a poem of "singular horror, but of horror mixed with a certain, hard, grim beauty." It is "a relief from the present run of pretty-pretty poetry."

A72._____. Review of *The Women at Point Sur, Independent*, CXIX (October 15, 1927), 389.

Mixed review. Emphasizes sick, insane quality. Action is so exaggerated it approaches humor. "Flashes of real poetry, of insight, of strong, masculine phrase. But I find, too, so complete, so utter an absence of humor, so preposterous an exaggeration of physical functions, that I am debarred from serious appreciation."

A73. _____. Review of *The Women at Point Sur, Star* (Minneapolis, Minn.), October 15, 1927, news section, p. 14.

Favorable minor midwestern review discussing heroic qualities. "The bold epic phrasing of Mr. Jeffers' poetry—its awesome beauty and compelling psychology—reach their most effective fusing in this impressive narrative poem."

A74. _____. "A Rising American Poet," *World-Herald* (Omaha, Neb.), July 24, 1927, magazine section, p. 6.
    Favorable minor review. An example of grass roots reception; questions themes. "A powerful, disagreeable poem. Almost novel length, and like a novel in its study of character development and character decay."

A75. _____. "Robinson Jeffers Has a New Poem," *Times* (Davenport, Iowa), July 9, 1927, p. 3.
    Favorable minor review. Compares Jeffers to O'Neill. Reviews plot. "Not a pretty tale this, nor handled prettily by the poet whose verse meets the dark and cruel demands of the narrative. . . . "

A76. _____. "Violent Verse of Robinson Jeffers," *Republican* (Springfield, Mass.), February 5, 1928, p. 7f.
    Adverse review from a leading Massachusetts newspaper. This volume contains "some sonorous lines, but rarely are his images impressive, and the narrative, apart from its daring, does not excite the interest."

A77. Beck, Clyde. "The American Lyre: Some Varied Strains," *News* (Detroit, Mich.), August 21, 1927, home section, p. 16.
    Minor mixed review. "Mr. Jeffers' genius, if genius it can be called, is that of chaos. . . . and his infernal imagery at times reads like the very Apocalypse of evil. At other times he is as opaque as Browning at his worst, or Blake at his most mystical.

A78. Brewer, William A. Jr. Review of *The Women at Point Sur*, *Chronicle* (San Francisco), December 4, 1927, p. 4d.
    Negative, minor review. *Women at Point Sur* does not come up to the standard set by his last year's volume. Excess horror overwhelms poetry, drama. "Perhaps Mr. Jeffers will strike a balance between the

three elements of his work which will give him permanently the place for which his undeniable talents have marked him."

A79. Crawford, Nelson Antrim. "Robinson Jeffers, Poet in the Sombre Cloth of Tragedy," *Sun* (Baltimore, Md.), September 17, 1927, p. 6.
    Despite Jeffers' obvious misanthropy, "one cannot but feel that 'The Women at Point Sur' is a great poem. It has the swift, undeviating inevitability of Greek tragedy plus rational exposition. . . . The characters are drawn with notable power and precision and with no trace of sentimentality."

A80. Davidson, Gustav. "A Mount Carmel Saga," *Forum*, LXXVIII (December, 1927), 956-957.
    Favorable review. This volume is "horror redeemed by beauty." Jeffers is neither as "tragic as Sophocles" nor so thoroughly as penetrating as Whitman. Nevertheless, he is as intuitive as Sophocles, and he has "keener grasp of the power and logic of words" than Whitman.

A81. Davis, H. L. "Jeffers Denies Us Twice," *Poetry*, XXXI (February, 1928), 274-279.
    A fellow poet offers a lucid judgment. The story lacks humanity, sympathy, pity, and love. Yet, "these years have never seen better than this, with its depth and beauty and barbaric splendor. . . . Every line of every page is a triumph. . . . If this be any less perfect than the choral poetry of Euripides, I can not see how."

A82. Deutsch, Babette. "Or What's a Heaven For?" *New Republic*, LI (August 17, 1927), 341.
    An important early admirer begins to cool. Rich subject, yet, "for all the lightning-like visions which streak certain passages with a glory, the poem leaves one with the feeling of having witnessed a Pyrrhic victory. Its profundities are too often obscure. Its drama is moiled with an irrelevant sordidness. There are too many persons, too many conflicts, that seem to have no organic relation to the whole. It is not sufficiently stripped and bare."

A83. Douglas, George. "Jeffers' Poem," *Bulletin* (San Francisco), August 27, 1927, section 1, p. 5.

Not completely favorable comment. None may deny that Jeffers is a poet, "a mad poet, if you will, but there is some madness in nearly all great poets." This is "a big, a powerful but an unlovely poem."

A84. Eisenberg, Emanuel. "A Not So Celestial Choir," *Bookman*, LXVI (September, 1927), 102.

Important critic finds "a misanthropy equalled only by Jonathan Swift." Nevertheless, it is an "electrifying poem and an unforgettable story, surging with vigor and heat and pain: but it is only for an eclectic minority of persons."

A85. Gessler, Clifford. "Robinson Jeffers A Giant Husky and Brawling," *Star-Bulletin* (Honolulu, Hawaii), October 15, 1927, p. 12.

Minor favorable criticism. Although there are bad lapses into prose-like lines, Jeffers "rises above these imperfections." He is one "who speaks with power."

A86. Gorman, Herbert. "Jeffers, Metaphysician," *Saturday Review of Literature*, IV (September 17, 1927), 115.

Mixed review in a major publication. "There is a core of intensive and exhalted poetry, but it is semi-smothered by a number of wilful urges, sexual obsessions, fogginess of utterance, undisciplined ardors, prophetic predilections." This book answers the question of whether Jeffers is a great poet. "He is not . . . he is an original poet and often the creator of highly-moving passages."

A87. H., F. C. "Passionate Music," *Columbia Varsity*, IX (October, 1927), 35-36.

Favorable review. Compares this poem to Greeks. The themes may be too strong for the older generation, but they express the ideas of the young. He "that comes reverently shall hear the singing of the Morning Stars that before was only given to William Blake in his madness to attend."

A88. Hansen, Harry. "The Dark Jeffers," *World* (New York), July 19, 1927, p. 11. Reprinted as: "Long Poem by Phenomenon of Nature," *Journal Post* (Kansas City, Mo.), August 7, 1927, magazine section, p. 11.

Important critic writes an unfavorable review criticizing Jeffers' lack of taste and restraint. Jeffers "writes much that is unsavory and uncalled for."

A89. Hartsock, Ernest. "Pastures on Parnassus," *Bozart*, I (September-October, 1927), 14.

Review in a Georgia literary journal. "An exciting and brilliant poem, climaxing in several catastrophes of terse and terrible realism. . . . In its unusual power of sustaining interest, and in its powerful descriptive rapidity, this is a significant book of poetry."

A90._____.. "The Women at Point Sur," *Journal* (Atlanta, Ga.), July 24, 1927, magazine section, p. 24.

Minor. This "is the longest and possibly the most powerful work yet offered by this solitary genius. . . . No poet except Edgar Lee Masters has used the American scene with such devastating results."

A91. Herzberg, M. J. "Jeffers Tells an Unpleasant Narrative of Crime in a Poem," *Evening News* (Newark, N. J.), September 3, 1927, p. 3x.

Generally unfavorable review. Sometimes vivid, but usually unpleasant. "He gives the reader in 'The Women at Point Sur' an analysis of several psychopathic temperaments in language so violent and raw as to destroy all artistic value." Good descriptions of the California coast.

A92. Hutchison, Percy. "Robinson Jeffers Attempts a New Beauty," *New York Times Book Review*, September 11, 1927, p. 5.

Former admirer find this not equal to earlier works. Cites Jeffers' lack of restraint and his honesty. "One carries away from a reading of Jeffers at least this; that one has been present at a birth-bed, and though one was not sure of the acceptableness of the offspring, and cringed in witnessing the throes, something not wholly unmomentous came into the world."

A93. Jones, Howard Mumford. "Dull Naughtiness," *News* (Chicago), August 3, 1927, p. 14. Reprinted in: *State Journal* (Columbus, Ohio), August 7, 1927, magazine section, p. 11.

Generally unfavorable review by important critic. "There are extraordinary passages," but in general an excess of sex, insanity and perversity. "My curiosity once satisfied, the book simply became absurd."

A94. Minot, John Clair. "Mid-Week Book Notes," *Herald* (Boston), July 13, 1927, p. 14.

Brief, minor review. This work "shows that he has been doing much thinking as he looked out over the Pacific. He tells his story in blank verse that is alive all the way."

A95. Morrow, Walter A. "Jeffers's Sardonic Smile at Futility of Life is Fanned into Mockery," *Daily Oklahoman* (Oklahoma City, Okla.), October 9, 1927, p. 15c.

Grass roots reaction. "It is poetry of a class. The intelligensia will read it and welcome it. The masses will not care for it. Perhaps he has looked into the future and psycho-analyzed the dawn. It is more probable that he has not."

A96. Neihardt, John G. "Hysterics," *Post Dispatch* (St. Louis, Mo.), July 9, 1927, p. 5.

Extremely negative review. The tale is "jumbled and pointless," and the manner is "overwrought." Only "devastating laughter" should be directed at this "incredible caterwauling."

A97. P., M. L. "Happily Not Many Will Read," *Post Standard* (Syracuse, N. Y.), July 13, 1927, p. 4.

Magnificent workmanship and imagery. Similar to the Greek dramatists and to Byron. "The reader can see before him all that the poet would describe—and he is fortunate if what he sees does not haunt him in his dreams."

A98. Payne, George M. "Intimate Views of Some Outstanding Books of the Day," *Times-Star* (Cincinnati, Ohio), October 15, 1927, magazine section, p. 26.

Brief minor review. "There is much in Jeffers's poem that is incomprehensible, but there is much that is wildly dramatic and beautiful, much that is tremendously stirring."

A99. Ramsay, Joan. Review of *The Women at Point Sur, Overland Monthly*, LXXXV (November, 1927), 340-341.

Mixed review in important western journal. Another voicing of Jeffers' "bitter credo." Praises descriptive power. However, "Jeffers uses his extraordinarily vivid expression only more completely to bring out the hideousness of his subject. . . . leaves one feeling exhausted, deadened, oppressed. If this is all that humanity is, why write at all, since it is only by humanity that it will be read."

A100. Rorty, James. "Satirist or Metaphysician?" *New Masses*, III (September, 1927), 26.

Mild disfavor from an early admirer. Bemoans metaphysical qualities. Characters are "dry puppets kept dancing by the power of an extraordinarily intense style," and "Jeffers' physical and mental isolation" is "unfortunate and dangerous;" yet it is "written, if anything, more magnificently than his other books. Jeffers is sane, and a poet whom it is possible to call great."

A101. Small, Harold A. "Between the Lines," *Chronicle* (San Francisco, Cal.), July 3, 1927, p. 10d.

Questions about Jeffers' themes. "The strained liftings of a giant under a bog trying to lift it up to the sky."

A102. Taggard, Genevieve. "The Deliberate Annihilation," *New York Herald Tribune Books*, August 28, 1927, p. 3.

Doubts from a fellow poet. An artist should fulfill his reader. However, "Jeffers has more strongly the desire to withhold fulfillment from his reader, to give him pain only, a desire that comes from the same source that compels his preoccupation with cruelty."

A103. Van Doren, Mark. "First Glance", *Nation,* CXXV (July 27, 1927), 88.

An early admirer questions Jeffers' themes. "I have read it with thrills of pleasure at its power and beauty, and I shall read everything else Mr. Jeffers writes. But I may be brought to wonder whether there is need of his trying further in this direction. He seems to be knocking his head to pieces against the night."

A104. Wilson, James Southall. "American Poetry—1927," *Virginia Quarterly Review*, III (October, 1927), 611-614.

Mixed review in an important journal. Jeffers "tells a story as complicated as any novel; a story that, for a reader with a stomach strong enough, has sustained interest and vigor. No one can question the mastery of sweeping lines, the strength of the phrasing, of the author of the poem. But to my sense it reeks with the stench of a decadent art."

A105. Yust, Walter. "Robinson Jeffers's Rich but Violent Narrative Poem," *Public Ledger* (Philadelphia, Pa.), July 2, 1927, p. 8.

Mixed criticism. The reader, like the victim of a clubbing, "realizes that it was at least forceful and arresting, though he may come to wonder whether it is his own idea of a poem or not, and question the club-man's good taste, and the quality of his artistic restraint, poet though he may be."

Cawdor and Other Poems
New York: Liveright
(1928)

A106. Anonymous. "The Poet of Terror," *World-Herald* (Omaha, Neb.), December 23, 1928, magazine section, p. 11.

Minor review. "There is a terrible power in the poetry of Robinson Jeffers, the poet to whom life is tragedy, and who sings the song of that tragedy in burning, intense and gigantic verse."

A107._____. "Recommended Books," *Yale Daily News Literary Supplement,* III (May 25, 1929), 3.
Included in list of recommended books.

A108._____. Review of *Cawdor and Other Poems, Argonaut,* CV (January 12, 1929), 12.
Favorable review in California journal. Jeffers deals with the characters "as inevitable victims of overwhelming tragedy. . . . 'Cawdor' is written in the same poetic form as the earlier works—a sweeping form admirably suited to the grandeur of the theme and to Jeffers' noble images."

A109._____. Review of *Cawdor and Other Poems, Union and Republican* (Springfield, Mass.), February 3, 1929, p. 7e.
Mixed reception. "Like 'Women at Point Sur,' 'Cawdor' is another indication that Jeffers works within a very limited sphere."

A110._____. Review of *Cawdor and Other Poems, American Mercury,* XVI (March, 1929), lvi.
Brief mixed review. "There are passages of illuminating beauty, especially in the shorter lyrical sketches, but as a whole the book is not equal to Mr. Jeffers' earlier work."

A111._____. Review of *Cawdor and Other Poems, Booklist,* XXV (March, 1929), 241.
Brief listing. "Reminiscent of Oedipus, yet entirely the personal creation of Jeffers, Cawdor is a powerful, tragic poem. The sixteen sonnets included in the book contain some fine poetry."

A112._____. Review of *Cawdor and Other Poems, Cleveland Open Shelf,* April, 1929, p. 54.

Sees this as the last poem of a trilogy including "Tamar" and "Women at Point Sur." "Written with the fierce power which marks [his] preceding volumes. Surrounded by the ocean, the Sierras and the magnificent redwoods, Jeffers sneers at an ugly little race of men which destroys itself with lust and hate." The shorter poems have "great beauty."

A113._____ . Review of *Cawdor and Other Poems. St. Louis Library Bulletin*, XXVII (May, 1929), 165.
Listing. "Completes a trilogy begun by 'Tamar' and 'The Women at Point Sur.' "

A114._____ . "Robinson Jeffers' Poem," *Transcript* (Boston, Mass.), December 15, 1928, book section, p. 7.
Unfavorable comment. This volume is incoherent and unpleasant. "There is neither beauty nor honesty in a work of this kind. None of the characters has any sincere relation to life. The shorter poems . . . have a distinct merit."

A115. Aiken, Conrad. "Unpacking Hearts with Words." *Bookman*, LXVIII (January, 1929), 576-577.
Mixed review by a fellow poet. "A kind of nightmare novel in a loose prose-verse. . . . for all its monstrosities and absurdities and excessive use of symbolism . . . a very interesting thing. If only Mr. Jeffers can hold himself down a little, be a shade less drastically and humorlessly melodramatic, one feels that he might give us something pretty astonishing. Even so, *Cawdor* is a fine thing, despite its bad lapses."

A116. C., G. H. Review of *Cawdor and Other Poems, Hound and Horn*, II (April-June, 1929), 318.
Harvard continues to condemn. "Jeffers lacks the power of self-criticism, the sensitiveness of emotion, the breath of interests that might have made him a competent prose writer. He has one great gift, keen physical senses, but they are tortured raw . . . general unhealthiness, copious barren phrases, and a deplorably verbose and stringy rhetoric."

A117. Deutsch, Babette. "Brooding Eagle," *New Republic*, LVII (January 16, 1929), 253.

An ardent early enthusiast cools. "There is sufficient evidence that Jeffers has lost none of his immense power. He has merely failed to use it throughout the book as terribly as he can."

A118. Hagemeyer, Dora. "The Eagle Flight in Cawdor," *Carmelite*, I (December 12, 1928), 13.

Minor review in local publication. "Perhaps the most superb piece of writing that Jeffers has ever done is that passage in Cawdor where he tells of the flight of the eagle's spirit to the sun. . . . Jeffers is a great poet."

A119. Hutchison, Percy. "Mr. Robinson Jeffers Brings Hamlet to California," *New York Times Book Review*, December 16, 1928, p. 2.

Unfavorable review by a leading New York critic. "Mr. Jeffers' weakness in completely vitalizing and visualizing the people of his tragedies militates against his work remaining in memory; and will militate against an enduring reputation. . . . There is not the same flaming beauty in the verse which so often illuminated Mr. Jeffers' two preceding tragedies. Is it that the poet has dwelt too long in . . . isolation?"

A120. Lal, Gobind Behari. "Cawdor Adds to Fame of Jeffers," *Examiner* (San Francisco, Cal.), January 27, 1929, p. 10e.

Minor comment by local reviewer. Jeffers "has carried his unique art to higher levels of sublime poetry than perhaps in any of his previous works."

A121. Murphy, Donald R. "Savage; Lovely," *Register* (Des Moines, Iowa), July 21, 1929, p. 8g.

Grass roots comment. " . . . the only American poet of major rank. . . . Jeffers is hard reading. At times his poems are unbearably painful: at times they go off into mystical flights in which the reader loses himself. Yet he seems to me to have extraordinary power. Reading him at his best is like witnessing a great natural force at work."

A122. Singleton, Anne. "A Major Poet," *New York Herald Tribune Books*, December 23, 1928, p. 5.
   Important reviewer finds that "Jeffers is writing the most powerful, the most challenging poetry of this generation."

A123. Van Doren, Mark. "Bits of Earth and Water," *Nation*, CXXVIII (January 9, 1929), 50.
   Early admirer praises. "His way is the way of the great tragic poets, whom Mr. Jeffers has been bold enough to take as his masters. Imitators of Euripides, Sophocles, and Shakespeare are usually ridiculous, but Jeffers is not because he is of their company. . . . "

A124. Zabel, Morton Dauwen. "The Problem of Tragedy," *Poetry*, XXXIII (March, 1929), 336-340.
   Generally favorable review by a leading critic. Jeffers is too obsessed with violence. "Cawdor has passages of magnificence not often found in poetry today." Magnificent nature, technically skillful narrative. Some characters too charged with purpose and passion, but others alive with sympathy. Prefers the shorter poems. "His line may often be blank-verse, but it can swell into a full diapason of great power."

Cawdor and Other Poems
English Edition
London: Hogarth Press
(1929)

A125, Anonymous. "The Battle Continues," *Nation and Athenaeum*, XLVI (November 23, 1929), 292-294.

Praises Jeffers' nature poetry. However, "it is the want of hope and humour (are they one?) that prevents him from being everybody's poet."

A126. Hillyer, Robert. "Nine Books of Verse," *New Adelphi*, III (March-May, 1930), 232-236.
A fellow poet condemns. Jeffers' works are not worth reading. "Yet in full justice, we should read a few . . . shorter poems."

A127. Quennell, Peter. "Recent Verse," *Criterion*, IX (January, 1930), 362.
Leading critic questions Jeffers' poetic skills. In comparing *Roan Stallion* to *Cawdor*, "*Cawdor* is as disturbing and as impassioned; Mr. Jeffers' verse is consistently vigorous and has occasional flashes of real beauty; but its beauties seem to me primarily the beauties which should belong to prose."

Dear Judas and Other Poems
New York: Liveright
(1929)

A128. Anonymous. "Jeffers' New Poems," *World-Herald* (Omaha, Neb.), December 22, 1929, magazine section, p. 11.
Minor comment. "Dear Judas" is a "poetic interpretation" of the biblical story. "The Loving Shepherdess" "is much the more tender of the two. . . . It is a poem of exquisite tragedy."

A129.———. Review of *Dear Judas and Other Poems*, *Star* (Minneapolis, Minn.), December 13, 1929, news section, p. 33.
Minor review. Summarizes plots of long poems. "Dear Judas"

presents "new and probable explanations of the mythical characters and acts of its protagonists."

A130._____. Review of *Dear Judas and Other Poems, Booklist*, XXVI (January, 1930), 151.

Listing. "Fine powerful verse, more easily read than 'The Women at Point Sur.' "

A131._____. Review of *Dear Judas and Other Poems, American Mercury*, XIX (March, 1930), xxvi, xxix.

Brief mention. Of "Dear Judas": "The narrative contains some fine passages, but it is less dramatic than 'The Loving Shepherdess.' . . . The volume concludes with half a dozen lyrical pieces of secondary interest."

A132._____. Review of *Dear Judas and Other Poems, English Journal*, XIX (September, 1930), 593.

Favorable, verbose praise in serious journal. "Colossal, indelible symphonies of a mad Dante are welling out of the massive strength of Point Lobos. To read Robinson Jeffers is to have a demoniacal vision of the chaotic Andes that make up the human spirit. He enters our spiritual crevasses with the easy steel spring of the mountain man and records every gigantic contortion of human bitterness and terror with the calm recording eye of Odysseus."

A133._____. "Tragedians," *Time*, XIV (December 9, 1929), 72.

Favorable review from major non-literary publication. Retells plots of long poems. "He is one of the few living poets who write extended tragedies. Some consider him the most impressive poet the U. S. has ever produced. His verse is long, unrhymed, irregular lines, usually powerful . . . sometimes majestic."

A134. Arvin, Newton. "The Paradox of Jeffers," *New Freeman*, I (May 17, 1930), 230-232.

Unfavorable, but hopeful, comment by prominent critic and biographer. He has not yet written a worthy successor of "Cawdor." Jeffers' poetry is too aloof, lacks affirmation. "But what is to keep Jeffers from writing such a poem?"

A135. Beck, Clyde. "Lofty Beauty of Two Poets," *News* (Detroit, Mich.), December 29, 1929, part 10, p. 6.
A common judgment for this volume. The title poem has, at best, an original point of view. "The Loving Shepherdess," however, "is a thing of restrained beauty which his readers will hardly expect from the poet of storm and terror."

A136. Black, MacKnight. "Robinson Jeffers, for First Time, Treats Theme of Sacrificial Love," *Record* (Philadelphia, Pa.), December 21, 1929, p. 10f.
Mixed comment. There are here no "pages as stirring as in 'Tamar' and 'Roan Stallion.' 'Dear Judas' seems to this writer to be one of the least successful of Mr. Jeffers' poems. But the simplicity, the beauty and the never sentimental sympathy of 'The Loving Shepherdess' make the present volume one which should be read by everyone who is interested in American poetry."

A137. Deutsch, Babette. "Sweet Hemlock," *New York Herald Tribune Books*, January 12, 1930, p. 4.
An early enthusiast offers restrained appreciation. "Those who care for truth and poetry will make this book their own. Those who do not will scarcely have troubled to read this inadequate praise for it."

A138. Dupee, F. W. Reivew of *Dear Judas and Other Poems, Miscellany*, I (March, 1930), 34-36.
Prominent critic finds that neither of the poems "will greatly advance the reputation of the poet." Of "Dear Judas," "the writing is by no means bald, but its texture is comparatively thin. In 'The Loving Shepherdess' ... there is more richness, but ... also long prosaic, almost barren passages." The characters in both are symbolic rather

than real. They begin "mad with disillusionment," thus precluding development. "Jeffers' pessimism is not a belief, it is an obsession."

A139. Eisenberg, Emanuel. "Jeffers Lends Rich Violence to Christ Legend," *Post* (New York), January 4, 1930, p. 65.

"Dear Judas" suffers in part from too much violence. "The Loving Shepherdess" is "a beautiful and moving poem, with that importance which is naturally attached to any of his long poems." Mentions "Birth Dues," as an excellent summary of Jeffers' philosophy.

A140. Hale, William Harlen. "Jeffers Refines His Fury," *Yale Daily News Literary Supplement*, IV (November 21, 1929), 1, 6.

High praise. "There is a vastness, a space-straining stature in this poetry that carries it far beyond most of what we have produced in the last fifty years." Finds qualities deriving from the Bible, the Greeks, Blake, Whitman and Milton.

A141. Howard, Don. "Book Parade," *Telegram* (Salt Lake, Utah), November 24, 1929, magazine section, p. 1.

Minor favorable review. " ... as massive and as untrammeled as his California hills. . . . It carries along with a vigorous swing, as clean and invigorating as the outdoors. . . . It has depth and feeling and power, and above all, drama. It has a quality of unerring psychology."

A142. Hughes, Richard. "But This Is Poetry," *Forum*, LXXXIII (January, 1930), vi, viii, x. Reprinted in: *Carmelite*, III (March 12, 1930), 8.

Favorable comment. "The Loving Shepherdess" is "another tragic and lovely story." "Dear Judas" is not Jeffers' most successful poem. "If his magnificent narratives were written in prose, his place among our foremost novelists would be indisputable, for he has in his writing those qualities of narrative imagination, of passionate drama, and of deep insight into character that go to make the great novelist." Blames Jeffers' lack of a wide audience on the poor taste of the American public.

A143. Humphries, Rolfe. "Poet or Prophet?" *New Republic*, LXI (January 15, 1930), 228-229.

Fellow poet praises Jeffers' power. However, "his weaknesses come from the same source as his strength, and they are almost equally formidable—a laxity of language; a proclivity for talking symbol, not sense; a scant artistic ruthlessness, particularly in knowing what to leave out; a romanticism gone somewhat rank; an inability to project character, or too loose an ability to project himself."

A144. Hutchison, Percy. "Robinson Jeffers Writes Two Passion Plays," *New York Times Book Review*, December 1, 1929, p. 12.

Leading reviewer calls "Dear Judas" amorphous and muddy, although the "surging line" remains strong. "The Loving Shepherdess," is "alone of serious consequence." Adds that "Jeffers, in his own, and often uncouth way, moves to pity and horror as few poets have done since the Greeks."

A145. Kresensky, Raymond. "Beloved Judas," *World Tomorrow*, XIII (February, 1930), 90.

"Dear Judas" confirms Jeffers' genius. Defends the "colloquial tone" of "The Loving Shepherdess." "With his use of poetic line, phrase, metaphor, and description, the poet gives expression to a spiritual understanding of tragedy."

A146.———. "Fire-Burning Cross," *Christian Century*, XLVII (June 11, 1930), 757-758.

Christian critic praises. That the crucifixion should interest Jeffers, this "apostle of negation," indicates the irresistible appeal of the theme.

A147. McWilliams, Cary. Review of *Dear Judas and Other Poems, Los Angeles Saturday Night*, X (January 25, 1930), 16.

Mixed words from California essayist. His poetry is prosy, but he has power. "It seems to me that 'The Coast-Range Christ' and 'The Tower Beyond Tragedy' are great poems when judged by the severest standards. 'Dear Judas' does not, however, maintain the high excellence of these earlier poems."

A148. Morrison, Theodore. "A Critic and Four Poets," *Atlantic Monthly*, CXLV (February, 1930), 24, 26, 28.

Generally favorable criticism in leading publication, although it is noted that excesses occasionally become grotesques. As for "Dear Judas": "What other profane writer has dreamt such a Christ, such a Judas, such a Mary, let alone setting them down in the glory of such poetry?" Of "The Loving Shepherdess": "Terrible and harrowing, but full of poetic beauty and power. Who would have his bowels of compassion wrung, let him read this."

A149. Nicholl, L. T. "New Poetry," *Outlook and Independent*, CLII (November 27, 1929), 509.

Praise and reinterpretation of Jeffers' philosophy. " 'Dear Judas' is flares and shadows and black blood; 'The Loving Shepherdess,' the book's other long poem, is like some low, sweet smelling bush growing everywhere among the rocks and breaking slowly into incredible white flowers; but the roots of the two poems are the same: love of every living creature, terrible consuming pity."

A150. S., W. B. "A New Christ," *Columbia Varsity*, XI (January, 1930), 26.

Discussion of Jeffers' successful break with tradition. Questions reason for putting "Dear Judas" in pseudo-present. "The Loving Shepherdess" is not particularly good "aside from some excellent descriptive writing, and a certain wistful attractiveness toward . . . Clare Walker." All of the shorter poems are good, but especially recommends "Evening Ebb."

A151. Schindler, Pauline G. "Poet on a Tower," *Survey Graphic*, XVII (April, 1930), 46.

High praise, especially for "The Loving Shepherdess" which "surpasses anything that has come from the pen of Jeffers."

A152. Snow, Francis. Review of *Dear Judas and Other Poems, Current History*, XXXI (January, 1930), 632.

Praise for the "entirely new orientation" in this biblical Passion Play.

A153. Swan, Addie May. Review of *Dear Judas and Othe; Poems,* *Times* (Davenport, Iowa), November 30, 1929, p. 3.

Grass roots praise for these departures from the usual Jeffers. The shorter poems, too, "are marked with a quiet and a peace that come oddly from Jeffers."

A154. Untermeyer, Louis. "Uneasy Death," *Saturday Review of Literature*, VI (April 19, 1930), 942.

A consistent admirer finds, in "The Loving Shepherdess," a "new tendency in Jeffers, in that for once he allows himself to be kind to his subject." Jeffers "sounds a major music in his long and short poems."

A155. Van Doren, Mark. "Judas, Savior of Jesus," *Nation*, CXXX (January 1, 1930), 20-21.

Mixed, cool review from an early admirer. " 'Dear Judas' is far from being one of Mr. Jeffers' best poems." Its "success depends after all upon our perception of a theory, and even upon our agreement with this theory; which at once removes the discussion of it from the field of criticism as I see that field. The setting, as might have been expected, is somber and fine, and utterances of the principal persons often reach a high level of rhetoric." Not always poetry. " 'The Loving Shepherdess' contains some of the best work that Mr. Jeffers has ever done. It is continuously pathetic, exciting and beautiful."

A156. Walton, Eda Lou. Review of *Dear Judas and Other Poems,* *Symposium*, I (January, 1930), 135-138.

Mixed comment. " 'Tower Beyond Tragedy' remains his greatest poem and 'Roan Stallion' his best book. And this is true despite the moving power of the second long poem in the book, 'The Loving Shepherdess,' " whose poetic quality is "far higher than that of 'Dear Judas.' His short poems have the failing of being prosaic and thematic, if not actually dogmatic. . . . his best passages are torches across a wilderness of thought."

A157. Winters, Yvor. "Robinson Jeffers," *Poetry*, XXXV (February, 1930), 279-286. Reprinted in: Zabel, M. D., ed. *Literary Opinion in*

America. New York: Harper & Bros., 1937 (Revised 1951), pp. 439-443.

Review of prime importance to Jeffers' critical reputation by violently unfriendly New Critic. "*Dear Judas* is a kind of dilution of *The Women at Point Sur*. . . . Mr. Jeffers' mouthpiece and hero, Jesus, is little short of revolting as he whips reflexively from didactic passion to malice, self-justification, and vengeance. The poem shares the structural principles, or lack of them, of *The Women at Point Sur*; and it has no quotable lines, save possibly the last three, which are, however, heavy with dross." "The Loving Shepherdess" "succeeds in being no more than a very Wordsworthian embodiment of a kind of maudlin humanitarianism."

Dear Judas and Other Poems
English Edition
London: Hogarth Press
(1930)

A158. Anonymous. "Poetry and Life," *Times Literary Supplement*, April 16, 1931, p. 302.

Finds great imaginative force in both poems. In "The Loving Shepherdess," Mr. Jeffers communicates the ecstasy and pathos of life, an intuition, too, of its essentially sacrificial nature beyond and through its transient cruelty and sordidness. . . . " A quality which "makes his poetry notable despite its frequent crudities of form and thought."

A159. ———. "Remembrance of Things Past," *Spectator Literary Supplement*, December 6, 1930, pp. 891, 893.

Impressive but crude. Work traced to "Walt Whitman and Mr. Masefield, in a curious Anglo-American combination. He is certainly a poet to be watched by those who have the time, and also the stomach, for such an alliance."

A160. Flint, F. S. "Verse Chronicle," *Criterion*, XI (January, 1932), 276-281.

Prominent critic offers brief, dubious praise. "Robinson Jeffers stands on a rock looking out over the ocean; and, in the grand manner of the prophets, tells sad stories of the death of Gods, Kings, and Shepherdesses. He is a lonely figure, chanting the ancient heroic virtues and pities in sweeping measures; and he is the only one of these twenty writers," covered in this article, "who has moved me. But that is, perhaps, only my bad taste."

A161. West, Geoffrey. Review of *Dear Judas and Other Poems*, *Adelphi*, New Series I (February, 1931), 432-436.

Moderate praise of the title poem. "The interpretation is not especially new in any particular, though free, but the drama of events is genuinely felt and, in parts, movingly rendered."

Descent to the Dead
Poems Written in Ireland and Great Britain
New York: Random House
(1931)

A162. Anonymous. "A Group of Recent Books," *Times* (Los Angeles, Cal.), February 7, 1932, p. 16.

Brief mention. Emphasis on "elegiac tone" of this volume by "that most disturbing of modern poets."

A163.———. "Jeffers Book of Poems Published," *Tribune* (Oakland, Cal.), December 27, 1931, p. 8s.

Minor local review. "He is the poet of the elemental who reads the stories of the rocks and the winds, an artist without compromise and those who see in his songs the work of gift of genius will exhibit this book as another clinching proof."

A164._____ . Review of *Descent to the Dead, Argonaut*, CX (January 22, 1932), 13.

Brief mention in California journal. "Supreme mastery of the craft and the idealism which must always be the foundation stone of true poetry are alike blended here in fine proportions."

A165. Alberts, Sidney S. "Jeffers' Trip to Ireland," *Contempo*, III (October 25, 1932), 1, 8. Reprinted in: *Carmelite*, V (October 20, 1932), 7.

Review by Jeffers' bibliographer. This volume is characterized by a "preoccupation with one subject, death." However, "in its more restricted field," it is "a volume of permanent worth." Jeffers' poetry "does not thrive in transplanting. For that reason . . . alone, *Descent* falls short of its Western companions. The touch is there, but the clay is different. . . . "

A166. Benét, William Rose. "Round About Parnassus," *Saturday Review of Literature*, VIII (January 16, 1932), 461.

Praise from an early admirer. "A beautiful book. But unlike most beautifully printed books now-a-days the poetry it contains is actually distinguished." Style is loose and prolix. However "he certainly possesses certain qualities of greatness. We have to judge him by higher standards than we apply to most poets. The range of his pondering and the power of his language necessitates that."

A167. Deutsch, Babette. "Comfort in Hell," *New York Herald Tribune Books*, January 31, 1932, p. 6.

Favorable review from one of the initial discoverers. "The mood is sustained throughout, with just sufficient variation to avoid monotony. Neither the form nor the content, if it is possible to divorce these in a work of art at all—will offer surprises to those who have followed this poet's progress. Here is simply a confirmation of his strength. He is one who has looked on life as on death and feared neither one."

A168. Gregory, Horace. "Jeffers Writes His Testament in New Poems," *Post* (New York), December 31, 1931, p. 9.

A Marxist critic praises. Jeffers' "elegies are among the best examples of Romantic poetry written by an American, and it is entirely possible that his boast of immortality will be justified by future generations of readers who will not fail to recognize his name."

A169. Humphries, Rolfe. "Two Books by Jeffers," *Poetry*, XL (June, 1932), 157.
Marxist critic complains of Jeffers' "arty" treatment of the rotten world he sees. He does not have the poetic quality to "cry his woes in the tones of Robert Frost or Hart Crane." He is, like so many others, "licked by modern life," suffering from a "paralysis of will so great that he can neither quit crying nor fight back."

A170. Hutchison, Percy. "New Books of Poetry," *New York Times Book Review*, January 31, 1932, p. 11.
Important critic praises the craftsmanship, but condemns the futility of the philosophical poems.

A171. Jack, P. M. "Bitter Dust," *Sun* (New York), December 18, 1931, p. 34.
Favorable eastern review. "There is a powerful and vital personality here, however it may mourn its lost youth and its own generation's decay: whether it is somber or bitter or querulous, it is so passionately and eventfully, making a great moment out of each line. No elegiac verse of our time is equal to this."

A172. Johns, Orrick. Review of *Descent to the Dead, Pine Cone* (Carmel, Cal.), January 15, 1932, p. 5.
Praise by fellow poet. "No living Irish poet, not Yeats himself, could have made them more authentic. The Irish weather is in these poems, the black stones and the gray waters, and the dead that live."

A173. Powell, Lawrence Clark. "Jeffers Abroad," *Carmelite*, IV (July 7, 1932), 6.
Important Jeffers critic praises. "Here again Jeffers appears as one of the great contemporary masters of written English, creating poetry in a

living idiom which is at once as homely as a peasant's speech and correct as a grammarian's discourse."

A174. Stuart, Gloria. Review of *Descent to the Dead*, *Carmelite*, IV (January 7, 1932), 5.
Local praise for new volume because, "he has left behind the needless morbidity of some preceding poems, he has used fine selection in his detail, he has lifted the veil of obscurity . . . and, finally, he has synthesized every quality of his inspired poetic concept into the supreme statement of his belief."

A175. Walton, Eda Lou. Review of *Descent to the Dead*, *Nation*, CXXXIV (February 3, 1932), 146.
Important critic complains of Jeffers' poor taste. However, his narratives have apt characterization, motivation, and dramatic sense. "But only in his lyrics does he show his command of the poetic line."

Thurso's Landing and Other Poems
New York: Liveright
(1932)

A176. Anonymous. "Books of Poetry Deal With Lyric and Epic Verse," *News* (Washington, D. C.), April 23, 1932, p. 11.
Minor praise. "The brutal force of a folk tragedy gains majesty with his varying verse forms, which for all the high tension, never gets out of control."

A177._____. "Harrowed Morrow," *Time*, XIX (April 4, 1932), 63-64. Reprinted in: *Pine Cone* (Carmel, Cal.), April 15, 1932, pp. 1, 9.

Important example of the extent of Jeffers' popularity. Front cover picture. Biography, plots, critical history. "Though critics, with few exceptions, have extrolled the splendor and intensity of Poet Jeffers's works, some women think that he spoils his poems with such outrageous themes. Even his wife complained. 'Robin,' said she, after he had finished 'Roan Stallion,' 'when will you quit forbidden themes?' Robin answered with an enigmatic smile." Nevertheless, the "outlines of the American continent and of its troubled inhabitants, grow colder and clearer under Poet Jeffers's western-starry light."

A178._____. "Poet Turns to Tragedy: 'Thurso's Landing' is Jeffers at Best," *Free Press* (Detroit, Mich.), June 5, 1932, section 3, p. 15.
Minor praise. In this volume Jeffers combines "the strength and beauty of his earlier works with a finished, yet casual, writing which sometimes was found lacking in 'Roan Stallion' and other of his earlier works."

A179._____. Review of *Thurso's Landing and Other Poems*, *Booklist*, XXVIII (June, 1932), 428.
Brief listing. The title poem "displays, as did the poet's previous works, vigorous beauty, passion, and a preoccupation with cruelty and violence."

A180._____. Review of *Thurso's Landing and Other Poems*, *English Journal*, XXI (June, 1932), 512.
Brief review finds affinity with Shakespeare and Aeschylus. The "supremely tragic" genius of Robinson Jeffers "clutches at the mysteries of life."

A181._____. Review of *Thurso's Landing and Other Poems, Forum*, LXXXVIII (July, 1932), vii.
Brief, favorable comment. "Of all Jeffers' narrative poems, 'Thurso's Landing' is perhaps the most human, the one which has the best chance of finding a popular audience. It is as grim and somber as 'Cawdor' or

'Women at Point Sur,' as full of tragic grandeur, but abnormal passions are for once subordinated."

A182_____. Review of *Thurso's Landing and Other Poems, Pittsburgh Monthly Bulletin*, XXXVII (July, 1932), 53.

Brief, unfavorable listing. The title poem "is on the whole more prosaic and unornamented, but not less brutal, than his earlier narrative poems."

A183. A., F. P. (Franklin Pierce Adams). "The Conning Tower," *Herald Tribune* (New York), March 26, 1932, p. 11.

Poet, journalist and wit makes brief mention, including an error (?) in the book's title. "So up and to the office, and read Thurso's Daughter by Robinson Jeffers, and I find him a mighty hard poet to read, but I find any poem of more than a hundred lines hard to read, especially when it is unrhymed."

A184. B., M. F. "An Allegorical Poem and Others by Robinson Jeffers," *Transcript* (Boston, Mass.), June 15, 1932, part 4, p. 2.

Mixed review rejecting morbidity. "In contemplation of the loveliness of nature, there is tenderness and appreciation and exhalted joy. Oh that this poet could view humanity, admitting its frailties, in the same manner! He knows compassion . . . but dwells, morbidly, on futility."

A185. Bancroft, Caroline. "Literary Lollypops," *Post* (Denver, Colo.), April 10, 1932, p. 16.

Trivia includes interesting quotation from A. E. Describes how, when asked, A. E. named Jeffers and E. A. Robinson as the greatest American poets. Miss Bancroft adds that the plot of the new poem is "banal in the same way that Shakespeare is banal—with such epic grandeur that the plot is forgotten."

A186. Belitt, Ben. "Cataclysmic Disaster and High Emotion," *Times-Dispatch* (Richmond, Va.), April 10, 1932, p. 6. Reprinted in: *News*

(Lynchburg, Va.), April 10, 1932, section 1, p. 7. *News-Leader* (Staunton, Va.), April 10, 1932, news section, p. 5.

Syndicated mixed review by poet-critic. "Thurso's Landing" wavers "between bald, unsublimated melodrama and the sculpturesque, subjective tragedy of the Greeks." Although it is "not the best of his poems," Jeffers "shines with especial brilliance" in comparison with Frost and E. A. Robinson.

A187. Benét, William Rose. "Jeffers' Latest Work," *Saturday Review of Literature*, VIII (April 2, 1932), 638. Reprinted in: Canby, H. S. (ed.). *Designed for Reading: An Anthology Drawn from the Saturday Review of Literature 1924-1937.* New York: Macmillan Company, 1937, 234-238.

An early admirer praises Jeffers' "pictoral eye," his ability to depict scenery, nature, animals. Jeffers' "people grow into roundness, the rock, earth, trees, flowers and animals in his country are alive. He is original in description without straining his similies and analogies. . . . "

A188. Brickell, Herschell. "The Literary Landscape," *North American Review*, CCXXXIII (June, 1932), 576.

Brief review. "The title poem in the Jeffers volume is a long narrative in blank verse, which again evidences that dark genius of Jeffers, a poet whose range is not wide, but a poet who has gazed into the abyss that surrounds the world, and discerned things in its blackness."

A189. Burns, Aubrey. "Will Against Will Clashes in Epic by Mount Carmel Poet," *News* (Dallas, Tex.), May 8, 1932, magazine section, p. 3.

Praise from grass roots. This is a poem "combining the best qualities of fiction, of poetry and of drama. . . . While it is yet too early for any definite estimation of Jeffers' ultimate place in poetry, it is the belief of this reviewer, that he is the major poet for which this century has waited."

A190. Cantwell, Robert. "Robinson Jeffers Better Novelist Than Poet," *World-Telegram* (New York), March 29, 1932, p. 23.

Unique opinion from novelist-critic who prefers Jeffers' ideas to his poetry. In a comparison of Jeffers and Lawrence: "Jeffers is the better novelist and Lawrence the better poet." "Thurso's Landing" is "a great story rather than a great poem and one feels that Jeffers has more to say to novelists than to poets." The short lyrics are weak.

A191. Childe, Myrtokleia. "Thurso's Landing: Jeffers in Familiar Setting," *Carmelite*, V (March 31, 1932), 8.

Ecstatic local comment. "Liking Jeffers, one would read this latest poem with keen enjoyment. Perhaps he has said it all before in a different guise. But he has written it in words that live, that cling to the rock of reality and reach into the sky of symbols."

A192. Coates, Grace Stone. "Bookshelf," *Frontier*, XII (May, 1932), 384.

Brief, minor comment. Jeffers interpretation of the characters in the "absorbing narrative" of the title poem is "penetrating and sound. . . . The nine short poems of the book are arresting and the volume concludes with a narrative poem of social import."

A193. Cooper, Monte. "Pain Matched by Courage," *Commercial Appeal* (Memphis, Tenn.), June 12, 1932, section 1, p. 18.

Favorable, minor review. " 'Thurso's Landing' is a poem of beauty and terror. Robinson Jeffers writes the most powerful and fearless poetry of any living American." The ten shorter poems are also "powerful and beautiful."

A194. Cunningham, J. V. "Modern Poets," *Commonweal*, XVI (October 5, 1932), 540.

Brief comment in review of ten poets' works. "Of the four ways of being middling—bad, dull, thin or imperfect," Mr. Jeffers chooses the first. He is a vendor "of loose emotion." His lines express only an "indistinguished exasperation." In this he is similar to Aiken, MacLeish and MacKnight Black and unlike Wilfred Owen.

A195. Deutsch, Babette. "The Hunger of Pain," *New York Herald Tribune Books*, March 27, 1932, p. 7.

An early admirer reacts with enthusiasm. Although this volume does not "touch the peaks of lyricism" reached in earlier works, the book has "urgency" and "power." He is comparable to Shakespeare and Homer and superior to O'Neill.

A196. Gregory, Horace. "Jeffers Again Hurls Indictment at Civilization," *Post* (New York), March 31, 1932, p. 9.

Although "Jeffers has mastered the art of telling a story," this important poet-critic issues a warning. "The Spenglerian gloom with all its philosophic fallacies threatens to engulf Jeffers entirely, and if the present volume indicates his final direction, he is well on the road toward intellectual and spiritual suicide."

A197. Hale, Adam de la. "Men Against Themselves," *Florida Times-Union* (Jacksonville, Fla.), April 24, 1932, p. 13.

Favorable minor comment comparing Jeffers to O'Neill. Praises "the long sweeping lines of human passion and dark hate."

A198. Hicks, Granville. "A Transient Sickness," *Nation*, CXXXIV (April 13, 1932), 433.

Marxist critic praises. "Perhaps the most human poem he has written, in the sense that its characters act from comprehensible motives. It moves swiftly, its lines terser and firmer than those the poet has hitherto composed, sweeping forward on the wings of an imagery even nobler than that we have known."

A199. Humphries, Rolfe. "Two Books by Jeffers," *Poetry*, XL (June, 1932), 157.

Mixed comment by Marxist poet-critic who compares Jeffers' and Shakespeare's "gorgeous rhetorical eloquence," and their "somewhat stagey misanthropy." But Jeffers' "shockers fail to come off for the same reason that O'Neill's do: for one thing, they are weighted with a too portentous symbolism; for another, he errs in transposing his mathematics into dramatic terms." He "often diagnoses in the universe the sickness that is original in him."

A200. Hutchison, Percy. "Robinson Jeffers' Dramatic Poem of Spiritual Tragedy," *New York Times Book Review*, April 3, 1932, p. 2.

Mixed comment by important reviewer. In comparison with earlier narratives, "it is more barren of passages of peculiar and exceptional beauty than one has been led to expect; on the other hand, as a human study this poem seems more pertinent to life. Balancing these two factors, then, 'Thurso's Landing,' while not Mr. Jeffers' most striking narrative, is his crowning achievement to date."

A201. Jack, P. M. "Cruelty and Power," *Sun* (New York), April 8, 1932, p. 33.

Favorable comment. "It is a finely thought out tale, told with rich rhetoric and a highly stylized dialogue. What is important is that it endures the telling. There is more to it than the breathless interest of narrative, though there is that in plenty."

A202. McDonald, Edward D. "Robinson Jeffers' New Work a Moving Search for Peace," *Record* (Philadelphia, Pa.), March 27, 1932, p. 7d.

Ambiguous review. " 'Thurso's Landing' will of course be read by those who read Jeffers at all. . . . the book will bring to these readers the old pleasure and excitement. To some of them will doubtless come also the old sense of disappointment that a lovely hope has been deferred."

A203. Morrison, Theodore. Review of *Thurso's Landing and Other Poems, Atlantic Bookshelf*, (September, 1932)

This pamphlet has unnumbered pages and no volume numbers.

Mixed comment. "Often . . . Jeffers reveals the force and pregnancy of the pure poet in him; and sometimes, amid the general violence of the story, he reveals the eye and hand of an unusual narrator. But the book is vitiated by a central weakness: the degree to which, in story, in temper, in language, in imagination, it is constructed of purely physical horror and agony."

A204. Pinckney, Josephine. "Jeffers and MacLeish," *Virginia Quarterly Review*, VIII (July, 1932), 443-447.

Novelist's review also includes comment on MacLeish's *Conquistador*. Emphasis on "sculpturesque," masculine and Saxon qualities. "It succeeds chiefly by a terrific objectivity."

A205. Reade, Mary Adda. Review of *Thurso's Landing and Other Poems, Peninsula Herald* (Monterey, Cal.), April 18, 1932, p. 10.

Minor local comment. "In *Thurso's Landing* not a page can be turned without tribute to the author's power of expressing his human, or inhuman conceptions."

A206. Rorty, James. "Symbolic Melodrama," *New Republic*, LXXI (May 18, 1932), 24-25.

Early admirer begins to question Jeffers' philosophy. "Jeffers thinks this is his best book; the reviewer agrees that it expresses better than earlier volumes what Jeffers has to express: the death-wish of a spent civilization. . . . A new literature is emerging, the work of poets ardently partisan for human life and the conquests of human consciousness. Their ardors are just as valid as Jeffers' enthusiasm for basalt and grave maggots."

A207. Towne, Charles Hanson. "A Number of Things," *American* (New York), April 1, 1932, p. 13. Reprinted in: *Herald and Examiner* (Chicago, Ill.), April 8, 1932, p. 9.

Praise in editor-essayist's feature column. Comparison to Whitman. In the title poem, his verse now and then explodes "in some of the gorgeous description which brings the reader up with a gasp." In the shorter poems, "Jeffers again reveals his strange power to evoke a scene, to bring to the brain a sense of loneliness and destruction."

A208. Trent, Lucia. "Jeffers Dips Pen into Acid Cruet," *Public Ledger* (Philadelphia, Pa.), April 16, 1932, p. 6.

Minor, unfavorable review stressing "the sadistic and antisocial material" in "Thurso's Landing."

A209. Untermeyer, Louis. "Five Notable Poets," *Yale Review*, XXI (Summer, 1932), 815-817.

Includes review of *Thurso's Landing* by a constant admirer. "Between Jeffers, the philosopher, and Jeffers, the poet, there is a significant dichotomy. The philosophy is negative, repetitious, dismal; the poetry, even when bitterest, is positive as any creative expression must be. . . . Here is an undeviating, full-throated poetry, remarkable in sheer drive and harrowing drama, a poetry we may never love but one we cannot forget."

A210. Walker, Helene. "Books," *State Journal* (Topeka, Kan.), May 24, 1932, p. 17.

Minor grass roots praise. Describes Jeffers as "a little on the type of Bill Hart." Jeffers' "position as a major poet, which was conceded with the publication of his first volume has been progressively strengthened with each succeeding book."

A211. Winters, Yvor. Review of *Thurso's Landing and Other Poems, Hound and Horn*, V (July-September, 1932), 681, 684-685.

Winters' condemnation is crucial to the history of Jeffers' critical disfavor in the next decades. "The doctrinaire hysteria of the earlier narratives is seldom to be found here. There is an attempt at some sort of coherent narrative, but the result is merely dogged and soggy melodrama. Mr. Jeffers' verse continues to miss the virtues of prose and poetry alike: it is capable neither of the fullness and modulation of fine prose nor the concentration and modulation of fine verse. There is an endless, violent monotony of movement, wholly uninteresting and insensitive, that may have a hypnotic effect upon a good many readers, much as does the jolting of a railroad coach over a bad road-bed. . . . The book is composed almost wholly of trash."

A212. Zorn, Gremin. "A Novel in Verse," *Press* (Long Island, N. Y.), April 10, 1932, p. 28.

Minor comment in which he is compared favorably to Faulkner. *Thurso's Landing* is "not the greatest of the writings of Robinson Jeffers." It is nevertheless outstanding. The title poem is "both rich in narrative and imagery."

Give Your Heart to the Hawks and Other Poems
New York: Random House
(1933)

A213. Anonymous. Review of *Give Your Heart to the Hawks and Other Poems, Transcript* (Boston, Mass.), November 18, 1933, p. 2.

Praise for one whose "words sing and surge like the earth. . . . One might almost find it possible to express the hope that Mr. Jeffers will be one at least to never embrace resignation in life."

A214._____ . Review of *Give Your Heart to the Hawks and Other Poems, Booklist*, XXX (December, 1933), 114.

Brief listing. "Poetry of violence and passion, but also of great beauty . . . heroic proportions."

A215. Canby, H. S. "North of Hollywood," *Saturday Review of Literature*, X (October 7, 1933), 162. Reprinted in his: *Seven Year's Harvest*. New York: Farrar, Strauss and Company, 1936, pp. 146-150.

Major editor and critic recognizes Jeffers' power. "In spite of its morbidity, and perhaps because of it, here is a poem that troubles the water as if there passed by some angel of judgment."

A216. Cerwin, Herbert. "Jeffers Again Portrays His Power in New Book of Poems," *Pine Cone* (Carmel, Cal.), November 3, 1933, p. 5.

Local praise for Jeffers' story-telling ability. " . . . the pen of this Titan of Carmel drips with sincerity—with a power that leaves one amazed and bewildered. . . . What a novelist this man Jeffers would have been. He can be so understanding, so humanly kind and in the next breath his sharp-pointed pen is delicately but painfully probing at the heart."

A217. Fletcher, John Gould. "The Dilemma of Robinson Jeffers," *Poetry*, XLIII (March, 1934), 338-342.

Important imagist poet writes a mixed review. "He will never achieve that apparently inevitable fusion of earthly and eternal interests which is what the world demands of its great poets." He has only some of the qualities that make "a Shakespeare, a Milton, an Aeschylus, or a Goethe." He can relate characters to a scheme of eternal values "in a way no American poet has yet done." Perhaps his highest distinction is that he is "deaf to the parrot-cries of the communists that there can be no poetry that does not . . . serve an obvious social purpose." However, he becomes less "interesting as he is obliged by the tenets of his own inhuman creed to make use of characters with strong streaks of neurotic obsession; or else to write pompous and inflated absurdity. . . . Unless he can find a new set of characters, we may see a total destruction of his poetry."

A218. Hutchison, Percy. "Sound and Fury in Mr. Jeffers," *New York Times Book Review*, October 15, 1933, p. 5.

Important critic questions Jeffers' love of cruelty, symbolized by the hawk, a love that is almost perversion. Finds appalling amounts of blood. "One wonders about these works of Jeffers: are they not, all of them, nightmarish rather than real, despite their apparent reality? But none can gainsay the effect produced at the moment; the reader is gripped and squeezed as in a vise. The poetry of Robinson Jeffers is unsure of survival; for succeeding generations, succeeding dances of death. But his is the most striking personality in verse today."

A219. Kennedy, Leo. "Descent to the Dead," *Canadian Forum*, XIV (December, 1933), 111.

Tempered praise. Little variety, though his "voice cries these few magnificent notes over and over again in the wilderness." Special praise for the short poems originally published as *Descent to the Dead.* "Robinson Jeffers has simply added to his bulk of remarkable poetry. He does not exceed himself nor fall short of previous work. This book reiterates that he is a great poet as poets go in our day."

A220. Matthiessen, F. O. "Yeats and Four American Poets," *Yale Review*, XXIII (March, 1934), 611-617.

Brief mention by major critic who views coldly the latest work. The title poem is "far less moving than several of his previous shorter poems." Notes "the fundamental confusion of Jeffers's thought, which in the end vitiates all of his tragedies."

A221. Rorty, James. Review of *Give Your Heart to the Hawks and Other Poems, Nation,* CXXXVII (December 20, 1933), 712.

Early admirer sours. "As craftsmanship" this "is in many respects one of Jeffers' ablest performances. But one starts unconvinced, for the tragedy is fraily premised on drunkenness and chance, and one ends, as too often in Jeffers' terrible stories, racked but unsatisfied."

A222. Walton, Eda Lou. "A Poet at Odds With His Own Civilization," *New York Herald Tribune Books*, October 8, 1933, p. 6.

Major review critical of Jeffers' distrust of civilization. Summarizes Jeffers' philosophy in general terms. Discusses him as a pantheist who hates machines and cities. Jeffers rejects both Marxism and Fascism because they "demean man whose greatness is in individualism. . . . Most men, however, moving with the age, will find in Jeffers no message and no solace. The poet, intrenched in his personal religion, will be more and more a voice in the wilderness, crying out to no purpose whatsoever."

A223. Zabel, Morton Dauwen. "A Prophet in His Wilderness," *New Republic*, LXXVII (January 3, 1934), 229-230.

Leading critic condemns Jeffers' futility and violence, comparing his attitude to Lawrence in fiction and O'Neill in drama. "His characters are indistinguishably desperate or willess as individuals, and are agencies for no morality but the anti-human revulsion that makes a running theme in all the poems." The treatment of California landscapes remains a virtue.

Solstice and Other Poems
New York: Random House
(1935)

A224. Benét, William Rose. **Review of** *Solstice and Other Poems,* *Saturday Review of Literature,* XIII (November 2, 1935), 20.

Early admirer finds Jeffers becoming redundant. "But he is wielding some of the grandest language of our time. He seems to have little flexibility in his temperment, but his stoicism is impressive."

A225. Deutsch, Babette. "In Love with the Universe," *New York Herald Tribune Books,* October 27, 1935, p. 8.

One of the initial admirers praises the grandness of the poetry in "Solstice." "The poem which opens Jeffers' latest volume restates his familiar themes, with no loss of power, and with the additional interest of a greater technical variety. . . . This is not the kind of poetry that inflames the heart against the brutalities of the strong, the greedy and the stupid. It is poetry that, fixing its eye upon the stars is less troubled by the human drama."

A226. Holmes, John. **Review of** *Solstice and Other Poems, Transcript* (Boston, Mass.) October 19, 1935, p. 4.

Mixed review. "If possible the rage and violence, the unreasoning and unhuman hatred are pitched a few notes higher than they ever have been pitched before." Finds "At the Birth of an Age" the "chief poem of the book, the one exciting item he gives up."

A227. Lechlitner, Ruth. Review of *Solstice and Other Poems, New Republic*, LXXXV (January 8, 1936), 262.

Condemnation of Jeffers' philosophy. "At the Birth of an Age" contains "confusing symbolism" and "Wagnerian thunder." Dismisses Jeffers with: "Not that he desires fascism, or communism either—oh no. Just plain annihilation of humankind (followed by peace) will do Mr. Jeffers nicely. Provided, I gather, that he can sit alone in his stone tower, surrounded by California scenery, while the whole disgusting business is going on, and dash off a last poem or two before Peace gathers him to her bosom."

A228. Matthiessen, F. O. "Society and Solitude in Poetry," *Yale Review*, XXV (March, 1936), 603-607.

Briefest mention by major critic. "His new volume reveals no new contours."

A229. Poore, C. G. "Three New Books of Poetry," *New York Times Book Review*, October 20, 1935, p. 21. Reprinted in: *Magazine of Sigma Chi*, LV (February, 1936), 27-28.

Important review compares Jeffers to Whitman, advises that one ignore the short poems. "But in 'At the Birth of an Age' we have a new conception of this arresting poet, a new Jeffers who has plunged deeper than heretofore. Whether, as time goes on, he will bring to the surface pearls of greater price, or only irridescent shells, time alone will tell."

A230. Rice, Philip Blair. "Jeffers and the Tragic Sense," *Nation*, CXLI (October 23, 1935), 480-482.

Mixed comment in major journal. *Solstice* contains some of his best poetry. His ideas closely resemble "good fascism" and Hitler, like Jeffers, also worships Woden. Jeffers' lust for pain "traces its descent to that perverted form of medieval asceticism which indulged in flagella-tion for its masochistic pleasure. . . . Mr. Jeffers' range is broad but his focus is narrow, and that universality of understanding to be found in great poetry is absent. His technical equipment, while considerable, has, I think, been overrated, for there is flabbiness as well as power in those long rhythms. . . . These things said, it remains undeniable that Mr.

Jeffers is one of the bulkiest figures of his time . . . and he is, above all, a superb story-teller."

A231. Thompson, Ralph. "Books of the Times," *Times* (New York), January 30, 1937, p. 15.
Favorable comment. "The title piece is a long and somewhat terrifying narrative of tremendous drive and sweep, the tragic story of a woman and her children and her husband. While Mr. Jeffers is essentially a dramatic poet, he is capable of ringing and magnificent music."

A232. Warren, Robert Penn. "Jeffers on the Age," *Poetry*, XLIX (February, 1937), 279-282.
Major novelist and New Critic offers negative comment. *Solstice* contains much self-imitation. The short poems are "turgid and feeble" and the narratives are "often deficient in the dramatic sense; and this deficiency is more than a trifling importance in a writer who sets out to be a dramatic and narrative poet."

Such Counsels You Gave to Me and Other Poems
New York: Random House
(1937)

A233. Anonymous. "California Hybrid," *Time*, XXX (October 18, 1937), 86-87.
Time reflects the changes in Jeffers' reputation. "Occasionally Poet Jeffers presents splendid glimpses, not of inhuman, but of nonhuman things. . . . Such glimpses however, are few and cursory. The book as a whole reveals no new juxtaposition of the parts of Jeffers' hybrid nature, but rather a wearied division between them—with the aging

prophet still hell-bent on emitting clouds of sulphur and smoke, and the poet simultaneously becoming more and more corner-loving and mealy-eyed."

A234._____. Review of *Such Counsels You Gave to Me and Other Poems, Booklist*, XXXIV (October 15, 1937), 66.
Brief listing. "Rugged, often beautiful, free verse."

A235. Bogan, Louise. "Landscape with Jeffers," *Nation*, CXLV (October 23, 1937), 442.
Unfriendly comment from a fellow poet who sees the characters "not so much puzzled and depraved as simple minded." Dislikes his "Presbyterian disgusts." However, his "great talents, allowed some humble relation to the race, which, whatever its faults, can at least laugh and change, might have escaped the limits that now increasingly distort them."

A236. Deutsch, Babette. "Jeffers' Tragic Drum-Roll," *New York Herald Tribune Books*, October 31, 1937, p. 8.
"The title poem . . . is written in the long, surging line, with the abrupt halt for moments of tension that is peculiarly Jeffers' own, and, like his other narratives, draws some of its strength from the poet's knowledge of medicine and astronomy. But though it has the suspense that a story needs, and is not without power and beauty, it does not rise to the height of his previous performances." This major mixed comment emphasizes Jeffers' integrity.

A237. Holmes, John. "Poetry Now," *Transcript* (Boston, Mass.), November 13, 1937, part 5, p. 3.
Mixed reception. "For all the heightened violence of the poem, or perhaps because of it, one is less impressed with this sixth book than with the other five." Yet, Jeffers, were he to "create an image of a man that all men may look to," could be "as great a poet as the critics say he is."

A238. Jack, Peter Monro. "Mr. Jeffers' New Version of an Old Scots Ballad," *New York Times Book Review*, October 17, 1937, p. 4.

Unfavorable discussion of faulty psychology of the major poem. It is "the extreme romanticism of a pseudo-science. . . . It will be said that Mr. Jeffers is to be congratulated for bringing a childish story to full maturity, and it will be said that the modern world is mirrored in his incestuous and degenerate violences; and all this may be true, but it is not well or truly written, in the sense, let us say, that 'The Waste Land' . . . is well and truly written." Prefers the shorter poems.

A239. R., J. Review of *Such Counsels You Gave to Me and Other Poems, Christian Science Monitor* (Boston, Mass.), November 10, 1937, p. 13.

Emphasis on Jeffers' philosophy. "Mr. Jeffers' poetry is negative and it is doubtful if, in the simple meaning of the word, it can be read for pleasure. But it can be read with profit."

A240. Rukeyser, Muriel. "Poet's Page," *New Republic*, XCIII (December 29, 1937), 234.

Important imagist poet views Jeffers unfavorably. His attacks on man's beliefs are "so mixed and meaningless, so half-true in their insistence, that, reading these shorter poems, one is tempted to accept only the half that rests on emotion for quality or place, setting aside every mental step." His "mess of ideas is shocking."

A241. Untermeyer, Louis. Review of *Such Counsels You Gave to Me and Other Poems, Saturday Review of Literature*, XVI (October 9, 1937), 11

Favorable review from important admirer. The pages of the title poem "are as emotional as they are modern, as passionate as they are perverse, as original in utterance as they are familiar in subject. . . . The other poems are less imposing, but they are scarcely less interesting. The shorter quasi-lyrics celebrate strength, the consolation of transient beauty, the solidity of sea-granite, and the will to endure against the horrors of new ways to give pain, new slaveries. Such elements do not make pretty verses, but they make impressive monoliths of poetry."

A242.———. "Seven Poets," *Yale Review*, XXVII (March, 1938), 604-609.

Curious inconsistency in Untermeyer's judgment of *Such Counsels You Gave to Me*. Mixed comments reflect possible second thoughts. Notes violence of title poem, though, "For all the resounding speeches . . . the stark old ballad remains the better poem." The shorter poems are "less horrific and more 'human.' "

A243. Van Wyck, William. *Robinson Jeffers.* Los Angeles: Ward Ritchie Press, 1938.

Highly laudatory. Emphasis on an explanation of Jeffers' philosophy. Pamphlet review. ". . . the first two poems are a bit disappointing inasmuch as they lack the catharsis which is necessary to sustain their themes. However, the shorter poems in the book give us a new Jeffers, the greatest Jeffers of them all." He is "a child of the sun whose wings are iridescent with the splendor of his father."

A244. Walton, Eda Lou. "Beauty of Storm Disproportionately," *Poetry*, LI (January, 1938), 209-213.

Emphasis in major journal on Jeffers' antisocial anarchism and his love of violence and power. He is "one of the last romantics, and his constant stressing of violence and evil is decadent because neither his scene nor his characters have anything but a mythical reality." He "repeats himself," and has "removed himself too far from his own age to be seriously listened to as a prophet."

The Selected Poetry of Robinson Jeffers
New York: Random House
(1938)

A245. Anonymous. "Nine and Two," *Time*, XXXII (December 26, 1938), 41.

Time, an accurate weathervane, definitely enters the hostile camp in this commentary on modern poetry. His work contains "semi-scientific platitudes, nonpoetical intensities, and—for the pay-off—mental exhaustion. . . . Because his words are impersonally grandiose instead of personally grand, Robinson Jeffers, who in another place and another time might have been a prophet, is here and now a vasty poetaster."

A246._____. Review of *The Selected Poetry of Robinson Jeffers*, *New Yorker*, XIV (November 19, 1938), 116.
Lists book. "Well arranged and edited."

A247._____. Review of *The Selected Poetry of Robinson Jeffers*, *Booklist*, XXXV (December 15, 1938), 130.
Brief mention. "Attractive format."

A248._____. Review of *The Selected Poetry of Robinson Jeffers*, *Pratt Institute Quarterly*, V (Spring, 1939), 23.
Included in a list of new recommended books.

A249. Brown, E. K. "The Coast Opposite Humanity," *Canadian Forum*, XVIII (January, 1939), 309-310.
Favorable judgment though regret voiced that all the long narratives could not have been included. Jeffers has become "a master of the short meditative lyric. . . . He has invented for poetry rhythms grander and more appropriate to huge and heroic conceptions than any other of his contemporaries can employ."

A250. Conrad, Sherman. Review of *The Selected Poetry of Robinson Jeffers*, *Nation*, CXLVIII (June 3, 1939), 651.
Condemnation of Jeffers' constant repetition of his philosophically narrow view based on "Spengler's cyclical decline of cultures, and behind that the final exhaustion of the universe resulting from the second law of thermodynamics. . . . He has loved neither art nor life enough. But here criticism must halt. For in the deepest sense Jeffers obviates human values, and criticism has no others."

A251. Fitts, Dudley. "Tragedy or Violence?" *Saturday Review of Literature*, XIX (April 22, 1939), 19.

Classicist and critic sees Jeffers as an act of nature. His "great virtues are the ability to tell a story and to sustain tremendous rhythms for long periods. His curious verse-form, a development of Whitman's is perfectly suited to narrative. In his descriptions of scenery he is always effective. What he lacks is restraint . . . and, above all things, humor."

A252. Jordan-Smith, Paul. Review of *The Selected Poetry of Robinson Jeffers, Times* (Los Angeles, Cal.), December 11, 1938, part 3, p. 10.

Favorable comment in major West Coast newspaper. "Not since Whitman have we had a more thoroughly American poet than Jeffers; not since Emerson one so philosophic." This is "a notable volume; . . . stately music, ready to be chanted."

A253. Miller, Benjamin. "The Poetry of Permanence," *Christian Century*, LXI (March 1, 1939), 288.

Favorable religious view stresses Jeffers' integrity, his adversion to humanism, and his sensuous mysticism. "Having cut himself free from all obsession with humanity and from an exclusive dependence upon science, he reaches toward the distinctively religious dimension. . . . Mr. Jeffers' intense poetic apprehension achieves a thorough-going pessimism regarding the human moral enterprise and a religious resource of considerable strength and courage found in 'breaking out of humanity.' "

A254. Schwartz, Delmore. "Sources of Violence," *Poetry*, LV (October, 1939), 30-38.

Sound negative criticism stresses Jeffers' dependence on nineteenth-century views on nature and the influence on him of the First World War. Jeffers' response is "hysterical. . . . To respond as Jeffers does by rejecting humanity and saluting the peace of death" is a "barren" and "false" conclusion. Hence, his poetry is "without interest and without value." His characters are "repetitive abstractions, and the long line of his verse is corrupted repeatedly by the most gauche inconsistencies of rhythm." He is "breaking away from literature as well as humanity in his poems."

A255. Worden, Perry. "Robinson Jeffers: Poet, Philosopher," in column: "Gleanings From History: Agua Mansa's Picturesque Finds," *Star-News* (Pasadena, Cal.), April 22, 1940, p. 9.

Minor statement of some biographical and bibliographical interest. Comment on the influence of Una Jeffers and the California coast on Jeffers' writings and notice of the acquisition of manuscripts by Occidental College. *Selected Poetry* is one of the "handsome attractions of the book-making season which many persons will desire to possess."

Be Angry at the Sun
New York: Random House
(1941)

A256. Anonymous. Review of *Be Angry at the Sun, Booklist*, XXXVIII (December 1, 1941), 110.

Brief listing. "Violence and passion are here, as in Jeffers' earlier poetry, but there is more awareness of world-wide dilemmas. Short poems, some reprinted from magazines, and one long narrative poem make up the volume."

A257._____ . Review of *Be Angry at the Sun, New Yorker*, XVII (December 6, 1941), 136.

Brief. "Jeffers sticks to his usual gloomy view of man's fate."

A258._____ . Review of *Be Angry at the Sun, Pratt Institute Quarterly*, VI (October, 1942), 17.

Listed among recommended books.

A259. Boyle, F. A. Review of *Be Angry at the Sun, Library Journal*, LXVI (October 15, 1941), 902.

Brief mention. "Brilliant blank verse with odd cadences, reminiscent of the poet's earlier work. . . . Recommended."

A260. Deutsch, Babette. "Poets and New Poets," *Virginia Quarterly Review*, XVIII (Winter, 1942), 132-134.

Early admirer detects fascist sympathies in Jeffers, particularly apparent in "The Bowl of Blood," the "not quite successful dramatic poem about Hitler consulting the seeress; but the volume as a whole rather bears testimony to the temper of an aging man in an unhappy world."

A261._____ . "The Worst for Being Timely," *New Republic*, CVI (March 23, 1942), 402.

Deutsch's enthusiasm palls somewhat. "The Bowl of Blood" is most striking. "In the main . . . Jeffers sticks to his old themes and his familiar style." The opening narrative could have been written twenty years ago and the title poem "reiterates the poet's aloofness from man's recurrent follies and crimes. Those lyrics which do not deal with current events are most notable, and one can but hope that current evil will not continue to obstruct the large vision which his singular power evokes."

A262. Frankenberg, Lloyd. Review of *Be Angry at the Sun, New York Herald Tribune Books*, November 30, 1941, p. 7.

Poet-critic and author deplores Jeffers' lack of selectivity. Compares him to a volcano, in which "the ludicrous is disgorged quite as easily as the monstrous. Nevertheless there has always been an impetus, a fever-pitch of words, that made up for other kinds of suspense. This carried his stories along at breakneck speed, preventing the immediate application of an analysis that might threaten his effects."

A263. Greenberg, Clement. "Robinson Jeffers," *Nation*, CLIV (March 7, 1942), 289.

Art critic writes negative review. "Mara" is especially bad. "How Jeffers won his reputation on the basis of his narratives I cannot see:

they contain some of the worst respectable poetry in English and couch a humanity too narrow ever to be taken very seriously in poetry or out of it." In the other poems "this narrowness does less harm, lacking the space in which to make itself felt."

A264. Holmes, John. "The New Books of Poetry," *New York Times Book Review*, February 22, 1942, p. 18.

Important review finds signs that Jeffers predictions are becoming reality. "This new book is, to be sure, a restatement of things he has said before, with the different light cast on the statements by the passage of time, but it proves in its greater immediacy simply that he was right many years ago, and has gone on being right."

A265. Kunitz, Stanley J. "The Day is a Poem," *Poetry*, LIX (December, 1941), 148-154.

Major poet-critic condemns "Mara" as a repetition of the other long narratives. Praises, however, "The Bowl of Blood," as a "magnificent accomplishment," and the "greatest masque since *Comus*." Fears Jeffers' possible fascism. He must, now that he "returns to the historical sense" accept "moral obligations and human values." If he doesn't, he'll "range himself on the side of the destroyers. It is a critical moment in his career."

A266. Miller, Benjamin. Review of *Be Angry at the Sun, Christian Century*, LIX (June 3, 1942), 729.

Religious viewpoint sees Jeffers as a justified prophet. He "has written what will in all probability stand as the strongest and most profound verse to come out of this war. With extraordinary sensibility to poetic tragedy and with the paradoxical strength of a passionate disinterestedness, he allows the monstrous decay and violence of these times to speak themselves out, and refuses to have any part in them. . . ."

A267. Roberts, R. E. "Lonely Eminence," *Saturday Review of Literature*, XXV (April 25, 1942), 8.

Favorable review. Singles out "The Bowl of Blood" as "a tense, taut piece of work, packed with imaginative understanding." Praises "Jeffers's profound pity for humanity and his skill in story-telling in 'Mara.' " "The whole book will confirm any intelligent reader that here is one of the few major poets now writing in English, a man who has his narrowness and his ubiquities but who is fit to sit down, as Yeats desired to sit, with 'Landor and John Donne,' for he has clung, as they, obstinately to his creed."

A268. Untermeyer, Louis. "Time and These Times," *Yale Review*, XXXI (Winter, 1942), 375-379.

Although some adverse criticism of the "philosophy of frustration," still this major admirer finds sufficient ground for praise. "To say that Mr. Jeffers repeats himself is to repeat an uncritical charge. What poet does not? Perhaps Mr. Jeffers has more right than most to insist on his misanthropy, for events are rapidly shaping humanity in his image." Finds "Mara" "one of the most vivid stories the author has ever told."

A269. Worden, Perry. "Robinson Jeffers: A New Poetry Wreath," in column: "Gleanings from History: Agua Mansa's Picturesque Finds," *Star-News* (Pasadena, Cal.), October 28, 1941, p. 4.

Minor California comment. This volume is "not inferior in parts to some of the best with which he has previously so enriched the literature of California."

Medea, Freely Adapted from the Medea of Euripides
New York: Random House
(1946)

A270. Anonymous. Review of *Medea, Bulletin of Virginia Kirkus' Bookshop Service*, XIV (February 1, 1946), 56.

Brief listing. "It will fall short of the wide general appeal. . . . At no point does he reach the intensity of horror and pity that the famous Greek poet achieves, even in translation."

A271._____. Review of *Medea, Booklist*, XLII (June 1, 1946), 313.
Listing. "The morbid, horror-filled theme is peculiarly suited to Mr. Jeffers' style."

A272. Bell, Lisle. Review of *Medea, New York Herald Tribune Weekly Book Review*, April 21, 1946, p. 19.
Praise for authenticity, dramatic force and language, which is "vividly in keeping with the barbaric tragedy. The reader of this version will not sense the operatic nature of Greek tragedy, but he will feel without question its tremendous dramatic impact."

A273. Bogan, Louise. "Modern Syndrome," *New Yorker*, XXII (May 11, 1946), 89-91. Reprinted in her: *Selected Criticism*. New York: Noonday Press, 1955. pp. 302-304.
Major poet finds that "to compare this 'free adaptation' of his Euripides with a straight translation is to be brought up against the most shocking symptoms of our literature and life." Jeffers' nightmare world has become our reality.

A274. Commins, Saxe. "Medea—The Perennial," *Key Reporter*, XI (Summer, 1946), 4.
Favorable comment praises vigor and eloquence of Jeffers' *Medea.* "The Jeffers version . . . loses none of the intensity and violence of the original, nor any of its psychological penetration." Jeffers' characteristic strong, long line "helps to sustain the narrative flow of the tragedy."

A275. Freedley, George. "Plays in Print," *Library Journal*, LXXI (May 15, 1946), 760.

Brief squib, in toto: "Freely adapted from Euripides by one of our foremost poets, this is distinguished writing. Recommended for drama collections."

A276. Kennedy, Leo. Review of *Medea, Chicago Sun Book Week*, April 21, 1946, p. 13.
Brief squib. "Jeffers, who is at his brooding best when exploring such misanthropic themes, is convincing both as poet and dramatist in this play."

A277. Meyer, G. P. "Medea in California," *Saturday Review of Literature*, XXIX (July 13, 1946), 20.
Mixed. Finds Jeffers "more archaic and deeply primitive" than Euripides. Jeffers is obsessed by cruelty, violence, and death; but although he fails to observe classic Greek concision, "being naturally inclined to the long, looping rhythm-baffling line, with its temptation to redundancy, he is still the maker of images, and can speak out with beautiful clarity as well as force."

A278. Mizener, Arthur Moore. "The Medea of the Rocks," *Nation*, CLXIII (August 31, 1946), 246.
New Critic and biographer lodges a protest at the liberties Jeffers takes with the original; admits however that this is "a far more successful piece of drama than most versions of Greek plays." Jeffers has made the play colloquial, realistic, and simplified.

A279. Stauffer, Donald A. "California Euripides," *New York Times Book Review*, April 21, 1946, p. 7.
Adverse comments from major humanist, critic and Princeton English professor. Bathos. Flat, loose poetry. "The play might act well, for with proper lighting and an ambitious actress it could explode uncompromising horror in the heart. But it is neither a great tragedy nor a good poem. It is a melodrama that falls between two styles."

The Double Axe and Other Poems
New York: Random House
(1948)

A280. Anonymous. "And Buckets o'Blood," *Time*, LII (August 2, 1948), 79.
Popular magazine condemns Jeffers' isolationist stance on World War II. "What gives these sentiments interest is that behind them is Jeffers' one great violent insight into the nature of things—an insight that has kept him going as a poet for twenty years, has formed his famous style, and made him a faintly theatrical, gloom-wrapped figure in U. S. poetry." The poetry's weakness is that it implies "that no human kindness or decency would survive modern warfare," which turns what "might have been a tragic moral struggle into a necrophiliac nightmare."

A281._____. "Chapter and Verse," *Time*, LII (July 5, 1948), 32.
Brief squib. Random House's preface gives "the persuasive powers of poetry . . . thumping recognition."

A282._____. Review of *The Double Axe and Other Poems, New Yorker*, XXIV (September 4, 1948), 75.
Brief mention. "Since Jeffers is antihuman, his gruesome puppets have only melodramatic impact and no 'appeal.' " Condemns publisher's preface.

A283._____. "Two Books of Verse," *Bulletin from Virginia Kirkus' Bookshop Service*, XVI (June 1, 1948), 276.
Comic sarcasm. Detects a note of fascism in Jeffers. *The Double Axe* is "the latest Robinson Jeffers' cocktail,—one part Sophocles, one part Lone Ranger, a dash of William Faulkner, and plenty of bitters. . . ."

Purile and violent rodomontade. To this reviewer his popularity is a puzzle; but he has his followers, and they will like this volume no doubt."

A284. Anderson, Stanley. "Robinson Jeffers Nods as World Marches By," *Press* (Cleveland, Ohio), August 3, 1948, p. 20.

Minor. Condemns Jeffers' political views. His "violent political isolationism is divorced from what the people think. . . . Jeffers is breathing, but he is asleep."

A285. Brigham, R. I. "Bitter and Skillful Treatise in Verse," *Post-Dispatch* (St. Louis, Mo.), August 1, 1948, section 6, p. 4f.

Violent condemnation of *The Double Axe*, its author and potential admirers. Jeffers is "hopelessly isolated from life and unbalanced in his thinking." Warning to readers: "Only the most devout followers of the right wing nationalists, the lunatic fringe, and the most ardent of Roosevelt haters could, after reading 'The Double Axe,' welcome the return of Robinson Jeffers."

A286. Cross, Leslie. "Robinson Jeffers vs. Mankind," *Journal* (Milwaukee, Wis.), October 24, 1948, section 5, p. 4.

Deplores the political views expressed in *The Double Axe*. "In this truculent book, Robinson Jeffers . . . makes it clear that he feels the human race should be abolished," and although "the poetry is stirring and eloquent," it "leaves a bitter taste."

A287. Dudley, Uncle (Ward Greene). "The Double Axe," *Globe* (Boston, Mass.), September 5, 1948, p. 2a.

King Features Syndicate editor praises the poem's philosophy. This "may be his best work. . . . This poet writes with a sword-blade dipped in blood, but the blood is that of our own slaughtered young men."

A288. Ferril, Thomas Hornsby. "The New Poetry," *Chronicle* (San Francisco, Cal.), November 7, 1948, This World section, p. 11.

Western poet-essayist feels Jeffers, in his love of nature, passion for God, and hatred of violence, has a "saintly kinship" with St. Francis. However, "some quirk has shunted it off obliquely to the end that we have one of the most powerful word-craftsmen of our time dipping his pen in international pus in an effort to write what, philosophically, amounts to a cosmic sequal to 'Black Beauty.' "

A289. Fitts, Dudley. "The Violent Mr. Jeffers," *New York Times Book Review*, August 22, 1948, p. 10.
Adverse criticism from a noted classicist. Praises a few passages in the shorter poems, "But they are scarcely enough to redeem the apoplectic shouting of the rest." Finds *The Double Axe*, "like his recent paraphrase of 'Medea,' largely a failure. Indeed, the virtues and faults of one book are very like those of the other."

A290. Fitzgerald, Robert. "Oracles and Things," *New Republic*, CXIX (November 22, 1948), 22.
Translator, poet and classicist dismisses Jeffers' efforts. "The attitude is childish and childishly easy; once assumed, it will turn out a Jeffers Lyric an hour for anyone who wants to try it, but it is a sorry exhibition for a responsible poet to have made."

A291. Gannett, Lewis. "Books and Things," *Herald-Tribune* (New York), July 30, 1948, p. 13.
Critic, essayist, pacifist finds *The Double Axe* "standard Jeffers— wild, strong, bitter, eerie stuff."

A292. Gray, James. "Robinson Jeffers in Pose as Isolationist Poet Laureate," *Dispatch* (St. Paul, Minn.), July 28, 1948, p. 12.
Novelist and literary editor feels that "whatever Jeffers' gifts may once have been, the ability to write verse has deserted him, temporarily at least. No lines quite so blunt, heavy-footed and prosy ever masqueraded as poetry quite so unpersuasively."

A293. Hackman, Martha. Review of *The Double Axe and Other Poems,
Voices*, CXXXVI (Winter, 1949), 54-56.
    Condemns the unrelieved violence and horror of the title poem. The
short poems are "repetitous and flat." He has lost his "old sweep and
power" and "the path he has chosen seems to be leading at present
through very barren country."

A294. Humphries, Rolfe. "Jeffers and Pound," *Nation*, CLXVII
(September 25, 1948), 349.
    Important poet-critic condemns Jeffers' philosophy of inhumanism.
Still, Jeffers can "feel with such emotion, and describe with dignity and
power, the California landscape around Monterey country. 'The Double
Axe' is characteristic of Jeffers, a long narrative poem with horrible
characters, and deeds of lurid violence on practically every page. Not
much evidence of change or growth. . . ." However, "Jeffers' command
of language does invest his work, I think, with an air of stature and
dignity beyond the philosophy's deserts."

A295. Lechlitner, Ruth. "A Prophet of Mortality," *New York Herald
Tribune Weekly Book Review*, September 12, 1948, p. 4.
    Important review concerned primarily with Random House's dis-
claimer. "In America, a democracy, in the year of peace 1948, why, the
reader may well ask, the compulsion on the part of its publishers,
whatever personal disagreement there may be, to disavow publicly
certain views of its author?" Calls Jeffers "a distinguished American
Poet."

A296. McCarthy, John Russell. "Jeffers' Anti-War Fervor," *Star-News*
(Pasadena, Cal.), July 25, 1948, book section, p. 35.
    Minor. This book is Jeffers' "most important statement to his
fellows" and America should listen to him, "especially now on what
may be the eve of a third and possibly annihilating World War." Jeffers
leaves "no doubt about his fervor." His "poetry is still there in places,
though too often the lines are prose."

A297. McDonald, Gerald. Review of *The Double Axe and Other Poems*, *Library Journal*, LXXIII (June 15, 1948), 948.

Brief, but opinionated. "His violent, hateful book is a gospel of isolationism carried beyond geography, faith and hope. . . . Although shocked and horrified by the views expressed, I still think the writer should be given a hearing."

A298. Meyer, Gerard Previn. Letter to editor. Review of *The Double Axe and Other Poems*, *Saturday Review of Literature*, XXXI (September 11, 1948), 24.

Reply to Rodman review: see A303. "Mr. Jeffers and those of his ilk, wherever and in whatever form they write are not 'irresponsible.' They are 'responsible' for much of the totalitarian madness that has been loose upon the world, which has led so many human beings to death or dispossession." How can Rodman "condemn a point of view so strongly . . . and then praise its expression?"

A299. Myhre, Paul. "Tongue of Doom, A Poet Sits in Judgment," *News* (Cleveland, Ohio), August 18, 1948, p. 9.

Brief mention. "This is distressing poetry" which may offend, "but it is magnificent poetry."

A300. Palmer, Hugh. "Typical Jeffers Misanthropy," *Herald* (Boston, Mass.), August 4, 1948, p. 23.

Minor. Although this contains Jeffers' "same dismal misanthropy," at its best "the poem gives evidence of power, eloquence and sublimity and a soaring freedom of verse. Some of the nature descriptions are breath-taking in their beauty and nobleness of concept."

A301. Powell, Lawrence Clark. "Poet Cries Out Loudly Against Wars and Man," *Times* (Los Angeles, Cal.), August 1, 1948, p. 3.

A trusted admirer finds little to praise in *The Double Axe*. "The most violent antiwar poetry ever published in this country. . . . The narrative poem is weak in plot and characters and almost barren of the poetry of place which ennobles Jeffers' best work. Several passages are in prose."

He argues well in this medium. However, "poetry that argues is rarely read after a season, except by students."

A302. Rockwell, Kenneth. "Robinson Jeffers' Exciting Verses," *Times Herald* (Dallas, Tex.), July 18, 1948, section 4, p. 6.

Texan reviewer finds *The Double Axe* is "poetry and dynamite" and contains long lines which "sting like poisoned whips. . . . more people will buy the poem and will talk about it than about any book of verse that has been published in years." Truly, Jeffers is "one of the masters of our time."

A303. Rodman, Selden. "Transhuman Magnificence," *Saturday Review of Literature*, XXXI (July 31, 1948), 13-14.

Important poet, editor and critic praises the poetry and condemns the "irresponsible" philosophy. "Jeffers, whatever one may think of his philosophy, remains as close to a major poet as we have. . . . He belongs in the ranks of Dryden and Byron, Whitman and Lindsay, not in the company of Milton, Keats and Eliot." It is sad that "he feels compelled to add more than his quota of hatred and violence to the hatred and violence abroad in the world, while he sits in the properly inhuman stone tower of his waiting exultantly for the Bomb."

A304. Rosenheim, Ned. "One Tiger on the Road," *Poetry*, LXXIII (March 1949), 351-354.

Argues that Jeffers has subordinated action, character and technique to the philosophical content of the work. "That the merit of his work should be, in great measure, a function of the merit of his belief is, in this case, necessary. And that the shocked protest . . . should determine . . . critical response is inevitable."

A305. S[cott], W[infield] T[ownley]. "War-Fed Verse Against the Race," *Journal* (Providence, R. I.), July 18, 1948, section 6, p. 8.

Minor discussion of Jeffers' inhumanism. Although "much in human affairs justifies Jeffers' above-the-battle contempt," one may be "suspicious of his beautiful hawks and all that such animal-loving may signify (it's too easy). . . . Meanwhile, I continue to believe Jeffers to be the most impressive poet now writing in English."

A306. Stork, Charles Wharton. "Jeffers' Seething Poetry," *Inquirer* (Philadelphia, Pa.), July 18, 1948, book section, p. 3.

Brief. *The Double Axe* is "perhaps his best," and although he may repel many readers, "there is an underlying sanity in him that deserves a hearing."

A307. Thompson, Ann Mae. "Poet Gloomy in New Verse," *Star-Telegram* (Fort Worth, Tex.), September 5, 1948, section 2, p. 7.

Moderate praise. "Apart from its gloomy outlook and its controversial political implications, or maybe because of them, the poem makes fascinating and entertaining reading and, from a purely literary standpoint, is above the average in contemporary poetry."

A308. Tribble, Edwin. "There Is an Axe in the Root of the World," *Star* (Washington, D. C.), July 25, 1948, p. C-3.

The language is "again a blend of that haunting, Sibelius-like tone which is his alone—an effect something like an orchestra of nothing except violins and drums," but his "world-be-damned" message, his "sustained hatred" display a deep cynicism which "repulses, rather than attracts, disciples."

A309. Upton, John. "Have You Read . . .?" *Pine Cone-Cymbal* (Carmel, Cal.), July 23, 1948, p. 10.

Despite "gritty subject matter," Jeffers creates moving poetry, says this minor local review. "A thoroughly competent craftsman, he attains in this volume some of the vituperative heights of Dean Swift without sacrificing beauty of line or concept."

Hungerfield and Other Poems
New York: Random House
(1954)

A310. Anonymous. "Brother to Boulders," *Time*, LXIII (January 25, 1954), 112.

This volume contains all the qualities his admirers have liked in the past. "But they are echoes. . . . Even as echoes, Jeffers' themes and poetic voice can still provoke and disturb. He moves among death, violence and pessimism as naturally as other poets celebrate love and ecstasy. . . . Optimists, those who put their faith in humanity, believers in God, in fact most people, will find little comfort anywhere in Jeffers' work."

A311.———. "He Falls Short in Newest Works," *News Leader* (Richmond, Va.), March 15, 1954, spring book section, p. 9.

Minor, brief. Jeffers "shows himself as a fretful, aging man. . . . But if Jeffers fails in his longer pieces, he does capture his old brooding intensity in several of the shorter poems."

A312.———. "Hungerfield and Other Poems," *Call-Bulletin* (San Francisco, Cal.), February 20, 1954, p. 8.

Brief mention. "He has lost none of the consummate skill which in the past placed him in the forefront of his contemporaries."

A313.———. "Perspective of the Star," *Journal* (Providence, R. I.), April 11, 1954, section 6, p. 10.

"He is still our greatest American poet." Compares him to Whitman, Wordsworth and Swift. "Jeffers has attained complete mastery of his long line. . . . This latest segment, while it is a satisfactory book in itself, and while it may be something of a last performance, could also serve as an introduction to the oeuvre of Robinson Jeffers."

A314._____. "Poems of Passion and Violence," *Argonaut*, CXXXIII (January 29, 1954), 18.
Brief general evaluation. "There is an elemental and sometimes wild power in Jeffers' poetry, but it offers, instead of consolation or affirmation, only a resigned despair."

A315._____. Review of *Hungerfield and Other Poems*, *Bulletin from Virginia Kirkus' Bookshop Service*, XXI (December 1, 1953), 778.
Brief general evaluation. "Jeffers seems old. His talent, rooted in nature and nature's powers, seems to be running out. There is a curious narrowness of vision, a lack of self renewal which was always inherent in his poetry. But he still has a following."

A316._____. Review of *Hungerfield and Other Poems*, *Volusia Review*, I (1954), 43.
Comment in Bethune-Cookman College, Datona Beach, Florida, journal. This work "still speaks out in an authentically virile tone for the values of beauty, independence and endurance." The title poem is "of savage tenderness and bitter acceptance."

A317._____. Review of *Hungerfield and Other Poems*, *Courier-Journal* (Louisville, Ky.), January 24, 1954, section 3, p. 9.
"The two longer poems . . . will please Mr. Jeffers' admirers. They are well done and each includes his special brand of physical violence. The fourteen shorter poems are spotty."

A318._____. Review of *Hungerfield and Other Poems*, *Mercury News* (San Jose, Cal.), January 31, 1954, p. 13.

Minor, brief. "Old familiar themes ... the constant repetition ... makes him seem a little worn and less interesting than he was."

A319._____. Review of *Hungerfield and Other Poems*, *Bookmark*, XIII (March, 1954), 129.
Listing. "A collection of striking verse."

A320._____. Review of *Hungerfield and Other Poems*, *Booklist*, L (March 1, 1954), 255.
Brief squib. "While there are flashes of brilliance, the over-all impression left the reader is that the poet is reaching the end of his inspiration."

A321._____. Review of *Hungerfield and Other Poems*, *Quicksilver*, VII (Spring, 1954), 19.
Jeffers "writes with undiminished power the wildly beautiful rhythms of conflict and agony and flame which have given him first place among modern poets in the minds of many. But at 67 he sees life as futility."

A322. _____. Review of *Hungerfield and Other Poems*, *Globe-Democrat* (St. Louis, Mo.), March 28, 1954, p. 8f.
Minor. "This is Jeffers at his best, and that best is a lonely peak others try to scale."

A323._____. Review of *Hungerfield and Other Poems*, *College English*, XV (May, 1954), 489.
Brief listing. "The usual Jeffers violence. The shorter pieces are not misanthropic, but see men as inconsequential. Beautiful landscapes."

A324. _____. Review of *Hungerfield and Other Poems*, *New Yorker*, XXX (May 8, 1954), 148.

Mention. "His language has moments of rightness and power, but his overwhelming taste for violence often reduces his meaning to nonsense and his music to a sort of melodramatic roar."

A325._____. Review of *Hungerfield and Other Poems, United States Quarterly Book Review*, X (June, 1954), 197.

"Mr. Jeffers, although he is too much out of love with the 'sick microbe' man, to write important tragedy, is still a powerful lyricist within the limits of his overmastering subject."

A326._____. Review of *Hungerfield and Other Poems, Post Roundup* (Denver, Colo.), August 1, 1954, p. 16.

Minor. "Here we have an old man, thoroughly weary and disillusioned, writing on today's themes with the sensitivity and flashing fire of a poet in his twenties! . . . This is great poetry, not the obscure and muddied sort nor the simpering sing-song kind but understandable outpourings from a great, hearty and brilliant mind."

A327._____. Review of *Hungerfield and Other Poems, Time*, LXII (December 20, 1954), p. 75.

Brief listing. This volume "remained true to the pessimism that has long been Jeffers' trademark; it also included some ringing tributes to nature."

A328._____. "Robinson Jeffers," *Star* (Washington, D.C.), December 5, 1954, Christmas book section, p. 10.

Brief listing. "More of the same brew."

A329. Derleth, August. "Minority Report," *Capital Times* (Madison, Wis.), February 18, 1954, p. 11.

Noted poet and novelist mentions that "Jeffers has neither grown nor retrogressed; he is peculiarly alone on the American literary landscape. . . . If this is not great poetry (I do not think it is), certainly it is moving and memorable."

A330. Eckman, Frederick. "Additional Jeffers Poems Collected," *News* (Dayton, Ohio), January 31, 1954, section 2, p. 7.

Minor. "Robinson Jeffers is the only accomplished narrative poet now writing in English." The title poem "does not show any marked technical advance. . . . but it does not, on thy other hand, indicate any decline in his powers."

A331. Ferling, Lawrence (Pseud. Lawrence Ferlinghetti). "For Jeffers the Purpose of Poetry, Is 'To Feel Greatly,' " *Chronicle* (San Francisco, Cal.), March 14, 1954, p. 17.

" 'Hungerfield' leaves the reader, above all, a powerful composite image of love and death, a burning image of nature, an apprehension of the natural coupled strangely with the supernatural."

A332. Fitts, Dudley. "Gigantic Bad Dreams," *New York Times Book Review*, January 10, 1954, p. 18.

Major. Noted classicist feels "the successful moments in the long poems are relatively few and always percarious. . . . It's a relief to turn . . . to the few animal and nature poems. Some of these are marred by preaching, others by politics, still others by simple hatred. Nevertheless, the language here is generally under control; one feels the yesness of real poetry."

A333. Fretz, Gene. "Somber, Except–," *Arkansas Gazette* (Little Rock, Ark.), January 17, 1954, section F, p. 6.

Minor. "The title poem . . . is a vivid, lengthy but gripping story. . . . His 'The Cretan Woman,' in play form, is fine free verse. . . . If Jeffers is mournful, he is brave."

A334. Gibbs, Alonzo. "Darkish Tower and Double-Reed," *Voices*, CLV (September-December, 1954), 54-56.

Notes that Jeffers' prophecies have current relevance. "Surprisingly enough many will find Jeffers' horrific tales and dark forebodements less shocking than they were twenty years ago, not because the poet has grown older but because his audience, exposed to the world's scientific and psychotic terror, has grown up." Best are "Jeffers' shorter poems wherein he is more himself and less the bogey-man."

A335. Gregory, Horace. "The Disillusioned Wordsworth of Our Age," *New York Herald Tribune Book Review*, January 24, 1954, p. 5.

Important critic, poet, and admirer of Jeffers' poetry detects a new maturity in Jeffers. "Something that is not resignation, yet has the serenity of self-knowledge, enters the fourteen short poems of the book. In taking the road beyond middle age few American poets have stepped so far with a more deeply expressed humility and courage. ... Jeffers' contribution to the poetry of our day is of mature inspiration and accomplishment. His position is secure and singular."

A336. Hayden, Robert. "A Poet Continues Bitter View of Man, Life," *Tennessean* (Nashville, Tenn.), April 18, 1954, p. 15-D.

Minor adverse review. The title poem "is only partly successful, for its personae are masks on neuroses rather than human types." The play is "marred by the frequent banality of its diction, the obtrusiveness of its colloquialisms. The shorter lyrics ... are less distinguished than some Jeffers has written earlier."

A337. Hedley, Leslie Woolf. Review of *Hungerfield and Other Poems, Inferno*, X (1954), 35.

Favorable review in a little magazine. "Few critics dare approach because they simply are not capable of understanding him." *Hungerfield* is a chapter in the one great book he "has been writing of his life. If he repeats, a great deal he has to observe bears repetition." "De Rerum Virtute," "Carmel Point," and "The Beauty of Things" "all climb beyond the quibbling philosophism of our floundering moderns. These three poems enter the periphery of greatness."

A338. Jacobsen, Josephine. "Two New Volumes of Poetry," *Sun* (Baltimore, Md.), January 29, 1954, p. 20.

Minor. Often Jeffers is "funny in an appalling and accidental way." He is too "heavy, didactic." Yet, "Nature ignited to drama ... gives Jeffers's work, in its bulk, a mountainous impressiveness."

A339. Joost, Nicholas. "Dramatic Playwriting in Poet Jeffers' Book," *Tribune* (Chicago, Ill.), January 24, 1954, p. 6.
Hungerfield is "a notable literary event of the new year." "The Cretan Woman," alone, "would prove Jeffers one of our finest living playwright-poets."

A340. Jordan-Smith, Paul. "Jeffers' Poems Show Balance," *Times* (Los Angeles, Cal.), January 17, 1954, part 4, p. 6.
California notice. The criticism of Jeffers' coldness and remoteness are false. "There is fire enough in the man and his poetry," and "from first to last in the new volume we know a poet who suffers and shares the tragedy of every man."

A341. Mc., D. "Poet Uses Symbols with a Preciseness," *Post* (Charleston, S. C.), January 29, 1954, p. 8b.
Praises Jeffers' precise use of familiar symbols. "The technique is more precise, too." The poetry never slips back "into strong rhythmic prose, as much of his earlier work did."

A342. McCarthy, John Russell. "Poems by Jeffers," *Star-News* (Pasadena, Cal.), March 7, 1954, p. 63.
Minor. Plot summary. "Some of the old fire, usually in the nature passages, is here."

A343. McCormick, John. "Poet and Anti-Poet," *Western Review*, XIX (Autumn, 1954), 65-72.
Finds little change in Jeffers since *Tamar*; no development apparent in *Hungerfield*. Volume is partially redeemed by two splendid short poems, "The Old Stonemason" and "The Deer Lay Down Their Bones," and by "The Cretan Woman." Notes that "Jeffers can still write brief verses of power.... Despite his lapses and despite his inverted sentimentality, Jeffers is not a trivial poet. The appalling sincerity of his coldness and hatred do much particularly in the briefer and less ambitious verse, to compensate for the absurdities."

A344. McDonald, G. D. Review of *Hungerfield and Other Poems, Library Journal*, LXXIX (March 15, 1954), 79.

Brief favorable comment. "Jeffers looks upon the sea, the great stone cliffs of nature and the hawks wings in the air above, and there is grandeur in his vision. When he beholds man he sees only the spoiler and viper. . . . He is the one poet who has found his major theme in almost total misanthropy, but he gives his people enough stature and dignity to attain tragedy."

A345. Nemerov, Howard. "Contemporary Poets," *Atlantic*, CXCIV (September, 1954), 66-68.

Famous poet and novelist finds title poem least successful part of work because the action lacks motivation. "The Cretan Woman" is "very moving and skillfully told. The only difficulty seems to be that the convention of poetic speech will not hold up for the more problematic aspects of character. . . . I wish, too, that the blatantly unnecessary message for today could be left out of Aphrodite's final speech."

A346. Poore, Charles. "Books of the Times," *Times* (New York), January 23, 1954, p. 11.

Hungerfield is written in an elegiac tone. It is "truly Jeffers at his best, a volume of furious threnodies. . . . He's said everything he has to say eloquently before, and he's saying it better than ever right now."

A347. Rodman, Selden. "Knife in the Flowers," *Poetry*, LXXXIV (July, 1954), 226-231.

Important poet-critic disapproves of the characters in *Hungerfield*. Especially in "The Cretan Woman," they are mere puppets, vessels of generalized passions, one-dimensional. The imagery is unrelieved sadism. Jeffers' glory is his ability to reiterate his stoic dirge "supremely well." Also, "Jeffers is an excellent story-teller, the best . . . of all poets writing in English today. . . ."

A348. Spearman, Walter. "Tar Heel Writers Cover a Variety of Subjects," *Observer* (Charlotte, N. C.), January 24, 1954, section C, p. 16. Also in: *Citizen Times* (Asheville, N. C.), January 24, 1954, section B, p. 5.

Brief. "Characteristic Jeffers fare, passionate and violent. . . . Some dozen shorter poems round out the volume but add little to Jeffers' reputation."

A349. Untermeyer, Louis. "Grim and Bitter Dose," *Saturday Review*, XXXVII (January 16, 1954), 17.

Favorable criticism from an important admirer. Although the reader will recognize all the familiar Jeffers elements, hawks, tides, keen winds, "he will not fail to be roused. Jeffers has not lost the gift of biting language and the ability to communicate the phantasmagoria of terror." Particularly praises the tribute to Una which frames the title poem. Speaking of Jeffers' philosophy: "This is bitter medicine grimly administered—bitterer since we are earnestly assured that the world will be well only when our sick civilization dies."

A350. Wolfe, Ann F. "Tragedy and Grief Treated Through Robinson Poems," *Dispatch* (Columbus, Ohio), February 28, 1954, p. 15.

Minor. "The title poem is characteristic Jeffers. . . . Some of his passages are magnificent." A few of the short poems are "equal to his best."

A351. Z., M. "Robinson Jeffers Writes New Volume of Poetry," *Independent Journal* (San Raphael, Cal.), April 10, 1954, magazine section, p. 2.

Minor. "His fierce, dramatic poetry that searches for an answer to the lonely, tortured human experiences is stilled with resignation."

The Beginning and the End and Other Poems
New York: Random House
(1963)

A352. Anonymous. "Homesick for Death," *Time*, LXXXI (May 3, 1963), 114.

His last poems "rank below his best," because "stripped of the beauty of language," his "sentiments seem merely sour. . . . But there are occasional flashes of the old genius." Summary of Jeffers' accomplishments: "For obvious reasons, this forbidding poet was never very popular. . . . But at his misanthropic best, he was one of the greatest American poets, whose verse often has the fire of a wrathful God. . . ."

A353._____. Review of *The Beginning and the End and Other Poems*, *Book Buyer's Guide*, LXVI (April, 1963), 63.
Summarizes subject matter. Advises, "Good Sales for poetry."

A354._____. Review of *The Beginning and the End and Other Poems*, *Newsday* (Garden City, N. Y.), April 27, 1963, p. 35.
Brief listing. "Some are equal to his best."

A355._____. Review of *The Beginning and the End and Other Poems*, *Beloit Poetry Journal*, XIII (Summer, 1963), 38.
Listing. ". . . though Jeffers' images changed to keep pace with the changing madness of the world, his subject matter and attitude never did. . . . A worthy final volume."

A356._____. Review of *The Beginning and the End and Other Poems*, *Booklist*, LIX (July 15, 1963), 922.
"Mirrors Jeffers' cosmic and tragic view of life and recapitulates many of the themes voiced in his earlier works. . . . preoccupation with old age and death . . . moving portrait of his five-year-old granddaughter."

A357._____. Review of *The Beginning and the End and Other Poems*, *Booklist*, LIX (September 1, 1963), 34.
"Short poems . . . which can be read with appreciation and understanding by young people."

A358._____. Review of *The Beginning and the End and Other Poems*, *Post* (Washington, D. C.), December 1, 1963, p. 24.
Brief. "Written with stern power and beauty."

A359._____. Review of *The Beginning and the End and Other Poems*, *New York Times Book Review*, December 1, 1963, p. 76.

Brief listing. "A posthumous collection which remains constant to the poet's vision that the world is beautiful and only man is unworthy of his Creator."

A360._____. Review of *The Beginning and the End and Other Poems*, *Wisconsin Library Bulletin*, LX (March-April, 1964), 151.

Complete review: "The summation of a long poetic career."

A361. Alexander, Irene. "Jeffers' Last Works," *Peninsula Herald* (Monterey, Cal.), May 16, 1963. p. 34.

Lengthy, favorable minor review. Briefly explicates several of the poems. Jeffers is "one of the most celebrated as well as controversial poets of this century."

A362. Antoninus, Brother (William Oliver Everson). Review of *The Beginning and the End and Other Poems, Ramparts*, II (Christmas, 1963), 95-96.

Jeffers' disciple praises the last poems of his master. "If the sense of wonder and awe that occasioned the early great breakthrough are gone . . . yet the energy remains, the undeviating capacity to say what is meant without equivocation. And that is great enough for any man to go out on."

A363. Bennett, Joseph. "The Moving Finger Writes," *Hudson Review*, XVI (Winter, 1963-1964), 624-633.

"This volume . . . contains some of the best work Jeffers has produced. . . . Jeffers is smart enough, when he has to be; and that animal vigor, that ear for blood and disaster, carry him along. . . . Here is a bloody barbarian who can sing, and who has got his plow wedged deep under the edge of reality. I think this book deserves to be read."

A364. Bewley, Marius. "New Poems," *Partisan Review*, XXX (Spring, 1963), 140-142.

Jeffers' knowledge of science harmed his poetry. Only when he writes about animals, which he doesn't do enough, does he seem to be human. The animals and birds redeem these last poems. "Nevertheless there are in the present volume, as always, moving passages, and even whole poems. . . . Jeffers held the consciousness of man in contempt but thought he knew the great scientific and cosmic laws and forces behind and beyond that consciousness. . . . It makes Jeffers seem old-fashioned now. The position is reversed today, when we are deeply interested in consciousness, but are not at all sure we know much about its objects."

A365. Clough, F. Gardner. "Last Words from Tor House," *Orange County Post* (Newburgh, New York), July 4, 1963, p. 4.
Minor. "These are the poems of old age, but they have lost none of the fire and courage and wisdom and a terribly stark love of Earth's beauty."

A366. Davis, Douglas M. "Important Poetry of 1963," *National Observer* (Washington, D. C.), December 23, 1963, p. 16.
List includes this volume as "The last poems by a major American writer."

A367. Dickey, James. "First and Last Things," *Poetry*, CIII (February, 1964), 320-321. Reprinted in his: *Babel to Byzantium: Poets and Poetry Now.* New York: Farrar, Straus and Giroux, 1968, pp. 187-189.
Extremely important balanced summary of Jeffers' accomplishments by a well-known poet. Jeffers' poetic prophecies are again finding favor. "As obviously flawed as he is, Jeffers is cast in a large mold; he fills a position in this country that would simply have been an empty gap without him: that of the poet as prophet, as large-scale philosopher, as doctrine-giver. . . . One cannot shake off Jeffers' vision as one can the carefully prepared surprises of many of the neatly packaged stanzas we call 'good poems.' . . . It is extraordinarily strange how the more awful and ludicrous aspects of the atomic age have come to resemble Jeffers' poems. Few visions have been more desperate, and few lives organized around such austere principles. It seems to me that we must honor these things."

A368. Hughes, Daniel. "Poetry's Larger Views," *Nation*, CXCVI (June 29, 1963), 551.

Unfavorable review of Jeffers' last poems. An important periodical. "There are moments of energy, sudden gatherings of reminiscent powers, but the verse is tired, the poems have become cosmic finger exercises, macrocosmic imitations as petty as the snapshot art we would escape. One does not feel here the autumnal last words of a major poet."

A369. Lane, Lauriat, Jr. "The Greatness of Robinson Jeffers," *Fiddlehead*, LVIII (Fall, 1963), 67-68.

Last poems occasion a prediction: "Robinson Jeffers has been long out of fashion, both his themes and his way of writing, but this final collection reaffirms that as time goes by he will have to be placed among the major American poets of this century." This volume "maintains the seriousness and eloquence that Jeffers has always had at his best."

A370. Levy, William Turner. "The Theme Is Always Man," *New York Times Book Review*, May 5, 1963, p. 5.

High praise. "Wonderfully unexpected poems of personal record. ... For the most part his focus remains cosmic, and he sees the universe as a great heart through which pulsate all the energies that exist. ... Robinson Jeffers in old age remains constant to the youthful vision which served for a lifetime to keep him at one with the splendor of a world he found so beautiful that man alone seemed unworthy of his Creator. His answer will not be ours, but he instructs us how our minds might be exalted in beauty—and so share in the divine quality and fabric of all creation."

A371. Morrison, Lillian. Review of *The Beginning and the End and Other Poems, Horn Book*, XXXIX (October, 1963), 521.

Magazine reviews new books for children. Jeffers' last poems have "something positive" to give to young readers. "A cosmic consciousness, a great love for the beauty and splendor of inanimate nature, and a rugged majestic line characterize his work. Unexpectedly there are some personal poems here, strong, tender. . . ."

A372. Morse, Samuel French. "Poetry 1963," *Wisconsin Studies in Contemporary Literature*, V (Autumn, 1964), 237-249.

High praise. This volume "is an eloquent rejoinder to those who, ten, or even twenty years ago, wrote Jeffers off as a blind misanthrope, a baffled naturalist out of tune with his century. The brooding pessimism . . . is far more compassionate than the arrogant complaints and the raucous self-pity that the younger 'Outsiders' have discovered. . . . The images here, although strongly and sparsely etched, evoke great sympathy. This last book sends one back to the earlier poems to discover how much of a piece Jeffers' work is."

A373._____. "Two Masters," *Virginia Quarterly Review*, XXXIX (Summer, 1963), 510-513.

High praise. These last poems prove how remarkable Jeffers' accomplishment has been. Deplores the "undeserved neglect" he has suffered. Praises Jeffers' integrity, conviction, eloquence, and fierce indignation. "Most of these last poems—even those that seem no more than notations and fragments—reveal a grasp of form and idea that is the work of a master."

A374. Schevill, James. "Eliot, Jeffers—Other Poets," *Chronicle* (San Francisco, Cal.), March 8, 1964, This World section, p. 29.

These last poems of Jeffers are "disappointing. They contain too many flat statements." They are "too didactic to measure up to his best work. . . . It is time for a new edition of his best narrative poems so that the extent of his achievement can be recognized. At his best he helped to regain for poetry some of the dramatic power that it has lost to fiction and drama."

A375. Scott, Winfield Townley. "The Undeserved Neglect," *New York Herald Tribune Books*, June 16, 1963, p. 10.

New England poet praises Jeffers' dignity, honor, beauty, "stern power." Analysis of Jeffers' critical reputation. Compares him favorably to Yeats. Jeffers is "far more important in American poetry than the critics in latter years have supposed." Probably he was overrated at his zenith. "Yet there is no question but he has been underrated in recent decades." He suffered because "of transitory and minor" trends in fashions. This last volume contains "the poems of an old man; relaxed, a little prosy, strong as ever, very moving."

A376._____. "Listening for the Different Voice," *Saturday Review*, XLVI (October 26, 1963), 36.
   Largely a reworking of the previous review. Adds that Jeffers' prophecies are attaining a new relevance. "The neglect of Jeffers, even the scorn of Jeffers, in the past three decades constitutes the major scandal of contemporary American poetry."

A377. Smith, Ray. Review of *The Beginning and the End and Other Poems, Library Journal*, LXXXVIII (April 15, 1963), 1675.
   Brief. "Jeffers' themes are unchanged, though more personalized, probably because of the death of his wife, Una. . . . The impressive final poems of a great poet, recommended for all libraries."

A378. Smith, William Jay. "Titanic Stance," *Harper's Magazine*, CCXXVII (September, 1963), 112.
   Jeffers' "Titanic stance . . . is often marred by touches of shrillness and self-pity. But when he is writing objectively, as he often does in these poems of the natural scene . . . no one has ever equaled him. A poem like 'Birds and Fishes' is as fine as anything he ever wrote."

A379. Spender, Stephen. "Rugged Poetry Imbued with Spirit of the Hawk," *Chicago Sunday Tribune Magazine of Books*, May 12, 1963, p. 3.
   Important favorable review by a major poet. Disagrees with Jeffers' philosophy but praises his "technical and intellectual resources," his

rare ability to incorporate science into poetry. Jeffers' poetry "is not poetry to live with, because it lacks intimacy." But "these last poems of Jeffers ... are extremely moving. They may well be his best poetry. . . ."

A380. Toelle, Gervase. "Familiar Lament," *Spirit*, XXX (September, 1963), 115.

Harsh criticism for Jeffers' failure to heed Yvor Winters' scolding in 1930 for his "suicidal bent." Unfortunately, Jeffers has been "consistent in both quality and quantity throughout his life." These final poems "add up to a failure . . . a waste of time to write or to read. Like the false god of Jeffers' nightmares, his poems must work to no purpose at all."

A381. Worthington-Smith, Hammett. "Robinson Jeffers: Twentieth Century Spokesman," *Atenea*, I (1964), 89-91.

Minor favorable review. Jeffers' "ability to work with real issues in a highly creative manner cause one to realize that he is not only a poet, as the popular mind conceives a poet, but something more—a preacher-prophet, a Socrates."

The following are reviews of major dramatic productions of Jeffers' works. Only those reviews or portions of reviews are included in which Jeffers is specifically mentioned. Minor productions (revivals off-Broadway, touring productions, and readings) are dealt with under article listings (Section B) for the years in which they were produced.

Tower Beyond Tragedy
University of California Player's Production
Opened November 8, 1932

A382. Holden, W. Sprague. "The Bloody Stones of Mycenae," *Argonaut*, III (November 11, 1932), 5-6. Reprinted in: *Carmelite*, V (November 24, 1932), 4.

Play compares favorably with O'Neill's "Mourning Becomes Electra." The excellence of language "is Jeffers' great strength. His Orestes has identified himself with agelessness, sunk himself into the cosmos beyond humanity but which still is the greatest humanity. . . . This is art which is greatest in its implications; in this sense is Jeffers a true maker."

A383. Nathan, P. S. "Jeffers' Drama Triumphs in Premiere," *Post Enquirer* (Oakland, Cal.), November 9, 1932, p. 7.

"Acting of surprisingly fine quality, intelligent staging and the superb beauty of the play itself made for a rare evening's entertainment."

A384. Thompson, Lloyd S. " 'Tower Beyond Tragedy' Offered by U. C. Players," *Examiner* (San Francisco, Cal.), November 12, 1932, p. 10.

"The performance heightened my admiration for Jeffers without settling for me the question of whether he is a towering genius of poetry and philosophy or just a magnificent medicine man. His work is so supercharged with emotion that it sometimes renders one a little suspicious of it."

A385. Soanes, Wood. "Jeffers Play in Premiere Acclaimed," *Pine Cone* (Carmel, Cal.), November 18, 1932, p. 6.

Praise from local newspaper. Jeffers "has already been recognized as America's major poet and his 'Tower Beyond Tragedy' admitted as one of the few worth-while contributions to literature in this decade, but its scope was broadened materially in its dramatic adaptation."

A386._____ "Student Actors Produce Poetic Drama of Electra," *Tribune* (Oakland, Cal.), November 9, 1932, p. 26.

The third act, "burdened down with speeches whose loveliness was marred by their length and whose action was impeded by the requirement for persistent flights of elocution, came as a distinct anti-climax to the preceding sequences wherein the ancient tragedy was sent thundering over the footlights."

A387. Warren, G. C. " 'Tower Beyond Tragedy' Done at U. C."
Chronicle (San Francisco, Cal.), November 10, 1932, p. 9.

"The uglier passions of mankind, murder, adultery, vengeance, incest,
are the themes treated in the play, their hideous aspects clothed
decently in Jeffers' sensuous poetry, which, however, suffered somewhat in its delivery by the student players, who lost something in the
cadence and rhythm of the swelling verse."

Tower Beyond Tragedy
Del Monte Summer Theater, Carmel, California
Opened July 5, 1941

A388. Hobart, John. "The Story Beyond the Tower," *Chronicle* (San
Francisco, Cal.), July 13, 1941, This World section, p. 18.

The play's pithy language "is its major glory." The first two acts
prove "that Jeffers has an innate instinct for the theater. The episodes
march magnificently forward, with a passionate fierceness that overwhelms the spectator."

A389._____. " 'Tower Beyond Tragedy': Robinson Jeffers Has
Written Drama Too Magnificent to Languish Between Book Covers,"
Chronicle (San Francisco, Cal.), July 7, 1941, p. 13.

"It has the shape and substance of mighty tragedy. . . . The words
. . . are extraordinary, just as words; but Jeffers' special triumph is that
he has used them always dramatically."

Dear Judas
Adapted by Michael Meyerberg
New York Production
Opened October 4, 1947

A390. Anonymous. "Another Judas," *Newsweek*, XXX (October 20,
1947), 91.

Unfavorable. "Now the poet Jeffers attempts to confute the weighted verdict of history in a new play called 'Dear Judas,' which presents Judas—and Christ—in a different and, to put it mildly, nontheological light. . . . Actually, the play is more dull than shocking. The poetry is often obscure."

A391._____. Review of *Dear Judas, Forum*, CVIII (December, 1947), 371.

Mixed unfavorable. "This notion," that Judas betrayed Christ when Christ lost humble humanitarianism, "could have served as well as any other for a poetic play, and it did provide some glowing moments especially toward the end of the drama. That the play failed rather distressingly is the result of woeful mismanagement of the adaptation for the stage."

A392._____. "New Play in Manhattan," *Time*, L (October 20, 1947), 73.

Unfavorable. "What Robinson Jeffers wrote in *Dear Judas* was simply a dramatic poem; putting it on the stage does nothing whatever to turn it into a play."

A393._____. "Theater," *New Yorker*, XXIII (October 18, 1947), 55-57.

Highly unfavorable. "Of the many attempts to interpret it a little more mystically, probably the most elaborate, though not necessarily either the most eloquent or plausible was a poem called 'Dear Judas' written in 1929 by Robinson Jeffers. . . . There can easily be many opinions about the artistic merits of Mr. Jeffers' poem (I find it involved and literary, full of curiously uncompelling images . . .), but I don't think there can be any question about its unsuitability for the stage."

A394. Atkinson, Brooks. "The New Play in Review," *Times* (New York), October 6, 1947, p. 26.

Mixed. "Mr. Jeffers did not write his poem for statement in the theatre. Although the phrasing is poetic in sharp, modern lines, the poem is a rationalization of a sacred theme and difficult to understand. . . . By enthusiasm and imagination Mr. Meyerberg has tried to lift it out of the study into splendor and beauty. If 'Dear Judas' were an inspired work of art, he might have succeeded wholly."

A395. Barnes, Howard. "The Theater Betrayed," *Herald Tribune* (New York), October 6, 1947, p. 26.

"Mr. Jeffers mystical apologia for Iscariot has been given mannered and muddled theatrical projection in 'Dear Judas.' "

A396. Chapman, John. "Dear Judas' a Stilted, Unmoving Version of Deeds at Gethsemane," *News* (New York), October 6, 1947, p. 30.

Unfavorable. "The sonorous pomposities and pompous sonorities" of Jeffers' poem have no purpose in the theatre. It is "neither uplifting nor annoying."

A397. Coleman, Robert. "Dear Judas Proves a Soporific," *Mirror* (New York), October 7, 1947, p. 24.

Unfavorable. "Take along a cushion or two. You will doze more comfortably. Sleeping tablets are superfluous."

A398. Freund, Philip. "A Word of Praise," *Times* (New York), October 12, 1947, section 2, p. 2.

Letter praising Atkinson for "his uniquely just and appreciative criticism of 'Dear Judas.' . . . It is not very heartening that his fellow critics found a work of this stature to be dull and obscure. Can it be that they are not interested in hearing what a great poet has to say on a theme that is deeply engrossing to most of mankind; or that they ask to have every word instantly clear to them? Not all ideas can be communicated as popularly as that."

A399. Garland, Robert. "No Power and Glory in Ideological Play," *Journal-American* (New York), October 6, 1947, p. 11.

Mentions Jeffers as the original author of the poem, while giving blame to Meyerberg for play's failure. " 'Dear Judas' is inoffensive to a Christian, ineffective to a critic, and, to this Christian critic, the profane translation of a sacred story, arty, pretentious and uncalled for."

A400. Hawkins, William. "Choir in Pit Takes 'Dear Judas' Honors," *World-Telegram* (New York), October 6, 1947, p. 22.

Unfavorable. "It does not seem likely that Robinson Jeffers wrote this work with any idea of its being produced as a drama. The language is poetic, often even lofty, but it is also very obscure. This is the sort of text that should be read, studied and reiterated to be understood." In the theatre it is confusing.

A401. Kronenberger, Louis. "A Poem Wholly Fails to Get by as a Play," *PM Exclusive* (New York), October 7, 1947, p. 19.

"*Dear Judas* does not belong in the theater, and can hardly help falling flat there."

A402. Morehouse, Ward. "Dear Judas is Awkward and Unimpressive upon Stage of the Mansfield," *Sun* (New York), October 6, 1947, p. 18.

" 'Dear Judas' is iconoclastic and anti-scriptural and it is also very tedious and undramatic.

A403. Nathan, George Jean. "Dear Judas." In his: *Theatre Book of the Year: 1947-1948.* New York: Alfred A. Knopf, 1948, pp. 77-80.

"The Jeffers verse, occasionally not without a felicity in phrasing, more generally misses the ring of beauty, the vibrance and the silver irony that the drama demands. As it stands, it is overladen with monotony and underladen with that spark, whether genuine or fraudulent, without which Biblical drama languishes, either critically or commercially, into failure."

A404. Phelan, Kappo. "The Stage and Screen," *Commonweal*, XLVII (October 31, 1947), 71.

Condemns attempt to censor play. "It will certainly be simpler to assess the dramaturgy of Robinson Jeffers in the forthcoming 'Medea' rather than attempting to unravel the motives and values behind the late strange Meyerberg production of his 'shocking poem.' "

A405. Pollock, Arthur. " 'Dear Judas,' New Version of the Bible Story, Opens at Mansfield," *Eagle* (Brooklyn, N. Y.), October 6, 1947, p. 14.

Unfavorable. "Robinson Jeffers' words, as brought to the stage by Mr. Meyerberg, are a confusion of trite phrases, old verbiage reshuffled, with little marrow in them, not much sense."

A406. Watts, Richard, Jr. "Drama About Judas Theatrically Dull," *Post* (New York), October 6, 1947, p. 31.

The play seemed "not only tedious drama but considerably less than first-rate poetry," and it "emerges as a dull and pompous stunt."

Medea
New York Production
Opened October 20, 1947

A407. Anonymous. "Critics Give 'Medea' Their Rare Praise," *Peninsula Herald* (Monterey, Cal.), November 1, 1947, p. 3.

Description of critical success of *Medea*. Extensive quotation from the New York critics. Praise "was extended to Jeffers, the renowned American poet."

A408._____. Review of *Medea, Life*, XXIII (November 17, 1947), 112-114.

"To prepare Medea for modern audiences Poet Robinson Jeffers freely adapted the original version, made it seem less like the inevitable tragedy of two ill-fated lovers and more like the study of a neurotic termagant."

A409._____. "Half-New Play in Manhattan," *Time*, L (November 3, 1947), 68.

"More in the limelight was Poet Robinson Jeffers for his quite free, sometimes florid, but generally effective adaptation. . . . The whacking Broadway success of *Medea* has made up to Jeffers the recent Broadway failure of a dramatization of his poem, *Dear Judas*. The sixty-year-old poet thinks now that he might even try writing an original play 'if I knew what to write about.' "

A410._____. "Magic by Medea," *Newsweek*, XXX (November 3, 1947), 76.

"As far as the writing goes, Robinson Jeffers has done a dignified and rhythmic job of adapting the Euripides original."

A411. Atkinson, Brooks. "At the Theatre," *Times* (New York), October 21, 1947, p. 27.

Rave notice. "Mr. Jeffers' free adaptation, as it is called, spares the supernatural bogeyman of the classical Greek drama and gets on briskly with the terrifying story of a woman obsessed with revenge. His verse is modern; his words are sharp and vivid, and his text does not worship gods that are dead."

A412._____. "Medea for Moderns," *Times* (New York), October 26, 1947, section 11, p. 1.

Mr. Atkinson is a consistent Jeffers admirer. "As a modern-minded writer, Euripides would be the first to agree that after 2,378 years 'Medea' needs a little play-doctoring. Robinson Jeffers has performed that service with the alacrity of a surgeon. Although he has retained the legend and the characters, he has freely adapted 'Medea' into a modern play by dispensing with the formalities, editing most of the woe-woe out of the chorus speeches; and in the interest of melodramatic suspense he has not announced every five minutes exactly what Medea is going to do. . . . Mr. Jeffers has kept most of the speeches short, which is a blessing in or out of the theatre; and his literary style is terse, idiomatic and sparing. The imagery is austere and brilliant."

A413. Barnes, Howard. "Miss Anderson's *Medea*," *Herald Tribune* (New York), October 21, 1947, p. 24.

Favorable. "When the two feminine stars are on stage, giving the Jeffers lines their poetic and evocative quality, 'Medea' has the stuff of splendor."

A414. Beaufort, John. "Robinson Jeffers' Medea on Broadway," *Christian Science Monitor* (Boston, Mass.), October 25, 1947, p. 10p.

Favorable review with mention of the sinewy and "throbbing verse" of Jeffers' adaptation.

A415. Beyer, William. "The State of the Theater: New Blood," *School and Society*, LXVII (February 28, 1948), 163-164.

Favorable. "Robinson Jeffers has done an excellent adaptation of the Euripides original, and his verse is pithy, terse, vivid, and illuminating without extraneous elaboration, hewing to the emotional line consistently. Euripides would quite likely have been a modern himself."

A416. Brown, John Mason. "Genuine Virtuosity," *Saturday Review of Literature*, XXX (November 22, 1947), 24-27. Reprinted in his: *Seeing More Things*. New York: McGraw-Hill Book Co., Inc., 1948, pp. 231-237.

"Mr. Jeffers has not attempted the impossible task of prettifying the Medea story. He has employed his poets' skill to streamline the text, to bring it closer to the contemporary stage, to rid its speeches of those stylistic villainies of which E. P. Coleridge was guilty in his translation. Mr. Jeffers' language, though not always satisfactory, has about it—at its best—a driving, iron quality that Gilbert Murray's more liquid version cannot claim. What it loses as poetry, it gains as theatre."

A417. Chapman, John. "Hell Hath No Fury Like Medea's When Miss Anderson Gets Going," *News* (New York), October 21, 1947, p. 45.

Jeffers has made "a splendid version of one of time's great tales of horror," but Miss Anderson "shot her bolt in the first act and had no reserve of ammunition for the second." Yet, the play won thirteen curtain calls.

A418. Coleman, Robert. "Medea of Jeffers Lacks Unity," *Mirror* (New York), October 21, 1947, p. 26.

One of the few mixed reviews. Jeffers' free adaptation is "eloquent," although Jeffers makes Euripides seem "repetitious and flowery."

A419. Cray, J. B. "Olympia Judgment," *Times* (New York), February 15, 1948, section 2, p. 3.

Letter to drama editor. "Judith Anderson's magnificent acting in Robinson Jeffers' version of 'Medea' was interrupted by anemia. Are we to take this as a slap of dramatic criticism from Olympus? Could it be that those choruses Mr. Jeffers dropped out of Euripides' script had a reason for being there? Anyway, if we are to go on omitting passages from our presentations of the Greek classics, may we not have to require theatregoers to furnish blood with the purchase of a ticket?"

A420. Garland, Robert. "431 B.C. Play a Triumph for Judith Anderson," *Journal-American* (New York), October 21, 1947, p. 10.

"Robinson Jeffers has strayed but slightly from the Corinthian history . . . as related by Euripides. . . . He has wisely, it seems—neither avoided nor stressed the piece's witchcraft and the magic chariot of the tortured one's escape is left waiting at the gate."

A421. Gibbs, Wolcott. "The Lady, the Professor, and the Cop," *New Yorker*, XXIII (November 1, 1947), 44.

Mixed reception. "Robinson Jeffers has done away with some of the supernatural visitations that complicated the original, but otherwise, overornamental and studiously poetic, his text isn't much help."

A422. Gilder, Rosamond. "Actors All," *Theatre Arts Magazine*, XXXI (December, 1947), pp. 10-12, 36. Reprinted in her: *Theatre Arts Anthology*. New York: Theatre Arts Books, 1950, pp. 669-672.
  Favorable. "In his *Medea* . . . Robinson Jeffers has created a terrifying image of evil. . . . a powerful rendering of this song of hate."

A423. Hawkins, William. "Judith Anderson Sets New High in 'Medea,' " *World-Telegram* (New York), October 21, 1947, p. 24.
  Rave review concentrating on Judith Anderson's performance.

A424. Kronenberger, Louis. "Judith Anderson Gives Her Finest Performance," *PM Exclusive* (New York), October 22, 1947, p. 15.
  "Mr. Jeffers' adaptation is generally a good one. Here and there something obtrudes as too 'poetic' or too odd; Mr. Jeffers is a little too much at home in Corinth, having rather a taste for the Corinthian style. But in the main his Medea has real movement and force."

A425. Morehouse, Ward. "The New Play: 'Medea' a Harrowing Drama, Magnificently Played by Judith Anderson," *Sun* (New York), October 21, 1947, p. 24.
  "There is beauty of language in the Robinson Jeffers adaptation. . . ." *Medea* contains "soaring verse" and is a "fine contribution" to the New York theatre.

A426. Nathan, George Jean. "Medea." In his: *Theatre Book of the Year: 1947-1948*. New York: Alfred A. Knopf, 1948, pp. 77-80.
  In "Honor List," *Medea* is listed as "Best Play" and Judith Anderson as "Best Female Acting Performance." "Jeffers' free, de-goded rendering of the great tragedy is a more than acceptable performance—much superior theatrically to the Gilbert Murray translation."

A427. Phelan, Kappo. "The Stage and Screen," *Commonweal*, LXVII (November 7, 1947), 94.

"It is necessary to say at once that Robinson Jeffers' 'free adaptation' of Euripides has resulted in an astonishing collaboration: a great performance. If the advance promotion stories are true, and Judith Anderson did indeed solicit the poet for his version of the 'barbarian bride,' he has, reversibly, solicited from her a most stern accomplishment. I think the result is monumental. . . . As I am most of all interested in poetry, Jeffers' several slow ascents into the formal simile—particularly as paused and articulated by Miss Anderson— seemed to me current history."

A428. Pollock, Arthur. "Medea, Anderson and Gielgud Get a Wonderful Reception," *Eagle* (Brooklyn, N. Y.), October 21, 1947, p. 8.

"Mr. Jeffers has made Greek drama easier to follow than it was the way the Greeks left it, but the words he finds for it are rather naked. He does not enrich it. He hollers."

A429. Shaw, Irwin. "Cavalry at Corinth," *New Republic*, CXVII (November 3, 1947), 36.

O'Neill chose plays that would make good American repertory theater "out of the works of the ancient Greek dramatists. O'Neill's artistic and commercial acumen has been confirmed in the production of Robinson Jeffers' adaptation of Euripides' Medea."

A430. Watts, Richard, Jr. "Judith Anderson Superb in Jeffers' 'Medea,' " *Post* (New York), October 21, 1947, p. 30.

". . . the simple, direct, striking and eloquent verse of his 'Medea' is both dramatically and poetically satisfying. It is in just the right mood. . . ."

A431. Wyatt, Euphemia van Rensselaer. "The Horror of Hatred," *Catholic World*, CLXVI (December, 1947), 263-264.

"Jeffers' verse is free and modern, terse and direct and what a boon to the theater after the contorted versification of Gilbert Murray."

A432._____. Review of *Medea, Catholic World*, CLXIX (June, 1949), pp. 228-229.

"Robinson Jeffers' version of Euripides in modern rhythms is certainly the finest for our theater."

Tower Beyond Tragedy
New York Production
Opened November 26, 1950

A433. Anonymous. "ANTA Launches Its New Series with Jeffers Play," *Christian Science Monitor* (Boston, Mass.), December 9, 1950, magazine section, p. 5.

"As for Mr. Jeffers, his colorful, free-wheeling dialogue may at times offend the otherwise music-lulled ear with some explicitly anatomical reference. His imagery may seem a trifle glib, hollow, and repetitious—a hawk in several instances being lugged in where a handsaw might serve as well or better. But, on the whole, his voice is as welcome as it is unwonted among the accustomed literary traffic of the Broadway stage."

A434._____. Review of *Tower Beyond Tragedy, Time*, LVI (December 4, 1950), 65.

"What is mostly the matter . . . is that it seldom seems like a play at all. It is merely an undynamic stage treatment of Jeffers' well-known dramatic poem on the House of Atreus. Though it chronicles the matricide of Clytemnestra, the murders of Agamemnon, Aegisthus, and Cassandra, and more than dabbles in adultery and incest, it is too choked by imagery ever to ignite, is too highbustedly declamatory ever to terrify."

A435._____. Review of *Tower Beyond Tragedy, Theatre Arts*, XXXV (February, 1951), 15.

Mixed. It "is more modern than Greek, but not only because of his so-called psychological approach. . . . It is the solution proposed for Orestes . . . that marks the work as contemporary. . . . choral effects serve no stage purpose. They are stressed unwisely."

A436._____. "The State of the Theatre: ANTA Storms Broadway," *School and Society*, LXXII (December 23, 1950), 416-419.

Favorable. "Poet and actress complement each other perfectly, and Jeffers' rugged and sinuously masculine verse, with its wide-swinging rhythms and evocative, emotionally charged imagery and its sense of eager urgency and immediacy, is unleashed to incisive, sensuous life in Judith Anderson."

A437. Atkinson, Brooks. "Judith Anderson Opens ANTA's Series in Jeffers' 'Tower Beyond Tragedy,'" *Times* (New York), November 27, 1950, p. 29.

"Written in lines of fire that make an ancient theme seem immediate and devastating . . . Although Mr. Jeffers has taken his theme out of Aeschylus, he is a modern poet who thinks in terms of human beings. He has concentrated the horrors of Agamemnon's tribe in a compact, tingling, and shocking tragedy that moves swiftly down the bloody corridors of time. The poetry is never self-conscious. . . . Mr. Jeffers has squandered all his passion on the people and the events without academic genuflections to traditions."

A438._____. "Queen of Tragedy," *Times* (New York), December 10, 1950, section 2, p. 5.

Atkinson continues to praise. "Robinson Jeffers . . . is a modern poet who represents modern thought and emotion and substitutes fire for the ceremonial grandeur of Aeschylus and Euripides. He is more interested in the personal torment of the characters than in consulting the whims of the Greek gods. To lovers of modern poetry this is a happy dispensation, for Mr. Jeffers goes straight to the heart of the matter in clean and pulsing verse. . . . Mr. Jeffers has written 'Tower Beyond Tragedy' in a mood of white heat. It is an intensely personal tragedy in his telling."

A439. Barnes, Howard. "ANTA's New Venture," *Herald Tribune* (New York), November 27, 1950, p. 14.

Mixed. "Since the poetry rarely soars, it inspires very little emotional response, unless it is backed up by superlative acting."

A440. Chapman, John. "Judith Anderson in a Heroic Role," *News* (New York), November 27, 1950, p. 43.

Favorable. ". . . the first dramatist, Aeschylus, got a taut and skillful treatment at the hands of the poet Jeffers." His "lines sound strong and true."

A441. Clurman, Harold. "From the Sublime to the Enjoyable," *New Republic*, CXXIV (January 8, 1951), 12.

"Jeffers' poem—written in verse that makes a brazenly joyless music-like sound without echo, as if all feeling were buried deep in stone—is an expression of a desire to transcend the pain and violence of ordinary humanity so as to become one with the moral impassivity of nature's eyeless forces."

A442. Coleman, Robert. "Judith Anderson Gives Telling Performance," *Mirror* (New York), November 28, 1950, p. 38.

Unfavorable. " 'Tower Beyond Tragedy,' though by a distinguished poet, somehow failed to impress, stimulate and move us as much as it might have."

A443. Gibbs, Wolcott. "The Mycenae Story," *New Yorker*, XXVI (December 9, 1950), 62, 64.

"Mr. Jeffers' verse, which, to my ear, has something of the majestic turbulence of a battle in progress, is really the only suitable way to do justice to so much dark passion and almost inconceivable butchery."

A444. Hawkins, William. "Poem-Based Play Powerful Theater," *World-Telegram and Sun* (New York), November 27, 1950, p. 20.

"Our most exciting actress and most distinguished theater poet joined their skills for a second time," and gave the American Theater Academy a "start of distinction."

A445. Kerr, Walter. Critique of *Tower Beyond Tragedy*, *Commonweal*, LIII (December 22, 1950), 279.
Because Jeffers "uses the action of the play to explain his philosophy," he robs the "action of that independent vitality which could give it life." The result is a dull play which contains "only meaningless actions."

A446. Marshall. Margaret. Review of *Tower Beyond Tragedy*, *Nation*, CLXXI (December 23, 1950), 683.
Although the reviewer did not see it, she questions ANTA's choice of this play as its opener. "The Jeffers poem is something less than great, and, again, I find it difficult to understand the choice."

A447. McClain, John. "Thousands of Attractive Words About Very Little," *Journal-American* (New York), November 27, 1950, p. 10.
"The language was soaring. . . ." However, "It takes Mr. Jeffers several thousand attractive words to unwind" the plot, which is "a great deal of talk about very little."

A448. Nathan, George Jean. "Tower Beyond Tragedy." In his: *Theatre Book of the Year: 1950-1951*. New York: Alfred A. Knopf, 1951, pp. 136-138.
"There are some moments of pregnant dramatic passion in the retelling, but there are not enough of them to atone for the drier narrative stretches and for the predominant feeling that a good library poem has been slaughtered to provide our first tragic actress with a Greek theatrical holiday. . . . While the minimum of good is of course independently to be sanctioned, the preponderance of bad condemns the work as a whole."

A449. Sheaffer, Louis. "Judith Anderson Returns to Ancient Greece with 'Tragedy,' " *Eagle* (Brooklyn, N. Y.), November 27, 1950, p. 8.

"Mr. Jeffers, I'm sorry to say, brings no fresh illumination or any great amount of eloquence and beauty to his new version of the old legend."

A450. Watts, Richard, Jr. "Judith Anderson's Clytemnestra," *Post* (New York), November 28, 1950, p. 48.

"It is clearly the work of a poet with fine rhetorical gifts, but it is not the work of a genuinely effective dramatist." Unlike *Medea*, this play "indicates that the author is still uncomfortable in the theatrical medium."

A451. Wyatt, Euphemia van Rensselaer. Review of *Tower Beyond Tragedy, Catholic World*, CLXXII (January, 1951), 308.

The production, "all in all is a fine one but Jeffers does far better in adapting the Greek poets than in attempting to reinterpret them. His muse is too apt to disrobe herself."

The Cretan Woman
Washington, D. C. Production: Opened May 4, 1954
New York, N. Y. Production: Opened July 7, 1954

A452. Anonymous. Review of *The Cretan Woman, Saturday Review*, XXXVII (June 5, 1954), 25.

"While Mr. Jeffers can readily be forgiven the lack of searching analysis for the essential truth of the legend that Jean Anouilh brings to a story like 'Medea,' he is expected to express the fierce and compelling strength of those barbarous forces, unleashed love and hate. This he does too diffusely."

A453. Atkinson, Brooks. "Cretan Woman," *Times* (New York), September 5, 1954, section 2, p. 1.

Continued praise. "He writes with relentless grandeur. He has a severe, uncompromising style with natural imagery ideal for Greek themes. If Mr. Jeffers were tempermentally more optimistic, he would probably have a larger reading public in America where angry rebellion against our hopeful folkways is not exactly relished, and if he were widely read, his literary genius would be more widely appreciated."

A454._____. "Jeffers Tragedy," *Times* (New York), May 21, 1954, p. 17.

"Mr. Jeffers is no genius at dramatic craftsmanship, but he can write craggy verse and flintlike phrases.... The contemporary significance ... is nebulous, if not beside the point.... Certainly the baleful tone of the Phaedra legend becomes Mr. Jeffers, who has never been guilty of feeling hopeful about life, and who writes with a kind of defiant independence and candor. Put 'The Cretan Woman' down as a refreshing exercise in the power of the spoken word."

A455. Bager, Roger. "The Cretan Woman; Absorbing," *World-Telegram and Sun* (New York), July 5, 1954, p. 16.

"... there was excitement for the listener, as this absorbing tragedy in the classical style disclosed its grim contents...."

A456. Bilowit, Ira J. Review of *The Cretan Woman, Show Business*, July 12, 1954, p. 6.

"Jeffers has maintained the inherent 'Greek tragedy.' "

A457. Carmody, Jay. "Arena Presents Premiere of Jeffers' 'Cretan Woman,' " *Star* (Washington, D. C.), May 5, 1954, p. 40.

"Like his 'Medea' of seven seasons ago, Mr. Jeffers' new play is in verse that is hot, turbulent and unashamedly candid." However, the whole play and subject "has about it a curious unreality."

A458. Coe, Richard L. "Phaedra Has New Twist at Arena," *Post* Washington, D. C.), May 5, 1954, p. 38.

Jeffers seems to believe that lust "is frequently confused with love. . . . He says it with dramatic heat and the Arena players do well by his fruity lines." This is Mr. Jeffers' "compelling quixotic variation on a favorite theatrical theme."

A459. Coleman, Robert. "The Cretan Woman Scores with Good Diction, Fine Setting," *Mirror* (New York), July 9, 1954, p. 27.

Favorable critique. " 'The Cretan Woman' is a taut, compact drama that boasts some lofty and eloquent verse by Jeffers. It calls for fine diction and powerful voices. It is fortunate that most of its interpreters have these gifts."

A460. Crist, Judith. " 'The Cretan Woman' Opens at Provincetown Theater," *Herald Tribune* (New York), July 8, 1954, p. 16.

"Mr. Jeffers is primarily a poet, not a playwright, and his soaring poetic and passionately sweeping version of the Phaedra legend requires performance and production that can meet the challenge of the script. That challenge was met only fleetingly last night."

A461. F[unke], L[ewis]. "Jeffers' Play," *Times* (New York), July 8, 1954, p. 18.

"It is an elemental story and in Mr. Jeffers' version it is straightly hewn, full of storm and fury."

A462. Hayes, Richard. Review of *The Cretan Woman, Commonweal*, LX (September 10, 1954), 558.

The play "captures ambiance, the hard clear thrust, the dramatic line at once noble and ravaged. Everywhere, too, it is flooded—and rightly—with the crystal air of Mr. Jeffers' Carmel, strewn with passionate boulders of his world-before-time." Although it contains "vulgarities" and lacks "moral spaciousness," it is "a challenge on the highest level of our contemporary dramatic literature."

A463. McClain, John. "Free Version of Tragedy," *Journal-American* (New York), July 8, 1954, p. 12.

"This is Mr. Jeffers' rather free interpretation of a Greek tragedy, but for my money he'd have been better off leaving the whole thing alone."

A464. Herridge, Frances. "Robinson Jeffers' Play is No Play," *Post* (New York), July 8, 1954, p. 32.

"Its powerful poetry almost blasted us out of the tiny village theater. Such emotings are unbearable in anything smaller than the Met."

A465. Wyatt, Euphemia van Rensselaer. Review of *The Cretan Woman*, *Catholic World*, CLXXIX (September, 1954), 469-471.

"Mr. Jeffers' verse is vigorous and at moments soars although his ideas are earthbound. After spattering with mud the Grecian Galahad, Hippolytus, Jeffers turns the Queen into a peasant and makes the great hero, Theseus, capable of butchering his son. It is Greek *au Grand Guignol.*"

B

ARTICLES ABOUT ROBINSON JEFFERS

1922

B1. Anonymous. "Pictures of Peninsula Penmen and Their Principal Products," *Pine Cone* (Carmel, Cal.), June 29, 1922, p. 7.

Brief initial mention in local newspaper. An article on Carmel literary figures is introduced by Jeffers' poem, "Let Us Go Home to Paradise." Mention, complete: "Robinson Jeffers is a writer of lyric and narrative poems, which clothe common experiences in beauty."

B2. Bostick, Daisy F. "Carmel and the Creative Arts," *Pine Cone* (Carmel, Cal.), July 6, 1922, p. 6.

Early recognition. In a listing of local writers, Jeffers is included as someone whose works "have sung its [Carmel's] praises."

1925

B3. Moore, Virginia. "Two Books," *Voices*, V (November, 1925), 70-72.

Brief mention in review of *Continent's End*. "Robinson Jeffers, of *Tamar* fame, contributes the title poem and four others, all arresting."

1926

B4. Anonymous. "Another Volume of Poetry," *Pine Cone* (Carmel, Cal.), May 22, 1926, p. 8.

Notice of forthcoming publication. "Another volume of poetry by Robinson Jeffers will be published by Boni and Liveright next spring. A very large sale has been enjoyed by 'Roan Stallion' which the publishers brought out some time ago."

B5.———. "August Contributors," *Overland Monthly*, LXXXIV (August, 1926), 241.

A California publication's complete comment on Jeffers' contribution to this issue, a poem entitled "The Beach": "Robinson Jeffers, we feel like only mentioning his name! He is one of the world's most famous and perhaps one of the best known poets of the day. Jeffers is an artist of words which few can touch with the written word."

B6.———. "Californians in 1926 List," *Pine Cone* (Carmel, Cal.), December 31, 1926, p. 6.

Brief mention in discussion of literature of 1926. Harold Smith of the San Francisco *Chronicle* is quoted as saying that, "Robinson Jeffers rose brillianty over the horizon of poesy with *Roan Stallion, Tamar and Other Poems.*"

B7.———. "Carmel–Secret Garden of the Gods," *Pine Cone* (Carmel, Cal.), October 8, 1926, pp. 1, 7.

Brief mention in article on Carmel: "It is the home at present of some of the best known names in the writing and art world and is the mental cradle of at least one name that is destined to become immortal in American letters–Robinson Jeffers, the poet."

B8._____. Comment on "Noon," *Literary Digest*, XC (August 7, 1926), 32.

Reprint of poem, with following complete comment: "Here is a mid-summer noon in some cloudless country. It is among *New Republic's* unusual poems."

B9._____. "Deluxe Edition of 'Tamar' To Be Aided by Artists," *Pine Cone* (Carmel, Cal.), November 5, 1926, p. 1.

Slight comment by an art critic. One Madame Ann Dane, a visitor to Carmel, knows the artists who are to illustrate the forthcoming edition of *Tamar.* She says they know California and "they also know and thoroughly appreciate the beauty of the great poem."

B10._____. "Greatest American Poet," *Pine Cone* (Carmel, Cal.), May 22, 1926, p. 6.

Trivia of possible biographical interest. "Benjamin de Casseres, author and critic, of New York, and Mrs. Casseres, were recent guests of Mr. and Mrs. Robinson Jeffers. George Sterling, California poet, was also the guest of the Jeffers over the weekend. Mr. de Casseres says of Robinson Jeffers, that he is 'the greatest modern poet.' "

B11._____. "A Little Poetry," *Nation*, CXXIII (October 20, 1926), 391-392.

Brief critical aside in an article on current publishing. Notes that publishers like to trim down size of poetry books, or anthologies. ". . . nothing could be more absurd than a state of mind which would refuse a hearing to writers with the dimension of Robinson Jeffers and William Ellery Leonard. 'Tamar' and 'Two Lives,' the outstanding volumes of poetry published here last year, were not pamphlet stuff; they had length of body and height of reach such as only unlimited space can encourage."

B12._____. "Local News Notes of Interest," *Pine Cone* (Carmel, Cal.), June 11, 1926, p. 3.

Brief news squib of possible biographical interest. "George Sterling, California's most prominent poet, who was one of the original settlers in the artists and writers colony here, is in Carmel this week as the guest of Mr. and Mrs. Robinson Jeffers. While here, a trip was made into the Big Sur country."

B13._____. "One Poet Writes of Another in Sterling's Tribute to Jeffers," *Pine Cone* (Carmel, Cal.), October 22, 1926, p. 1.

Favorable minor comment from the town that considered itself the home of both poets. Review of Sterling's book. See C5. This book "will be of marked interest—of personal interest—to all Carmelites and lovers of the village that has been identified with the careers of both men."

B14._____. "Pagan Horror from Carmel-by-the-Sea," *Monitor*, LXVII (January 9, 1926), 8.

Interesting conservative approach to Jeffers' themes. "Robinson Jeffers has the power of Aeschylus, the subtlety of Sophocles. Shelley and Swinburne played at being pagans. This man's work is ruggedly pagan. It is no tour de force. He is intrinsically terrible. The first point to note is that he could not have produced such horror, had he not a pagan background in California and throughout America. Greater is our fright to note that our country has become so pagan as to produce such a writer. In college we read Greek poets, but the Greek pagans were turned to dust. The modern pagans are alive. The second point to note is to watch and pray. Some will accuse us of advertising Jeffers. He has already been advertised by papers shamefully read in Catholic homes. This is a warning to watch and prevent our children from having their souls scarred by the reading of this modern pagan giant's corruption. This is not a matter of preventing curiosity, but of saving them from a devastating decadence."

B15._____. "Pine Needles," *Pine Cone* (Carmel, Cal.), May 15, 1926, p. 14.

Of possible biographical interest. Gossip column. George Sterling is weekend guest at the Jeffers' home.

B16._____. "The Roan Stallion in French," *Pine Cone* (Carmel, Cal.), October 1, 1926, p. 8.

Of possible biographical interest. Notice that Jeffers has received a copy of "his brilliant poem," in its French translation done by Eugene Jolas.

B17._____. "Sterling's Loss Is Keenly Felt by Associates, Carmel Friends," *Pine Cone* (Carmel, Cal.), November 19, 1926, p. 1.

Jeffers' tribute to Sterling, following Sterling's suicide. Preceded by: "Robinson Jeffers, internationally known poet, whom Sterling had visited a few weeks before his death, was deeply moved."

B18._____. "Terrors of Tamar," *Examiner* (San Francisco, Cal.), September 26, 1926, p. 5f.

Of possible biographical interest. Drawing by Alexander King accompanies paragraph describing Jeffers as a poet who has "skillful imagination," and who stirs little from his home. Notes that Sterling is preparing a book about him.

B19. Bassett, W. K. "Wherein One Poet Talks Not and Another Shoots Squirrels," *Carmel Cymbal*, I (June 15, 1926), 3, 11.

Trivial, error-filled interview with Jeffers and George Sterling, including a description of a visit to "Falcon Tower," where "the tearing lines of 'Roan Stallion' found material form."

B20. Burgess, R. L. "One Hundred and Three Californians," *Poetry*, XXVII (January, 1926), 217-221. Reprinted as: "A Very Great Californian," *Evening News* (San Jose, Cal.), February 1, 1926, section 1, p. 6.

Review of *Continent's End, An Anthology of California Poets.* Ed. by George Sterling, Genevieve Taggard, and James Rorty. Brief mention of Jeffers. "Then our big man, Robinson Jeffers, whom we Californians are so proud of New York's having discovered in romantically belated fashion, is awarded the deserved honor of conferring the title on the collection from one of his own poems, in which, printed decoratively opposite the title-page, he is the spokesman of us all."

B21._____. "The Seaward Print of Unreturning Feet: A Tribute to George Sterling," *Overland Monthly*, LXXXIV (December, 1926), 379, 409, 412.

Brief mention in a memorial tribute to Sterling. "Till Jeffers came, Sterling was always the one great poetic figure associated with Carmel. . . . Oh, good St. George of Bohemia, how grandly you saluted this younger brother of poetry, and with what utter lack of petty jealousy you proclaimed Jeffers' greatness to all who would listen, and to many who would not."

B22. Fitch, W. T. "Is There Literary and Artistic Culture in California?" *Overland Monthly*, LXXXIV (December, 1926), 391, 408.

Deplores the scornful attitude New York critics display towards California writers and challenges the effete east with Jeffers, an example of the flowering of California letters. Quotes Edgar Lee Masters: "Now this California poet Jeffers is truly Grecian. How deeply saturated with the marvellous beauty of this state! He thrives in the open. He has first hand understanding of the things he sings of—nature, soil, the plain folks around him."

B23. Hagemeyer, Dora. "How Jeffers and Lawrence 'Do' the Atmosphere," *Carmel Cymbal*, I (May 18, 1926), 6, 11.

Minor local study. Both writers see nature subjectively. Of Jeffers: "So little is he concerned with the importance of things in themselves that it is in the fine abstraction . . . that he achieves a majesty only comparable to Whitman."

B24. Humphries, Rolfe. "Hail Cal-i-forn-i-aye!" *Herald Tribune* (New York), February 7, 1926, p. 9.

Brief initial comment by prominent Marxist critic in a review of *Continent's End*. "There are good poems by Robinson Jeffers, who is at his best when he is least Whitman."

B25. Kuster, Edward. "After 8:30," *Pine Cone* (Carmel, Cal.), July 16, 1926, p. 8.

Of biographical interest. Critical comment by Una Jeffers' first husband. "Two men of outstanding genius came to Carmel recently to visit a third. The three trekked about our shores and hills for a week—Carmel was vaguely aware of them, but was too busy with its 'fussy excitement of action' to give them much heed. To their relief, no doubt. To me, this visit of Edgar Lee Masters and George Sterling at the home of Robinson Jeffers has a wide—indeed a dramatic—significance."

B26. Lal, Gobind Behari. "Once Upon a Time There Was a Poet—And He Lived Up in a Big Tower," *Examiner* (San Francisco, Cal.), November 14, 1926, p. 4n.

Of possible biographical interest. Anecdotal and trivial. Discusses and compares Jeffers' and Sterling's life styles. They both "shun the 'herd movements' of the animal known as man." Concludes that "Next to George Sterling as a poet of the highest magnitude comes Robinson Jeffers."

B27. Monroe, Harriet. "A Travel Tale," *Poetry*, XXVIII (June, 1926), 150-157.

Brief mention by the poet and founder of *Poetry*. Mentions that while in Carmel, an "exciting event was a talk with Robinson Jeffers," whose poetry contains "rhythms as bold as the plunge of the Pacific on Carmel's rocks."

B28. Sterling, George. "A Tower by the Sea," *San Francisco Review*, I (February-March, 1926), 248-249. Reprinted as: "Sterling on Jeffers," *Carmel Cymbal*, I (June 15, 1926), 9.

Lavish praise of Jeffers' strong line by a friend and fellow poet. Finds him superior to Frost and E. A. Robinson. "The disclosure of Jeffers' greatness has been as brilliant as that of a *nova*, or new star, without the latter's fate of subsequent diminuation."

B29. Turner, Ethel. "Continent's End: An Anthology of Contemporary California Poets," *San Francisco Review*, II (July-August, 1926), 40.

Review of *Continent's End*. Extremely brief mention of "the truly great Robinson Jeffers."

B30._____. "George Sterling," *San Francisco Review*, II (November-December, 1926), 97-98.

Local California memorial to George Sterling, comparing him briefly to Jeffers who "struck fire from the rock," while Sterling "found along the white shore line only a fugitive and lonely beauty."

B31. West, George P. "Great New Poet, Jeffers, Arises at Carmel, Voices Real California Lure," *Call* (San Francisco, Cal.), January 2, 1926, pp. 9, 14.

Trivial general critique and biographical background. "Robinson Jeffers . . . is so far above and beyond all the men and women who play skillfully with words that his first book has left its readers breathless. They are breathless with the excitement of men who see a new planet, a new marvel of nature."

1927

B32. Anonymous. "Moral or Immoral," *Pine Cone* (Carmel, Cal.), April 15, 1927, p. 8.

Example of the moral turmoil created by Jeffers' poems. Editorial discussing Professor T. K. Whipple of the University of California who says a poem that affords a valuable experience is a moral poem. "Inevitably Robinson Jeffers' works come to mind; his widely discussed 'Tamar' and other verses from that pen that is rounding off lines that bid for immortality. The reader may form his own opinions of Jeffers' verse, in its social relations, for instance, by applying Professor Whipple's interpretation of morality and immorality in poetry."

B33._____. "Our Thinking Work," *Chicago Schools Journal*, IX (April, 1927), 317-318.

Favorable review of Sterling's book (see C5) which "presents facts which enable us better to understand the thought and way of life of this poet whose deeply reflective mind, strength of brain, wide experience, and scholarship have given his poems the power of epics."

B34._____. "The Phoenix Nest," *Saturday Review of Literature*, III (July 9, 1927), 968.

Announcement of *The Women at Point Sur*. Also following complete comment: "We admire Mr. Jeffers' work for many qualities, but it seems to be emphatically full of sexual hysteria, though it has more drive and intensity than most of the poetry written today. His 'Tower Beyond Tragedy,' remains to us his most striking work, though portions of 'The Roan Stallion' are astonishing."

B35._____. Review of Sterling's *Robinson Jeffers: The Man and the Artist, American Mercury*, X (April, 1927), xvi.

See C5. Complete comment: "This work is of slight value. The biographical section is fragmentary and inadequate, and Mr. Sterling's criticism is mainly extravagent eulogy. The admirers of Mr. Jeffers, indeed, bid fair to damn him with excessive praises."

B36._____. "Sterling's Essay on Jeffers," *Argonaut*, CI (February 19, 1927), 8.

Favorable review of Sterling book. See C5. "Mr. Sterling set himself the exciting task of making Jeffers known to the world. And he succeeded; for the work of the young Carmel Hellenic . . . is, now, thanks to Mr. Sterling's high praise, in the hands of all poetry lovers. There are bay leaves on Mr. Jeffers' brow, bay leaves that promise to remain perennially green."

B37. B., F. B. "Robinson Jeffers: A Study of the Work of An American Poet," *Transcript* (Boston, Mass.), February 19, 1927, book section, p. 3.

Review of Sterling book. See C5. Quotes liberally from Sterling. "Anyone who has read Mr. Jeffers' poems . . . has thrilled to them and stands ready to support the statement that he is one of the two or three outstanding poets of America."

B38. Bjorkman, Edwin. "An American Poet," *Times* (Asheville, N. C.), July 31, 1927, p. 13a.

Emphasis on beauty of the poetry and similarities to Euripides, Dante and Shakespeare, by prominent Swedish born critic. "In Mr. Jeffers we have a truly great poet."

B39. Bland, Henry Meade. "The Poetry of Today," *Overland Monthly*, LXXXV (December, 1927), 373-375.

Questions Jeffers' pessimism and use of violence. "The English language centuries ago was full of rough gutterals. These are dying out. Does he not realize a thought slipping easily off the tongue enters the mind with more sureness?"

B40. Broun, Heywood. Review of Sterling's *Robinson Jeffers: The Man and the Artist, Carmel Cymbal*, III (February 23, 1927), 16.

See C5. Ironic account of Jeffers' life style by a New York critic and essayist. "Here is a poet who appreciates the value of singularity, and an appealing madness runs through the story of his life." Concludes by quoting how Jeffers joined the Aviation Corps, but had to wait so long for a nose operation that the war ended. ". . . this arouses my admiration, for, I believe it establishes a world's record."

B41. Cestre, Charles. "Robinson Jeffers," *Revue Anglo-Américain*, IV (August, 1927), 489-502.

First European recognition by a major French critic. "Malgré des inégalités et des défaillances l'oeuvre de Jeffers porte la marque de la grande poésie. Quelle qu'ait été sur lui l'influence de Whitman pour le forme—peut-Être—dans une certaine mesure, de Poe pour le fond—il est original par la richesse du coloris, l'invention des subjects, l'intensité de la passion et l'élan de l'imagination. Il dépasse Whitman par l'observation objective, le relief du trait, l'harmonie du vers, la sûreté du sens artistique. Il est supérieur à Poe par l'humanité et par la vérité de l'émotion dramatique."

B42. Croissant, Albert. "An Occidental Poet," *Occidental Alumnus*, IX (March, 1927), 3. Reprinted in part as: "Oxy Graduate Gains Laurels," *Occidental* (Pasadena, Cal.), April 5, 1927, p. 2.

Trivial tribute to a famous Occidental College alumnus. "Because of his stern, sombre philosophy, his ruthless realism, and his fondness for shocking themes . . . Mr. Jeffers will never achieve the popularity of Longfellow or of Eddie Guest; but there will always be many, endowed with strong minds—and strong stomachs—who will appreciate him and acclaim him as one of the notable poets of the day."

B43. DeCasseres, Benjamin. "Robinson Jeffers: Tragic Terror," *Bookman*, LXVI (November, 1927), 262-266. Reprinted in: *Pine Cone* (Carmel, Cal.), March 16, 1928, pp. 12-13, 16. Reprinted as pamphlet: *Robinson Jeffers: An Artist.* San Francisco: John S. Mayfield, 1928.

The sort of hysterical hyperbole that inspired later adverse reaction. "There is not a superfluous line in all his poetry. It is an arterial, a ganglionic system, to remove one tiny bit of which would cause the story of the poem to bleed to death." Praises especially "Tamar," "The Coast-Range Christ," and "Fauna." "That portion of California . . . belongs as absolutely to Robinson Jeffers . . . as Wessex belongs to Thomas Hardy."

B44. DeLaguna, Frederica. "Robinson Jeffers, the Poet's Poet" (a paper read before the Ebell Club), *Ebell*, I (November, 1927), 7, 30-31.

Uninspired but thorough review of plots and themes of long narratives, emphasizing that "it is not good for a man to follow his soul into such black, despairing wrong. . . . I do not ask that art should sweeten life, but it must strengthen life. Jeffers' language has unrivaled beauty, but Jeffers is forcing his unguarded soul into a too-bitter consorting with unholiness. I believe he holds the capabilities of being the greatest poet of our age, but not the promise."

B45. Eisenberg, Emanuel. "The Lean Season," *Bookman*, LXVI (October, 1927), 222-223.

Passing mention of Jeffers in a discussion of current poetry. Though Jeffers "has attained magnificence and will scale greater heights than any other poet of this country, he is utterly unAmerican. His unremittant abhorrence for humanity's surely dispensable pettiness and the grim disbelief in any eventual good ... will always prevent the United States from accepting him as a supreme, genuine expression of its essence."

B46. Farrar, John. "This Stream of Poets," *Bookman*, LXV (March, 1927), 80-81.
Favorable review of Sterling book. See C5. "Robinson Jeffers is one of these poets that I must take on faith. I am willing to believe all that my friends say about him, and I have enjoyed some of his magnificent lines, yet, he still puzzles me."

B47. Field, Sarah Bard. "Memories of George Sterling," *Overland Monthly*, LXXXV (November, 1927), 334-335.
Prominent California poet's memorial tribute to Sterling. In discussing his friendship with Jeffers: "Nor has any other historic friendship included more tender humility in the giving and taking than this. Not since John the Baptist pointed to the young Christ ... has there been so large a gesture of exalted devotion as that with which George Sterling pointed to the luminous star of his own discovery." Anecdotal description of Sterling's initial enthusiasm.

B48. M'Clure, John. "Literature and Less," *Times-Picayune* (New Orleans, La.), November 20, 1927, p. 4.
Jeffers is sometimes monotonous, yet his poems are "strong and masculine. But the subject-matter of Mr. Jeffers' poetry lacks the sanity you find in the most excellent poetry."

B49. Pollard, Lancaster. "Jeffers as Example of Modernism: Magnificent Poetry of West Coast Writer in Important Revelation of Our Age," *Post-Intelligencer* (Seattle, Wash.), August 14, 1927, p. 6d.
Favorable critical comment on *Roan Stallion* and *The Women at Point Sur*. Emphasis on his vivid imagination. "If he can resolve his intellectual doubt ... Jeffers will become a poet of such surpassing eminence that he will stand ... in the company of the great of all ages."

B50. Roedder, Karsten. "Prose Extracts to Test Lyrical Qualities of Two Great American Poets—Jeffers Progresses as a Genius If Not a Poet of the Old School," *Citizen* (Brooklyn, N. Y.), July 3, 1927, p. 7.

One of the earlier critiques mentioning Jeffers' debt to Nietzsche. The Jeffers poem "is a sinister piece of work." Jeffers writes "as no poet should write except he happens to be a genius. Being something of the most genuine as well as most turbulent that has occurred within American literature before as well as after Walt Whitman . . . Jeffers can only be commended."

1928

B51. Anonymous. Critical Comment Quoting Church's Article in November 1928 *Carnegie Magazine, Press* (Pittsburgh, Pa.), December 11, 1928, section I, p. 2.

Compares Church's opinion (see B57), with De Casseres' (see B43). Thanks Church for saving the public's time which might have been wasted in reading Jeffers. "But of course (as we should all rejoice if Pittsburgh really produced the poet of the ages) we reserve the right to buy and read Jeffers if it should transpire that you [Dr. Church] are wrong and De Casseres right."

B52._____. "Not Wanted: A Poet Laureate," *Argonaut*, CIV (September 15, 1928), 2-3.

Reaction to Jeffers' themes provokes this ironic treatment of California Philistines, who are choosing a new poet laureate for California. "How would the pious Mr. Wright of San Jose, author of the prohibition enforcement laws, explain to his constituents a vote for Robinson Jeffers, whom competent critics rate first and almost alone among California poets, but whose themes find little favor in the decorous reading circles of the Santa Clara Valley?"

B53._____. "Pittsburgh's Poet Son Gets Belated Tribute," *Sun Telegraph* (Pittsburgh, Pa.), August 26, 1928, section 2, p. 13.

Describes the successful efforts of one Robert Garland to have

Jeffers' works placed in the Pennsylvania room of Pittsburgh's Carnegie Library. Extensive quotations from *Bookman* article (see B43), and De Casseres' letter (see B58).

B54._____. "Pondering," *Carmelite*, I (December 19, 1928), 13.
Of possible biographical interest. An anecdote of some "sophisticated New Yorkers" who came "to see the great poet," and who were embarrassed by Jeffers' silence.

B55._____. "Silent Men," *Pine Cone* (Carmel, Cal.), December 21, 1928, p. 8.
Of possible biographical interest. "Robinson Jeffers, our townsman, our neighbor, we honor for having the courage to live his life. We do not consider him unsociable, unneighborly, but a good citizen." In discussing *Carmelite*, December 12, 1928 (see B74): "It contains invaluable close-ups of one of the world's greatest and most concealed personalities. . . . Few of us are privileged to achieve terms of intimacy with a mountain. But a mountain casts a large shadow, and that we may see."

B56. Bynner, Witter. "The Judgment of His Peers," *Carmelite: Robinson Jeffers Supplement*, I (December 12, 1928), 5.
Brief critique by a fellow poet. "He should change his disgust into patience and become a real seer. . . . Jeffers begins always like a preacher with a text, and the text is usually beautiful, and then he deteriorates into anathema against the human race."

B57. Church, Samuel Harden. "A Pittsburgh Poet Discovered," *Carnegie Magazine*, II (November, 1928), 180-182.
Interesting grass roots reaction to Jeffers' themes. Reviews Jeffers' career. Because of the moral perversion in his long poems, "the essential beauty of literature has been sacrificed to a sordid photography of the baser elements of humanity." Jeffers, in some places shows imagination, "but not one of the longer stories in this volume can be read aloud in the family circle. . . . And is not good taste an indispensable part of great authorship?"

B58. DeCasseres, Benjamin. Letter to Editor, *Sun Telegraph* (Pittsburgh, Pa.), August 7, 1928, p. 3.

Urges recognition of Jeffers. "When America has achieved a great cultural life, Pittsburgh will be remembered for that alone [that it was the birthplace of Jeffers] —as Baltimore for Poe and Camden for Walt Whitman, are indissolubly linked."

B59. Ficke, Arthur Davison. "A Note on the Poetry of Robinson Jeffers," *Carmelite*, I (December 19, 1928), 17.

Tribute by fellow poet and rebel. Jeffers writes on the brink of madness. "Americans resent Robinson Jeffers blindly—because a secret part of them is aware of the terrible truth of all he writes." Jeffers' poetry "is undoubtedly one of the most daring explorations of the human spirit that has been attempted in our day. Whether you like it or not," there it is, "shocking and beautiful."

B60. Field, Sara Bard. "The Judgment of His Peers," *Carmelite: Robinson Jeffers Supplement*, I (December 12, 1928), 4.

Brief critique by a fellow poet. Jeffers is a "titanic poet" of pure heart. However, "Were I a god who could give this great poet one gift, it would be to open to him the deep secret of Joy. To me his one great lack is a need to know Socrates' teaching of equal counterparts."

B61. Garrott, Hal. "A Profane History of Carmel," *Pine Cone* (Carmel, Cal.), December 14, 1928, p. 35.

Mention of Jeffers as one who was inspired by Carmel country to become "America's greatest poet."

B62. Kantor, MacKinlay. "Plenty of Sex and Plenty of Bible," *Voices*, VII (February, 1928), 180-183.

Brief mention by important novelist and historian. Review of *A Miscellany of American Poetry: 1927* (in which poems of Jeffers appear). Many admirers are drawn only by his free use of sex.

Nevertheless, "Robinson Jeffers is sitting on the popular pinnacle where Masters and Lindsay sat a decade or two ago. We will pray that he signs a longer lease than they did."

B63. Lal, Gobind Behari. "Three New Poems by Jeffers," *Examiner* (San Francisco, Cal.), January 8, 1928, pp. 1a, 10e.
Minor review from local source. Page 1a is a picture of Jeffers' home. Lal discusses three poems published in *Poetry*. ". . . the people, having tasted of Jeffers' gold, want more from him."

B64. Masters, Edgar Lee. "The Judgment of His Peers," *Carmelite: Robinson Jeffers Supplement*, I (December 12, 1928), 3.
Brief critique by fellow poet and friend. Biographical data. Mentions "the magnitude of the genius which has given America 'Roan Stallion,' 'The Women at Point Sur,' and many poems of enduring memory."

B65. Mayfield, John S. "Robinson Jeffers Receives a Convert," *Overland Monthly*, LXXXVI (August, 1928), 279-280.
Lavish praise in article by DeCasseres' publisher. Describes the great number of requests the printers have received for the DeCasseres pamphlet (See B43).

B66. Morris, Lawrence S. "Robinson Jeffers: The Tragedy of a Modern Mystic," *New Republic*, LIV (May 16, 1928), 386-390.
Early lengthy study emphasizing Jeffers as voice of modern times. Compares him to Blake and Whitman. Best as a mad mystic, he becomes melodramatic when he intellectualizes. ". . . in the intensity of his struggle with the unattainable he has produced lines at a pitch unequalled in America at present. Jeffers seizes words by the throat and shakes them until they tremble with his passion."

B67. O'Day, Edward F. "George Sterling," *San Francisco Water*, VII (July, 1928), 9-12, 13.

Minor memorial article for a local son. Brief mention of Jeffers. Sterling "was so whole-heartedly pleased when Robinson Jeffers commanded an audience . . . that he could not bring himself to express publically his instinctive disapproval of the themes which finally drew attention to this strange, powerful singer of Carmel."

B68. Root, E. Merrill. "Three Singers Before Sunset," *Poetry Folio*, I (January-February, 1928), 1, 4.

Discussion of Jeffers as an exponent of nihilism. Jeffers is the most profound poet of this "America of Dreadful Night." He is "more mighty in his desolation than almost any other single poet of disillusion."

B69. Rorty, James. "The Judgment of His Peers," *Carmelite: Robinson Jeffers Supplement*, I (December 12, 1928), 13-14.

Tribute by one of Jeffers' first admirers. "I think Jeffers is one of the best poets alive," but "I don't share his philosophy. What of it? He writes with greater poetic intensity than any other living poet I have read."

B70._____. "Time and Western Man," *Carmelite: Robinson Jeffers Supplement*, I (December 12, 1928), 13-14.

Diatribe against California's treatment of its artists, using Jeffers as an example of that state's indifferent attitude. Jeffers is "not only a first-rate poet, but an indigenous California poet, embodying in his work both the qualities and the defects of his state. The qualities are the power and beauty of the California landscape." His treatment is undeserved.

B71. Rowntree, Lester. "Flora of the Jeffers Country," *Carmelite: Robinson Jeffers Supplement*, I (December 12, 1928), 10-11.

Surface analysis of Jeffers' use of California flora, stressing botanical data. "Things are portrayed as they really are and who can read 'Fauna' without a better understanding and stronger love for the wooded slopes and canyons that come, fold on fold, down to the ocean side."

B72. Sandburg, Carl. "The Judgment of His Peers," *Carmelite: Robinson Jeffers Supplement*, I (December 12, 1928), 5.

Brief appreciation by fellow poet, which is later to be much quoted. "Often I have the feeling that Jeffers is more than an equal of Balboa, for he too has discovered the Pacific Ocean. And to discover something as big as the Pacific Ocean, after others have also discovered it, requires eyesight and navigation ability requisite to the business of being a poet."

B73. Steffens, Lincoln. "Jeffers the Neighbor," *Carmelite: Robinson Jeffers Supplement*, I (December 12, 1928), 1-3. Reprinted in his: *Lincoln Steffens Speaking*. New York: Harcourt, Brace and Co., 1936, pp. 76-83.

Of bibliographical interest. Anecdotal account of Jeffers' life. "He puts in more cement than a good enough builder would; he puts, too, much cement into his poetry and his life and his family for the same reason that he likes to handle stone: because he has learned from nature to like to feel that he is building for ever and ever."

B74. Steffens, Lincoln, *et al. Carmelite: Robinson Jeffers Supplement*, I (December 12, 1928), pp. 1-16.

Entire issue devoted to Jeffers. Contains several essays by Jeffers and biographical anecdotes. Those articles with specific critical references are included here as: B56, B60, B64, B69, B70, B71, B72, B73, B76, B77.

B75. W., E. [Wilson, Edmund], Review of *A Miscellany of American Poetry: 1927, New Republic*, LIII (February 8, 1928), 330.

Brief favorable mention of Jeffers by a leading critic. "There are some apparently grandiose and loose, but really quite original and distinguished short lyrics by Jeffers: it may be that a California literature is possible, after all, and that Jeffers is the first genuine poet of the Pacific."

B76. Winter, Ella. "J. R. Jeffers, Stone-Mason," *Carmelite: Robinson Jeffers Supplement*, I (December 12, 1928), 6-7.

Local resident offers chatty biographical data. "When his poems are done he is as free of them as when the stone has hardened in the wall of the dining room. He never reads his own poems, never after they are in print; he very rarely looks at the reviews of his own works. . . ."

B77. Wood, Charles Erskine Scott. "The Judgment of His Peers," *Carmelite: Robinson Jeffers Supplement*, I (December 12, 1928), 5.

Brief tribute by a fellow poet of an earlier generaton. "I think Jeffers the largest of our living poets, the greatest English poet of today. . . . I do not know of any one else so little imitative—so dramatically imaginative."

1929

B78. Anonymous. Advertisement, *Pine Cone* (Carmel, Cal.), August 30, 1929, p. 36.

Interesting example of the extent of Jeffers' fame. Advertisement for "Half Acre Villa Sites," selling for $2,500, at San Remo, adjoining Carmel Highlands. A quotation from Jeffers' poetry and a photograph of redwoods is preceded by "Poet's Country—the poet Robinson Jeffers has laid the scene of one of his most beautiful poems in San Remo at the mouth of Mal Paso Canyon."

B79._____. "The Author of 'Dear Judas,' " *Transcript* (Boston, Mass.), September 14, 1929, book section, p. 4.

Trivial news article. Brief notice of *Dear Judas and Other Poems*. Mention of Jeffers' Irish trip, which is the first time in years he has been away from Carmel "with which all his poetry is associated."

B80._____. "Breezes Blowing in Kuster Home," *Pine Cone* (Carmel, Cal.), October 11, 1929, p. 1.

Of possible biographical interest. Dynamiting for road broke twenty-four panes of glass in Kuster's (Una Jeffers' first husband) home. "Investigation showed that the stone fortress of Robinson Jeffers close by escaped unscathed."

B81._____. "Jeffers or Bland," *Examiner* (San Francisco, Cal.), January 17, 1929, p. 34.

Editorial discussing the two possible choices for a State Laureate. "The well-known Jeffers is the Dante of America, because his genius has gone down into the profoundest pits of Hell and Purgatory."

B82._____. "Jeffers Plans Trip to Ireland," *Examiner* (San Francisco, Cal.), January 30, 1929, p. 3.

Of possible biographical interest. Describes Jeffers' travel plans. "All the work by which he has acquired national fame has been written during his residence in Carmel."

B83._____. "Little Portraits: Robinson Jeffers," *Register* (Des Moines, Iowa), July 21, 1929, p. 8g.

Trivial. Of possible biographical interest. Describes construction of Jeffers' tower, marriage to Una. Quotations from DeCasseres' article in November, 1927, *Bookman*; see B43.

B84._____. Notice of *Dear Judas and Other Poems*, *Bookman*, LXX (October, 1929), 188-190.

Of possible biographical interest. Reprints parts of DeCasseres' article; see B43. Describes Tor House, Hawk Tower and plans for Ireland trip.

B85._____. "People Talked About," *Pine Cone* (Carmel, Cal.), February 22, 1929, p. 9.

Of possible biographical interest. Describes post card Jeffers received from England advocating preservation of nature.

B86._____. Review of *A Comprehensive Anthology of American Poetry* edited by Conrad Aiken, *American Mercury*, XVI (April, 1929), xxvi.

Brief mention. Criticizes Aiken's choices. "Again, on what basis can Mr. Aiken justify the complete exclusion of Robinson Jeffers and Leonie Adams, and the large space he allots to Marianne Moore, Wallace Stevens, John Grow [sic] Ransome and Archibald MacLeish?"

B87._____. "Robinson Jeffers Gloomy Bard of Carmel," *Pine Cone* (Carmel, Cal.), December 20, 1929, p. 13, 28.

Of possible biographical interest. Portrait of Jeffers and Sterling on page 13 titled "Two Bards of Carmel." Article reports that Jeffers is coming back from Europe. Describes his life and work.

B88._____. "Robinson Jeffers Trip," *Democrat* (Sherman, Tex.), November 10, 1929, unnumbered book page.

Brief notice of Jeffers' trip to Ireland and notice of publication of *Dear Judas*.

B89._____. "Singers of the New Age: A Group of Distinguished Young Poets Who Have Found Fresh Material in the American Scene," *Vanity Fair*, XXXIII (September, 1929), 89.

Picture article on new poets. "The doomed nobility of Greek tragedy is powerfully reflected in the passion and terror of Robinson Jeffers' modern narratives in verse." These works "have identified him as one of the outstanding figures in American letters."

B90._____. "A Stop-Over at Carmel," *Pine Cone* (Carmel, Cal.), February 15, 1929, p. 10.

Trivial criticism. Of possible biographical interest. Describes Jeffers' decision to live in Carmel. "Some people do not know what all of Jeffers' poems mean, but that does not worry Jeffers or his friends. Millions did not understand every line of Robert Browning and Browning clubs sprang up all over the world; soon, perhaps there will be Jeffers clubs."

B91._____. "We Nominate for the Hall of Fame," *Vanity Fair,*
XXXII (June, 1929), 83.
   Brief picture article includes Jeffers. An example of his wide
popularity. "Because he is one of the first among contemporary
American poets; because he has embodied the vitality of the California
coast in his poems of tragic terror; because his epic works have won him
the title of 'the new Whitman,' and finally because his poem *Cawdor*,
recently published, is the final part of a powerful modern trilogy."

B92. Adamic, Louis. "Robinson and Una Jeffers: A Portrait of a Great
American Poet and His Wife, *San Franciscan*, III (March, 1929), 6, 29.
   Essayist and admirer offers biographical data. "He has unquestion-
ably grown since settling in Carmel in 1914. One can scarcely believe
that the John Robinson Jeffers who in 1913 published a third-rate
story in the *Smart Set* has become crystallized into Robinson Jeffers
who worte 'Tamar,' 'Roan Stallion,' 'The Women at Point Sur,' and
'Cawdor.' "

B93. Anderson, Kenneth. Letter mentioning disireability of Robinson
Jeffers as State Laureate, *Chronicle* (San Francisco, Cal.), January 18,
1929, p. 28.
   Suggests, ironically, that Dr. Henry Mead Bland of San Jose Teacher's
College be named state laureate instead of Jeffers. "Jeffers is only a
professional writer, and the author of 'Roan Stallion' and other poems,
which have been proclaimed as outstanding among the work of modern
American poets. Besides, Dr. Bland seems to need the honor more than
does Jeffers, and the latter would not greatly miss it."

B94. Brown, M. Webster. "A Poet Who Studied Medicine," *Medicine
Journal and Record*, CXXX (November 6, 1929), 535-539.
   Discusses Jeffers' knowledge of medicine as reflected in his poetry.

B95. Croissant, Albert. "A Poet of Distinction," *Occidental Alumnus*,
XI (May, 1929), 3-4.

Trivial attempt to discover Jeffers' philosophy. "There is something baffling and obscure about Jeffers' work, especially the long poems. His singular strangeness and turbulence colors every page. This, together with his use of symbolism, and his abnormal, terrible themes, makes it difficult for one to speak with confidence of his philosophy."

B96. Deutsch, Babette. "The Future of Poetry," *New Republic*, LX (August 21, 1929), 12-15.
Mention of Jeffers as a possible example of what future poetry will resemble. "In the work of Robinson Jeffers, a poet who is drawn, like Yeats, into the tangle of theosophical thought, one finds even more distinctly a vision of the universe large enough to inform a long philosophical poem. It is, in the case of Jeffers, a terrifying vision, but, steadfastly confronted, it has the reconciling gift of all truth. . . . It is not inconceivable that the poetry of the future should approximate this vision even more closely."

B97. Hale, William Harlan. "Robinson Jeffers: A Lone Titan," *Yale Literary Magazine*, XCV (December, 1929), 31-35.
Careful discussion of two of Jeffers' sources, the Greeks (immutable destiny) and Whitman (mysticism). The theme of his brutal works is mysticism based on despair. Jeffers' mind "is an intellect unmatched today for its severity, its solitude, its spontaneous expressions of human agony under the canopy of endless orbits. Jeffers has evoked from the depths of his being, and from the inmost nature of his lonely surroundings, a fierce dynamic conception of the world."

B98. Harper, Frank C. Biographical Note, *Press* (Pittsburgh, Pa.), January 9, 1929, p. 2.
Of possible biographical interest. Mention of DeCasseres' statement that Pittsburgh will be remembered as the home of Jeffers. Concludes with a quotation from a Jeffers letter in which the poet describes his connection with that city.

B99. Johnson, Edward S. "Greece and California," *Yale Daily News Literary Supplement*, III (January 23, 1929), 3.

Discussion of the influence of Greek dramatists. "Jeffers is doing for California what Robert Frost is doing for New England, and Carl Sandburg for Chicago. It is appropriate that the poet of that volcanic sea coast should be so much more intense, so much more serious than his contemporaries dwelling in the milder landscapes of the East."

B100. McWilliams, Carey. "Robinson Jeffers: An Antitoxin," *Los Angeles Saturday Night*, IX (August 3, 1929), 5.

Favorable but trivial discussion, by noted California journalist, of Adamic book (see C14), and of Jeffers' interpretation of death as an antitoxin for life. "There is, perhaps, no figure in modern American poetry who has provoked the same amount of critical attention as Robinson Jeffers. This state of affairs is just as it should be, for there is no figure of more importance."

B101._____. "When the Big Boys Were Small," *San Franciscan*, III (January, 1929), 31-32.

Jeffers included in a discussion of the early writing of several authors. "But 'ere passing too quickly into the realm of the new lust poetry, should enquiry not be made of its antecedents? Is it possible that the Roan Stallion was once a Shetland Pony?" Discusses *Flagons and Apples* as a "naive little volume of verse."

B102. Munson, Gorham Bert. "The Young Critic," *Bookman*, LXX (December, 1929), 369-373.

Brief mention by critic and founder of the literary magazine, *Secession*, states that some critics seek out an educated public or write as if such a public existed. "Is this last not clearly true in the papers on Sherwood Anderson, Upton Sinclair and Robinson Jeffers which Lawrence S. Morris has contributed to the *New Republic*?" Refers to B66.

B103. Palmer, Peggy. "The Matoor Mind: Bored Scribe Yearns for Vacation, Visits Carmel Poet," *Pine Cone* (Carmel, Cal.), June 14, 1929, p. 1.

Trivial humor. Describes visit of girl reporter to Jeffers, shortly before his departure for Ireland. "Well, the Jeffers live in a stone tower that Mister Jeffers bilt [sic] all by himself out of Rocks, and when I arrived there was a large sign on the door saying NOT AT HOME." Cartoon illustrating article pictures Jeffers and the girl. He: "I wrote the ROAN STALLION." She: "Ah-ha Mr. Jeffers! Then you *do* like horses."

B104. Rorty, James. Review of *An Anthology of World Poetry* by Mark Van Doren, *Nation*, CXXVIII (February 13, 1929), 197-198.

Brief mention by an early admirer. "The contemporary Americans represented are Santayana, Robinson, Amy Lowell, Frost, Sandberg, Lindsay, Ezra Pound, H. D., Robinson Jeffers, T. S. Eliot, and Edna St. Vincent Millay. These are surely the right names, and Mr. Van Doren has made excellent selections from their work."

B105. Vivas, Eliseo. "Robinson Jeffers," *New Student*, VIII (April, 1929), 13-14.

Seeks to correct the "rather hysterical acclaim" Jeffers' work has received. Because he lacks a "fundamental acceptance of the sense of human dignity," he cannot be rated with the greatest. "But if the citadel of his fame cannot be placed next to that of the Greeks, nor with that of Dante and Shakespeare, it must be placed not far from theirs. There is surely no doubt that his large poems have all the characteristics of lasting works."

B106. Walton, Eda Lou. Review of *The Fate of the Jury* by Edgar Lee Masters, *Nation*, CXXIX (July 17, 1929), 72.

Brief mention of Jeffers as partially responsible for the renewed interest in the long narrative poem.

1930

B107. Anonymous. "Books Chosen for White House," *Times* (New York), April 10, 1930, p. 34.
Books chosen by appointees of the American Booksellers Association include *Roan Stallion, Tamar and Other Poems.*

B108._____. "Forty Books of 1929 Selected as Notable," *Times* (New York), April 29, 1930, p. 18.
Dear Judas and Other Poems included in a list prepared for the International Institute of Intellectual Cooperation of the League of Nations, by the American Library Association.

B110._____. "Gessler Talk on Poetry," *Star-Bulletin* (Honolulu, Hawaii), April 7, 1930, p. 5.
An example of wide interest in Jeffers. In a lecture on "Tendencies in Contemporary Poetry," the first of two lectures, Clifford Gessler, literary editor of the *Star-Bulletin*, said of Jeffers that he "is the only outstanding poet to have evolved a definite philosophy, something approaching an answer to the questions the other metaphysical poets raise."

B111._____. "A Homesick Poet, Mr. Jeffers of Carmel," *Call-Bulletin* (San Francisco, Cal.), January 11, 1930, section 2, p. 28
Of possible biographical interest. Jeffers, "who has more 'power' than any poet his country has ever known," has returned from his Irish trip.

B112._____. "Huntsman, Spare the Gull," *Pine Cone* (Carmel, Cal.), December 19, 1930, pp. 13, 23.
Of possible biographical interest. Account of an incident in which Jeffers stopped hunters from shooting sea gulls near his property.

B113._____. "Jeffers Working on New Addition," *Pine Cone* (Carmel, Cal.), September 26, 1930, p. 5.

Of possible biographical interest. Jeffers' work on his dining room addition, started five years ago, is well underway. He is now working on the roof, which should be finished by next month. The sons help; Mrs. Jeffers offers suggestions.

B114._____. "New Car Bought by Poet Jeffers," *Pine Cone* (Carmel, Cal.), September 19, 1930, p. 6.

Of possible biographical interest. The Jeffers bought a new Ford. Their old touring car is being kept for carrying stones, while the new one will be for long motor trips up the valley.

B115._____. "Noted Poet is Carmel Visitor," *Pine Cone* (Carmel, Cal.), February 14, 1930, p. 4.

Of possible biographical interest. Edna St. Vincent Millay visited Carmel and included a visit to Robinson Jeffers.

B116._____. "On the White House Shelf," *Times* (New York), April 11, 1930, p. 26.

Brief mention of Jeffers in editorial. In illustrating how varied the list (see B107) is: "The poetry shelves are ample enough to hold James Whitcomb Riley and Robinson Jeffers."

B117._____. "The Poetry Column," *Pine Cone* (Carmel, Cal.), September 5, 1930, p. 8.

Interesting opinion from local newspaper in editorial praising the newspaper's own poetry column. "Carmel is, and has been, far-famed for its greater poets. The names of Sterling and Jeffers are universally known, and are linked for all time with Carmel. But our minor poets are entitled to appreciation. They sing less loudly, but sometimes more sweetly."

B118. Arvin, Newton. "The Paradox of Jeffers," *New Freeman*, I (May 17, 1930), 230-232.

Noted critic of American literature discusses the paradox that Jeffers hates man, but makes him heroic. Jeffers finds all human intercourse corrupt. Therefore he does not "accept men too genially for what they are." That would be "the one certain way to belittle them; only when the worst has been said can the best be momentously imagined. This is the strength of Jeffers' case against humanity: in a culture dominated by fake good-nature and shallow fellowship . . . he has . . . returned to something more primitive . . . something all men should be aware of before they babble of cooperation."

B119. Carew, Harold D. "Bard of the Tragic Muse," *Touring Topics*, XXII (August, 1930), 32-34, 55.

Favorable. Biography and brief, surface comment on Jeffers' poetry. "This man whose mind broods on life as a play of forces set over against the infinity of Time is a reincarnated Sophocles, a man whose name and works will undoubtedly survive his century even though his century does not understand him."

B120. Conklin, G. Review of *Our Singing Strength* by Kreymborg, *Bookman*, LXX (February, 1930), 685-686.

Mention of Jeffers. See C19. "The author has included thorough valuations of all the great and near-great figures from Anne Bradstreet to Robinson Jeffers. . . . Whitman and Jeffers he sees as America's greatest and most representative poets; a theory the expatriates (at home and abroad) will take delight in jeering at, but one which has considerable reason behind it: they are at once our most individual poets and our most universal prophets."

B121. Humphries, Rolfe. "More About Robinson Jeffers," *New Republic*, LXII (April 9, 1930), 222.

Letter to editor pointing out similarity between *The Brook Kerith* by Moore and *Dear Judas*.

B122. Johnson, Merle. "John Robinson Jeffers, 1887-(?)," *Publishers'
Weekly*, CXVII (April 19, 1930), 2143.
  Brief bibliography of Jeffers' first editions.

B123. Johnson, Spud. "She Did It," *Carmelite*, III (May 29, 1930),
1, 8-9.
  Of possible biographical interest. Describes Mabel Dodge Luhan's
successful campaign to bring Jeffers to Taos, New Mexico. "Carmel
should be interested and not jealous, for, after all, even if Jeffers never
writes another word about this coast . . . think how completely and
perfectly he has already expressed it, and made it live."

B124. Jolas, Eugene. "Literature and the New Man," *Transition*, 19-20
(June, 1930), 13-19.
  Brief mention in a longer article on trends in modern literature. On
poetry: "It is high time that we revise our notions of the beautiful and
its supposed antithesis. . . . Against more glacial and static beauty there
should be placed the monstrous, the grotesque. . . . It is here where
American poetry, with the exception of Jeffers, has not yet stepped out
of the Calvinistic atmosphere."

B125. Lehman, Benjamin H. "The Most Significant Tendency in
Modern Poetry," *Scripps College Papers*, II (1930), 1-12.
  One of the series of "lectures on significant tendencies in contemporary letters," delivered in November 1929, at Scripps College in
Claremont, Cal. Mention of Jeffers, who expresses a neutral view
toward nature, and whose work is an example of poetry's not
completely successful attempts to cope with modern science. "What I
miss in Jeffers is, then, the full and hearty affirmation of the universe,
in its human as well as its unhuman manifestations. Wanting this, he has
not realized the highest mode possible to the patterns of the neutral
universe which the artist is to trace." This mode will be the comic.

B126. MacDonald, Dwight. "Robinson Jeffers," *Miscellany*, I (July and
September, 1930), July: pp. 1-10; Sept.: pp. 1-24.

Review of Jeffers' career and the individual narratives. Emphasis on the dignity and elevation of his verse. "His poetry is the best which this country has so far produced. Not only is he the most brilliant master of verse among contemporary poets, but his is also incomparably the broadest and most powerful personality."

B127. McWilliams, Carey. "Swell Letters in California," *American Mercury*, XXI (September, 1930), 42-47.

Light, humorous mention. "Judging from the frequency of the Robinson Jeffers numbers of the *Carmelite*, there can be little doubt that the site of the future monument to Jeffers has already been selected by far-sighted deliverers of funeral orations and memorial speeches. Jeffers will probably escape, however, the dire fate of George Sterling, to whose memory a water company in San Francisco recently dedicated a slab in a reservoir. George probably cared less for drinking water than any poet of his generation."

B128. More, Paul E. "A Revival of Humanism," *Bookman*, LXXI (March, 1930), 1-11.

Extremely brief mention by noted humanist. Humanism "perceives that a literature depicting our adventures in such a universe [one without purpose] must degenerate into the clever futilities of an Aldous Huxley or the obscene rigmarole of a James Joyce, or, seeking to escape the curse of impotence, into the sadism of a Robinson Jeffers."

B129. Powell, Lawrence Clark. "D. H. Lawrence," *Saturday Review of Literature*, VI (April 12, 1930), 928.

Unfavorable mention in a letter to the editor by the most complete Jeffers critic. Art needs struggle and unrest. "Robinson Jeffers has endeavored to maintain a peaceful state and as a result, his art has suffered. It is premeditated, conscious, cold." This is contrasted with Lawrence's experience.

B130. Snow, Francis. Review of *Our Singing Strength* by Kreymborg, *Current History*, XXXI (January, 1930), 632.

See C19. Brief mention. "One of the most interesting chapters deals with Robinson Jeffers, contrasted as symbolic of a new age, with Whitman. Kreymborg takes the Whitman age, stemming from Emerson as representative of the virtues of the race; the Jeffers period as representative of its vices."

B131. Tate, Allen. Review of *Our Singing Strength* by Kreymborg, *New Republic*, LXII (February 26, 1930), 51-52.

Mention by a New Critic. "The new Shakespeare may combine, as Mr. Kreymborg hopes, the love of Whitman and the hate of Jeffers, and he may combine many other things. One may hope that he will not mistake the size of his vision for its intelligence and quality." See C19.

1931

B132. Anonymous. "Literary Intelligence," *London Mercury*, XXIII (January, 1931), 215.

Brief mention. "The Hogarth Press had the courage, three years ago, to set out to cut a cross-section through contemporary verse," and "many exciting finds have been made . . . and it is to be hoped that the editor will cut and come again, even though the series should not go much deeper, perhaps, than Mr. Robinson Jeffers."

B133._____. "Luhans Return for Long Visit," *Pine Cone* (Carmel, Cal.), April 15, 1931, p. 4.

Of possible biographical interest. Tony and Mabel Dodge Luhan are being entertained by the Jeffers. "After Luhan's visit last year, the Jeffers went with him and spent a number of weeks in Taos."

B134._____. "People Talked About," *Pine Cone* (Carmel, Cal.), January 2, 1931, p. 15.

Of biographical interest. Relates following anecdote: Friend gave the Jeffers two wine bottles when they left for Ireland. Mrs. Jeffers, forgetting prohibition, packed them in suitcase. Passed safely through several states. In a state checking for agricultural pests, their baggage was searched. Mrs. Jeffers feared headlines showing Jeffers arrested for liquor possession. When asked what the bottles contained, "Jeffers calmly looked at the wine . . . 'Only grape juice!' he flashed back." His calmness convinced the inspector and he was passed through.

B135._____. "People Talked About," *Pine Cone* (Carmel, Cal.), August 7, 1931, p. 13.
Of biographical interest. Various information about Jeffers' family. For example: son's favorite book is *The Brothers Karamazov*; they collected rocks from famous writers' homes while in Ireland; their trees were planted by writer friends; they own a pet blind bantam.

B136._____. "Robinson Jeffers: Bard," *Magazine of Sigma Chi*, L (May-June, 1931), 292-296.
Minor, mixed discussion of a fraternity "brother." Discusses Jeffers' fame; his lack of popularity "because of his forbidden themes and his cold aloofness." He is not like Whitman. "Indeed, the emergence of Jeffers, and that he is hailed as a major poet and prophet, is a severe commentary upon Whitman's dream of America. . . . It may be said that he stems from the Greeks . . . but he even goes beyond them in style and form as well as in dreadfulness of themes."

B137. Bushby, D. Maitland. "Poets of Our Southern Frontier," *Overland Monthly*, LXXXIX (February, 1931), 41-42, 58.
A discussion of the manner in which the East ignores western poets. Jeffers is a poet of "first rank" importance, "who has long been hailed as the Titan of Western poets," and whose rise has "reached its apex in 'Dear Judas.'" In that "psychology is the keynote of Jeffers' poetry," he "resembles to a marked degree E. A. Robinson and Masters," and his

"work has shown steady improvement and there is every reason to believe that this improvement will continue in his future creations; in this respect he outsizes Masters and Frost, both of whom are fully matured in their art." Of contemporaries, only Robinson might be a better poet than Jeffers.

B138. Calverton, Victor Francis. "Pathology in Contemporary Literature," *Thinker,* IV (December, 1931), 7-16. Reprinted in: Schmalhausen, Samuel Daniel (ed.). *Our Neurotic Age.* New York: Farrar and Rinehart, 1932, pp. 286-308.
Unfavorable comment by Marxist critic who sees Jeffers symptomatic of a dying civilization. Unlike the tragedies of the sane Greeks, Jeffers' tragedies are pathologic. He "envisions the world as a monstrous miscarriage of fate. . . . Jeffers is more than non-logical; he is alogical in his whole approach to life. . . ."

B139. Carr, Harry, "The Lancer," *Times* (Los Angeles, Cal.), April 28, 1931, section 2, p. 1.
Of possible biographical interest. Describes Antonio Lujan and his "particular pal," Jeffers, who "is recognized as one of the few really great poets of this generation."

B140. Cerwin, Herbert. "Twenty-four Hours a Day," *Pine Cone* (Carmel, Cal.), May 8, 1931, p. 5.
Minor mention in local newspaper. Jeffers and Sarah Bard Field would make good poet laureates. "Should some of their poetry, however, be read before the senate," some of the members "would leave their chambers suffering from delirium tremens."

B141. Dobie, Charles Caldwell. "The First California Authors," *Bookman*, CLXXII (February, 1931), 590-596. Reprinted in: *Pine Cone* (Carmel, Cal.), March 13, 1931, p. 11.
Brief mention in article on the Carmel colony by a prominent conservative interpreter of San Francisco: "Sterling became one of the

strongest assets in its bid for a valid reputation, to be succeeded by Robinson Jeffers, to whom Sterling generously yielded his poetic sceptre."

B142. Hicks, Granville. "The Past and Future of William Faulkner," *Bookman*, LXXIV (September, 1931), 17-24.
Prominent Marxist critic concludes article with favorable comparison of Jeffers to Faulkner. "Jeffers has a vision, which expresses itself in symbols of lustful deeds and bloody crimes; Faulkner has strangely focused powers of observation. Jeffers writes the poetry of annihilation, Faulkner the record of thwarted lives and savage deaths. . . . If he [Faulkner] had the dark genius of a Robinson Jeffers one could condone, even admire, his abandoning himself to the guidance of his more sensational talents. But no signs of that genius have appeared."

B143. Karo, Leila Mitchell. "Robinson Jeffers," *Present Day American Literature*, IV (March, 1931), 160-165.
Lengthy but trivial. General review of each of the major narratives with *Dear Judas* as least successful. "Those who have given him truly serious attention invariably have become convinced of his greatness and are now deeply aware that Robinson Jeffers possesses the art of a master."

B144. Lawless, Ray M. "Robinson Jeffers–Poet," *Present Day American Literature*, IV (March, 1931), 154-160.
Favorable, but unsuccessful, attempt at a balanced judgement of Jeffers. Reviews career and compares him to other poets. "In the pantheism, there is comparison with William Cullen Bryant. . . . In the realm of horror, Jeffers far surpasses Poe . . . in his probing into the darker secrets of the mind, Jeffers is to be compared with Eugene O'Neill. . . . As to their use of free verse, Jeffers shows much greater skill," than Whitman. His philosophy resembles Melville and Hardy. "It may be an exaggeration to say that the greatest poetic event in America in the 1920's is the arrival of Robinson Jeffers; but it is not easy to keep from making such a statement."

B145. Lehman, Benjamin H. "Robinson Jeffers," *Saturday Review of Literature*, VIII (September 5, 1931), 97-99.

Slightly revised edition of Lehman, "The Most Significant Tendency in Modern Poetry." See B125.

B146. Marchand, Leslie A. "Robinson Jeffers–Poet Extraordinary," *MS*, III (October, 1931), 3, 9. Reprinted in: *Carmelite*, IV (November 19, 1931), 11.

Favorable comment. "Downright persons will be troubled by the awfulness of his subject matter." However, "his figures and his descriptions win us out of mediocrity for a moment and we live in the intensity of freed desire."

B147. McWilliams, Cary. "The Writers of California," *Bookman*, LXXII (December, 1930), 352-359. Reprinted in: *Pine Cone* (Carmel, Calif.), January 16, 1931, p. 8.

Brief mention of Jeffers. "Carmel is famous today . . . because it is the home of Robinson Jeffers. Whatever one may think of Mr. Jeffers' poetry, or the chaotic commentary on his work, it is quite obvious that he towers above all of his California predecessors. The intensity of his feeling for the Carmel shore-line does not require emphasis."

B148. Mencken, Henry L. "Market Report: Poetry," *Americn Mercury*, XXIV (October, 1931), 151-153. Reprinted in: *Literary Digest*, CXI (October 10, 1931), 17.

Brief mention. Speaking of the "great dearth of talented new-comers," he adds, "Since Robinson Jeffers I can recall but one debutant who has really got any serious notice: to wit, Hart Crane."

B149. Powell, Lawrence Clark. "Leaves of Grass and Granite Boulders," *Carmelite*, IV (October 22, 1931), 8-9.

Favorable article by leading Jeffers critic. Comparison of Whitman and Jeffers. They both, "having started from a common point of wonder at seeing the race nearly home again to Asia, have gone their own ways—one to a sure conclusion that the Pacific empire will serve to justify all evolution; the other to the belief that as yet, the empire-builders have failed to fill the enormous stage."

B150. Walton, Eda Lou. "California's Place in the Literary Firmament," *New York Times Book Review*, August 9, 1931, p. 10.
Review of Edwin Markham's *Songs and Stories*. See C28. Brief mention. "Robinson Jeffers, the most famous of all the California poets, is very badly represented; Mr. Markham does not in the least understand what Mr. Jeffers is about."

1932

B151. Anonymous. "Novel in Verse," *Time*, XX (October 3, 1932), 47.
Review of W. R. Benét's *Rip Tide*. Brief Jeffers mention. In describing plot: "Poet Robinson Jeffers would have carried them on to incest."

B152._____. "A Poet's Son Turns Critic," *Post* (New York), April 22, 1932, p. 11.
Of possible biographical interest. Jeffers' son, Donnan, read his father's "Thurso's Landing," though his twin brother doubted it was "fit" reading. Donnan's opinion of the poem: "Well, I don't know anything about poetry, but it's a good story and well told."

B153._____. "Robinson Jeffers and His Sons," *Vanity Fair*, XXXVIII (April, 1932), 27.
Example of Jeffers' wide popularity. "In the eyes of many, Robinson Jeffers is America's greatest poet." His themes—"often cruel, always powerful—invariably subordinate mankind to the greater and more lasting verities of the natural universe."

B154. Bates, Ernest Sutherland. "Criticism in 1930," *Herald Tribune* (New York), January 24, 1932, p. 2.

Review of *American Writers on American Literature* edited by John Macy. Complete brief mention of Jeffers: Criticizes Louis Untermeyer for "far too neatly tying up Robinson Jeffers, George Sterling and the shade of Joaquin Miller in a single package."

B155. Brooks, Philip. "The Colophon's Casements Open on Antique Vistas," *New York Times Book Review*, June 5, 1932, p. 2.

Review of *Colophon*, III, #10 (May, 1932), part 10: Jeffers, Robinson. "First Book." Reprinted in *Breaking into Print*, by Various Authors. New York: Simon and Schuster, 1937. Complete comment on Jeffers: "One essay alone remains to uphold the honor of the moderns. It is a part of the 'confession' series, an account of his first book and others by Robinson Jeffers, and it will appeal strongly to his numerous following."

B156. Broun, Heywood. "It Seems to Me," *World-Telegram* (New York), December 28, 1932, p. 17.

Mention in an interview by well-known essayist. Edna St. Vincent Millay "can't think of a single great poem that's glad." For example, Jeffers, whom she considers great, " ' writes the most disillusioned, tragic, marvellous stuff.' "

B157. Canby, Henry Seidel. "The Pulitzer Prizes," *Saturday Review of Literature*, VIII (April 23, 1932), 677.

Mention by noted critic in discussion of the year's prizes. States that Jeffers should have been given the prize, even though *Dear Judas* is not his best work. Jeffers "belongs among the few poets of unquestioned eminence now practicing here."

B158. Cerwin, Herbert. "Familiar Sights," *Pine Cone* (Carmel, Cal.), April 15, 1932, p. 10.

Brief comment of possible biographical interest. Account of "Jeffers hiding out in his tower as dashing co-eds arrive to have him pen his name on his latest books."

B159. DeCasseres, Benjamin. "Robinson Jeffers," *University of North Carolina Daily Tar Heel*, XL (January 24, 1932), 1.

The most ardent critic praises once more. "An Aeschylus in Main Street. . . . . When I saw Jeffers at the top of his tower," writing poetry, "I had the feeling that the tower suddenly shot up and hit a star. . . . In fifty years only two living Americans will be read, Robinson Jeffers and James Branch Cabell."

B160. Eisely, Loren C. "Music of the Mountain," *Voices*, LXVII (December-January, 1932-1933), 42-47.

Favorable comment by leading critic in a discussion of Jeffers' treatment of the environment. Although Jeffers is not "an able turner of love lyrics" and possesses no "abiding faith in humanity," neither did Thoreau, whose stature has grown with the years. Jeffers is "an older Whitman gone down to the land's end, grown sadder, more sophisticated." He will not "suffer any more than a temporary obscurity in the flush of new enthusiasms. This was true of Thoreau, and it will be true of Jeffers."

B161. Gibson, W. H. "Robinson Jeffers: Pro," *Nassau Lit*, XCI (November, 1932), 11-16.

Reviews works with emphasis on "The Loving Shepherdess" and "Thurso's Landing," in both of which Jeffers shows unusual pity for human suffering. "If Jeffers can unite the various fine elements" of his poems, "and if he can expand and further develop such characters as Clare Walker and Helen and Reave Thurso, it is my opinion that his place among very great poets will be assured."

B162. Grover, Beth. "Robinson Jeffers Suffers From Being Lionized," *Pine Cone* (Carmel, Cal.), July 15, 1932, p. 7.

Of possible biographical interest. Since his success with "Thurso's Landing," Jeffers has had many more visitors than usual. "He'll probably have to move to a new island or construct a moat and drawbridge to keep himself from becoming lionized."

B163. Hazlitt, Henry. "Our Greatest Authors: How Great Are They?" *Forum*, LXXVIII (October, 1932), 245-250.

Mention of Jeffers, whose work "seems destined to endure because of its sheer narrative intensity and power." Those authors most likely to survive are Eliot, Frost and Edward Arlington Robinson, "followed by Jeffers."

B164. Horton, Phillip. "Robinson Jeffers: Con," *Nassau Lit*, XCI (November, 1932), 17-23.

Analysis by prominent critic and biographer, in terms of Jungian psychology. "Stewing in his own muddy emotionalism and insular idleness, he lags far behind the other poets of today who have the courage to face reality and the tremendously significant problems it is posing, as well as the maturity of intellect to grapple with them. . . . Jeffers deserves thorough condemnation and execration not only for what he has done, but more especially for what he has left undone."

B165. Jeffers, Una. "Strange Idyll," *Carmelite*, V (March 3, 1932), 9.

Of possible biographical interest. Review of *Lorenzo in Taos* (See C35) and description of Mabel Luhan's writing of the volume. Mention of Mabel's desire, before D. H. Lawrence's death, to have him meet Jeffers. " 'Those two could understand each other,' she said. I believe in her heart she knew it would be fun to watch."

B166. Loving, Pierre. "Whither the American Writer," *Modern Quarterly*, VI (Summer, 1932), 11-18.

Questionaire asking, among other things, which way American literature is headed. Although most of the writers questioned discounted the way of Jeffers, Loving states, "Even if they have no followers—Robinson Jeffers and Eugene O'Neill may survive as great writers—mirrors of their period, and a little more than mere mirrors."

B167. Masters, Edgar Lee. "The Poetry Revival of 1914," *American Mercury*, XXVI (July, 1932), 272-280.

A friend and fellow poet recognizes Jeffers, the innovator. Includes Jeffers in revival because *Californians* was published that year. In it

Jeffers "abandoned rhymes and old forms . . . and adopted a long rhythmical line of great beauty." He "has great imagination and it is motivated by a thinking mind of subtlety, courage and power. Being still in the heyday of his creativeness, the success to which he may go is beyond prediction."

B168. Nethercot, Arthur H. "Ways That Make Us Ponder While We Praise," *Voices*, LXVII (December-January, 1932-1933), 52-54.

Extremely brief mention. Edwin Arlington Robinson was the first in our generation to search for the small satanic "kink" in men's brains, but his quest was intellectual, not emotional, as with Jeffers.

B169. Robinson, A. C. "Jeffers' Mother," *Time*, XIX (April 25, 1932), 8.

Of possible biographical interest. Letter to editor by president of Peoples-Pittsburgh Trust Co., questioning the brief way Jeffers' mother was brushed aside in the April 4, 1932 review of *Thurso's Landing*. "To his heritage from her and her influence and training, Robinson Jeffers owes much, as well as to his able father." The writer is a member of the mother's family.

B170. Sanderson, E. "Ex-Detective Hammett," *Bookman* LXXIV (January-February, 1932), 518.

Brief mention in interview with the prominent detective novelist, Dashell Hammett, who "thinks Robinson Jeffers the best story-teller he has ever read, and the cruellest."

B171. Tate, Allen. "A Note on Donne," *New Republic*, LXX (April 6, 1932), 212-213.

Comment by a moderately friendly New Critic. Jeffers is part of our "historical consciousness" because he "performs a fusion of literary psychology with a fictitious primitivism. . . ."

B172. Thompson, A. R. "The Cult of Cruelty," *Bookman*, LXXIV (January-February, 1932), 477-487.

Mention. Jeffers is a greater master of the horrible than Faulkner. However, "I, too, relish Jeffers' power, and get a 'kick' out of him generally. But I find it impossible to read him continuously and preserve an aesthetic attitude toward him. His crude horror destroys the delicate balance of aesthetic distance."

B173. Winters, Ella. "Jeffers' Bust Comes Home," *Carmelite*, V (January 9, 1932), 8.

Of possible biographical interest. Description of a bronze bust of Jeffers made by Jo Davidson. "That poet sings, as the stone-mason he is also, builds, like a bird; it's all in a day's work. Only the bird he resembles is the eagle. . . ."

1933

B174. Brown, Leonard. "Our Contemporary Poetry," *Sewanee Review*, XLI (January-March, 1933), 43-63.

Syracuse professor and prominent critic reviews *The New Poetry*, edited by Monroe and Henderson. See C36. Included is a brief, but apt negative Jeffers critique. Mr. Jeffers is "one of the more lately arrived luminaries in the contemporary heavens." Feels the "classic qualities" of Jeffers' style are "so overladen with a dark melodrama that we come finally to suspect his so-called Greek temper." Hence, Jeffers is more "romantic" than "classical." The defect of the "Sandburg-Imagist-Jeffers generation of contemporary poets," is largely a "lack of intellectual effort." They do not know enough.

B175. Cerwin, Herbert. "How Authors Get That Way," *Pine Cone* (Carmel, Cal.), September 1, 1933, p. 1.

Of possible biographical interest. Discusses the sources of inspiration for Carmel's authors. "Robinson Jeffers gets his best lines for his poems when washing dishes. We're told that one of his best poems was composed while building a stone fence around his house on the Point."

B176. Jeffers, Una. "A Correction," *Nassau Lit*, XCI (January, 1933), 41.
Mrs. Jeffers complains, in a letter, that Horton's article (see B164) contained a factual error when it was stated that Jeffers had undergone psychoanalysis.

1934

B177. Anonymous. Review of Powell's *Robinson Jeffers, The Man and His Work, Booklist*, XXXI (December, 1934), 128.
See C46. Listing. "The author describes the poet's aims, methods, and achievements, and advances his reasons for believing him to be a great poet whose works will endure."

B178. Gregory, Horace. "Suicide in the Jungle," *New Masses*, XXV (February 13, 1934), 18-19.
Marxist critic compares O'Neill and Jeffers. Jeffers is a better poet, but he erred in associating himself with a corrupt society. He is a superlative nature poet, but more important, "He made us see the underside of a vast dream called American prosperity at a time when its golden cloud floated over us."

B179. Hatcher, Harlan. "The Torches of Violence," *English Journal*, XXIII (February, 1934), 91-99.

Comparison of the decade's two leaders in the "school of violence," by the novelist and later president of the University of Michigan. Jeffers, in poetry, and Faulkner, in the novel, see "the elements of terror and destruction" and dwell on them for their "morbid fascination!" The difference between the tragedy and pain of great literature and "Faulkner's buzzards, dead men, and ghoulish eyes, or Jeffers' pathological demons, hurt hawks, and libidinous symbolism" is the difference between "exalting human courage and fortitude in the face of inescapable evil and administering pain and shock as ends in themselves. . . . It is out of realism, war, and Freudianism, either singly or in combination, that the school of Jeffers and Faulkner has developed."

B180. Hutchinson, Percy. "The Poetry of Robinson Jeffers: A Sound and Careful Study of the California Poet's Work and of the Life and Personality Behind It," *Times* (New York), September 2, 1934, section 5, p. 2. Reprinted in: *Magazine of Sigma Chi*, LV (February, 1936), 20-23, 25, 27.

Review of Powell book. See C46. The book is "thorough and painstaking," albeit "uninspired as to style." Jeffers is "that very remarkable poet of the West," whose poetry has "thrilled, shocked, and astounded readers. . . ." Questions whether "contemporary studies of living authors can be wholly satisfactory—that is, of course, unless the object of the study is a colossus, and we question if Mr. Jeffers is quite that, startling literary figure though he undoubtedly is. . . . Jeffers will look very different a generation hence; he may have grown in stature, he may have shrunk, but he will be different."

B181. Powell, Lawrence Clark. "Robinson Jeffers on Life and Letters," *Westways*, XXVI (March, 1934), 20, 21, 34.

Of biographical interest. Description of several interviews with Jeffers, by leading Jeffers critic. Detailed discussion of Jeffers' literary tastes. Concludes: "He has thought too deeply, written too widely and deeply, to be understood generally by his own time. But there are those who have felt the impact of his genius, and I may venture to prodict that their number will be increasing as long as English is remembered."

1935

B182. Anonymous. "First Editions of Jeffers," *Pine Cone* (Carmel, Cal.), May 3, 1935, p. 2.
Minor local recognition. Lists and comments on all of Jeffers' works to 1935.

B183._____. "Robinson Jeffers Honored by College from which He Graduated 30 Years Ago," *Pine Cone* (Carmel, Cal.), May 3, 1935, p. 1.
Occidental College commemorates the graduation of "one of its most distinguished alumni, Robinson Jeffers, the Carmel poet of world renown."

B184. Busch, Niven. "Duel in a Headland," *Saturday Review of Literature*, XI (March 9, 1935), 533.
Biography and favorable survey, by the novelist and later screen writer, of Jeffers' pessimism as a possible alternative philosophy for our times. "I hope that when the spectral episode of man's life on earth has ended finally in all the disasters whose scientific and rhetorical values Jeffers knows so well, he'll still be on his headland, shouting reverberant defiance at his enemy the sky."

B185. Humphries, Rolfe. "Robinson Jeffers," *Modern Monthly*, VIII (January and February, 1935), 680-689, 748-753.
Marxist critic damns Jeffers' decadent pessimism. Jeffers expresses "belief representative of bourgeois upper-class philosophy as that upper class verges on dissolution. . . . He makes no effort to show that the present horrible frustrations, deformations and agonies of men are due to the fact that they are for the most part still living under the degenerating capitalism of the twentieth century," and by telling men that it is futile to protest against man's hard, inevitable lot, "he serves a very useful purpose to the governing class."

B186. Powell, Lawrence Clark. "Robinson Jeffers, '05," *Occidental Alumnus*, XVII (March, 1935), 5, 12.

Description of Occidental College activities to honor the thirtieth anniversary of Jeffers' graduation. Biographical notes on the poet's student days. "Robinson Jeffers' medical training was not useless. In our own day he has brought so rich a transfusion to the dwindled stream of poetry that the sectional, cultist and obscurist versifiers, with their tiny diluted phials of thin stuff are not needed."

1936

B187. Canby, Henry Seidel. "The Pulitzer Prize Winners," *Saturday Review of Literature*, XIV (May 9, 1936), 6.

Brief mention. Deplores the fact that Jeffers has been neglected again. "But the Central Committee has this year finally dropped from its announcement the statement that the prizes must go to the 'best books!' "

B188. May, Henry Farnham, Jr. "After Reading a Carmel Poet," *Poetry*, XLVIII (September, 1936), 318-319.

Minor poetic tribute contradicts Jeffers' philosophy:
"Go not to the hard gray solitude of stone
(Though rock lasts longer than men.)
. . . .
These things were never ours. Man, as the spray,
Lives in chaotic strife;
And from that chaos may not turn away—
Unless he turns from life."

B189. Moore, Merrill. "An Appreciation of Robinson Jeffers," *Magazine of Sigma Chi*, LV (February, 1936), 24.

Trivial tribute to a fellow Sigma Chi. "Everyone who reads modern verse has felt the power and directness of Robinson Jeffers' poems. He is blessed and cursed with an extraordinary ability to feel and to be articulate."

B190. Powell, Lawrence Clark. "The Man at Tor House," *Vomag* (Pasadena, Calif.), IV (March, 1936), 41-42.

Biographical interest. Scant critical judgment. "Robinson Jeffers is an important poet because of the exalted range and dignity of his thought. There is in all of his work a strain of nobility. . . . none can deny the simple forthright honesty and passion for truth implicit in everything Robinson Jeffers has written."

1937

B191. Anonymous. "Book of the Month Club Awards," *Publishers' Weekly*, CXXXI (February 6, 1937), 736-737.

Report on award and concurrence with committee choices. On Jeffers: "The award was made to Robinson Jeffers for his distinguished accomplishment as a poet through numerous volumes."

B192._____. "Four Forgotten Books Win $2,500 Prizes," *Times* (New York), January 30, 1937, p. 15.

Jeffers received most votes and was "the first one voted an award." One of the judges was Edna St. Vincent Millay. She said: "He has many admirers among poets, . . . but I think that I am his most enthusiastic admirer. I felt after reading the long poetic play in the beginning of 'Solstice' that his work showed great dramatic talent. His real genius is along dramatic lines." She considers Jeffers "one of the great American poets."

B193. DeVoto, Bernard. "Rats, Lice and Poetry," *Saturday Review of Literature*, XVII (October 23, 1937), 8.

Mention by prominent critic in an editorial dealing with modern literature's tendency towards despair. "Mr. Robinson Jeffers has not fully resolved the conflict. From where he perches with an old she-eagle on a cliff . . . struggle and flight seem just the same to him. . . . But once an eon the rock trembles . . . just enough to blur the edge of his conclusions . . . and the conflict rises up again."

B194. Flanner, Hildegarde. "Two Poets: Jeffers and Millay," *New Republic*, LXXXIX (January 27, 1937), 379-382. Reprinted in: Cowley, Malcolm (ed.). *After the Genteel Tradition*. Carbondale, Ill.: Southern Illinois University Press, 1964, pp. 124-133.

Compares the two. Judges "Tower Beyond Tragedy" Jeffers' best work. "There is a kind of willing insanity in many of his characters that robs them of the essence of real tragedy." However, some works are "supreme." Unfortunately, "the formula of tragic introversion becomes, after repeated use, worn out." Interpretive error in assuming that Jeffers recommends war as a cleansing force.

B195. Jones, Idwal. "Letters on the Pacific Rim," *Saturday Review of Literature*, XV (March 6, 1937), 22.

Extremely brief. In speaking of the "Carmel Group": "Many varied talents are attached to it, some of major importance, like Robinson Jeffers, and Professor Haakon Chevalier of the English Department of Stanford."

B196. Quercus, P. E. G., pseud. "Trade Winds," *Saturday Review of Literature*, XV (March 6, 1937), 22.

Briefly discusses DeCasseres' "skyrocket about poor Mr. Jeffers," which was "so frenzied that even the poet's own publishers never dared use it." Lists those to whom Jeffers was compared. See C16. "As we rather admire Jeffers at his best, we naturally resented this."

B197. Swallow, Alan. "The Poetry of Robinson Jeffers," *Intermountain Review*, II (Fall, 1937), 8-9.

Important Marxist traces Jeffers' failure to the fact "that he works so completely within the bourgeois culture." Still, he is a "fine poet, the best poet of his time and culture, . . . the only poet of hulking stature who has developed completely within the bourgeois culture." While "Eliot, Pound, Yeats, and the Marxians have been at cross purposes to the movement of decadent capitalism, Jeffers has expressed the driving forces . . . of that culture. Society is taking another road. Perhaps Jeffers has been fooish not to choose that progressive culture and develop within its dialectic. But being foolish does not completely destroy his effectiveness as a poet."

B198. Thompson, Ralph. "Books of the Times," *Times* (New York), January 30, 1937, p. 5.

Discussion of award choice by a member of the judging board that gave Jeffers the Book-of-the-Month Club award. "Robinson Jeffers has for years been writing poetry of a powerful and individual sort, and 'Solstice and Other Poems,' the volume by which he is represented in the contest is most impressive. . . . I hope it is not improper to reveal that in the balloting Edna St. Vincent Millay was one of Mr. Jeffers' staunchest advocates."

1938

B199. Davis, Harold. "Robinson Jeffers: A California Poet," *Pomona College Bulletin*, XXXV (March, 1938), 3-10.

An extra edition from the California college subtitled *Radio Talks* by various authors. An introduction to the poet by a prominent western critic. Includes biography and summary of narratives. Extensive quotations. "No modern poet has caught so well the moods of the ocean. . . . Mr. Jeffers can scrutinize as closely as the peering naturalist and is as sensitive to color as an artist." His work is "cosmic," and has "sustained and bare magnificence." His philosophy is "not bitter, not cynical. It is simply the long range view of things—and of man along with them."

B200. Sergeant, Elizabeth Shepley. "Sphinx in Taos Desert," *Saturday Review of Literature*, XIX (November 26, 1938), 12-14.
   Biographical interest. A discussion of Mabel Dodge Luhan's life. Includes brief mention of Jeffers as a visitor to Taos.

B201. Waggoner, Hyatt Howe. "Science and the Poetry of Robinson Jeffers," *American Literature*, X (November, 1938), 275-288.
   A discussion of the problem of poetry and science. Itemizes the individual sciences to which Jeffers is indebted. Feels science has moved on from Jeffers' determinism and has left him behind."

B202. Wann, Louis. "Robinson Jeffers—Counterpart of Walt Whitman," *Personalist*, XIX (Summer, 1938), 297-308.
   In an extremely lucid essay, Jeffers is contrasted to Whitman. The philosophies of the two are antithetical. Jeffers "has achieved a consummate expression of the divine beauty of the world about us."

1939

B203. Anonymous. "Critics Vote on Best Books of 1938," *Saturday Review of Literature*, XIX (April 22, 1939), 6-7.
   Results of a poll of reviewers and literary editors, in which Jeffers' *Selected Poems* received a winning eight votes as the poetry volume that should be awarded the Pulitzer Prize [John Gould Fletcher was the actual recipient that year]. Of *Selected Poems*: it "contains this poet's most distinguished work."

B204._____. "The Pulitzer Prizes," *Saturday Review of Literature*, XX (May 6, 1939), 8.

Brief mention. Although Fletcher is a good selection, "we have no choice but to revive the annual battle-cry in these columns, and protest once more that Robinson Jeffers has been neglected. The number of minor poets who have won Pulitzer Prizes in years when Jeffers had books in the field is a serious reflection on the standards of the poetry award."

B205. Brown, E. K. "Robinson Jeffers: The Tower Beyond Tragedy," *Manitoba Arts Review*, I (Spring, 1939), 4-17.

Discusses Jeffers' career. Summarized plots of the narratives. Emphasis on Jeffers' pessimism which finds "inexhaustible consolation in nature.... His poems are full of delicate notations of the beauty of California."

B206. Flewelling, R. T. "Tragic Drama—Modern Style," *Personalist*, XX (July, 1939), 229-240.

A comparison of Aeschylus' *Orestia* with "Tower Beyond Tragedy." Ancient drama based on belief in fate, in gods, and in man's divinity. Jeffers' poem is based on belief in science and man's helplessness. "It may seem a bit daring to compare Aeschylus with Jeffers, since a prophet is without honor in his own generation, nevertheless, it is the writer's opinion that the American comes off with a fair degree of credit. Not only so, but we believe that Jeffers offers the truer psychology of human emotions and the profounder solution."

B207. Gierasch, Walter. "Robinson Jeffers," *English Journal*, XXVIII (April, 1939), 284-295.

Detailed examination of Jeffers' themes of pessimism, incest, and transcendent nature, concluding: "Jeffers has created a world that most readers cannot like or believe in, but which they find it hard to resist. The power of his imagination and the sweep of his long lines are more effective than many prettified songs.... it seems scarcely possible that such a force can die."

B208. Haydon, A. Eustace. "Robinson Jeffers: Poet-Philosopher," *University Review*, V (Summer, 1939), 235-238.

Extravagant praise. Sees Jeffers as a prophet who preaches, stripping away all illusions and recognizing man's limitations. He is "superb when he portrays the splendors of cosmic immensities. If the sun should again become careless in the paths of the stars . . . Jeffers would be the perfect poet to write the epitaph of humanity in that fiery death and rebirth of worlds."

B209. Lind, L. Robert. "The Crisis in Literature," *Sewanee Review*, XLVII (January-March, 1939), 35-62.

Favorable mention of Jeffers in whose "death and hatred" the contemporary world is mirrored. Comparison with Swift. Jeffers writes with "Hebraic thunder." He seeks to express "in gigantic, fearful, almost grotesque symbols his cold hatred for humanity." As with the prophets, "intolerable spleen will not permit silence, though speech brings only the need for more and more speech, until the end is hysteria." He "illustrates the cul-de-sac into which contemporary history has fallen."

B210. Miller, Benjamin. "Toward a Religious Philosophy of the Theatre," *Personalist*, XX (October, 1939), 361-376.

Brief use of some comments by Jeffers and one of his poems, "The Answer," in an attempt to clarify the connection between the aesthetic and the religious experience.

B211. Taylor, Frajam. "The Hawk and the Stone," *Poetry*, LV (October, 1939), 39-46.

Deals primarily with *Tamar* and *Give Your Heart to the Hawks*, in a comparison with Nietzsche. Finds Jeffers' ultimate affirmation in nature. We find "many dark places in his poetry, and sometimes it will seem as if we have wandered into abysses of denial, but always it is important to realize that whatever else this poet may deny, he never denies the joy of living."

B212. Van Petten, Oliver. "Posterity's Poet," *Andrean*, III (Fall, 1939), 12.

Trivial, but interesting example of Jeffers' continuing popularity. Written by a student at St. Andrew's School, Middletown, Delaware. Feels Jeffers "stands to remain a pillar of classic art down the ages."

B213. Wronecki, Jeanne. "Un Poete Américain d'aujourd' hui: Robinson Jeffers," *Revue de France*, XIX (March 15, 1939), 283-286.

Jeffers is discussed as typical of post-World War I thought in America in this French recognition. "Les croyances philosophiques de Robinson Jeffers peuvent être discutées. Il demeurera toujours néamoins, un grand poète, car il a su voir la beauté des choses et la capter dans des vers . . . qui semblant couler de sa plume sans effort avec un inépuisable abondance."

1940

B214. Anonymous. "Robinson Jeffers Honored with PBK Membership at USC," *Pine Cone* (Carmel, Cal.), May 3, 1940, p. 2.

Trivial. Jeffers made an honorary Phi Beta Kappa, although at college he had never won this honor.

B215._____. "SC Publishes Jeffers' Early Poetry in 1905," *Southern California Daily Trojan* (Los Angeles, Cal.), April 25, 1940, p. 2.

Interesting early Jeffers material. Reprint of three poems printed in the 1905-1906 editions of the literary magazine while Jeffers was a U. S. C. student. Introductory material notes that he "is to become an honorary of the local chapter of Phi Beta Kappa," and that he "is prominent in the field of poetry."

B216. Carpenter, Frederic Ives. "The Values of Robinson Jeffers," *American Literature*, XI (January, 1940), 353-366.

First discussion by important Jeffers authority. Tries to find affirmative values in apparent denial and exaggerated despair. Defends Jeffers from charge of fascism. "Jeffers considers social action doomed to defeat. But his pessimism in this is not properly 'defeatist.' It rather suggests the pattern of fatalistic Greek thought, as opposed to Christian. . . . His manner of asking suggests the answer and his poetry has always implied it: the development of all man's powers and the discovery of truth are the new values of modern man. The experience of sorrow and pain becomes a positive value. And the old value of ignorant happiness is denied."

B217._____. "Death Comes for Robinson Jeffers," *University Review*, VII (December, 1940), 97-105. Reprinted in his: *American Literature and the Dream*. New York: Philosophical Library, Inc., 1955, pp. 144-154.

In this University of Kansas City publication, discusses Jeffers' attitude death as something neither to be desired nor dreaded, but accepted, even embraced. Concludes: "But any man—even a great poet—may sometimes imagine the music of death more sweet than reality, and praise it beyond proportion."

B218. Gilbert, Rudolph. "Robinson Jeffers' Huge Background," *Pine Cone* (Carmel, Cal.), April 12, 1940, p. 5.

Critique of the Schwartz (see A254) and Taylor (see B211) articles in the October, 1939 *Poetry*. An ardent admirer answers any hint of adverse criticism. If Schwartz doesn't like Jeffers, he should not review him. "A critic or a reader who does not grasp Jeffers' 'complex vision' implicitly or artistically outside of social morals and politics will never receive a message from his work." Jeffers offers "a heightening power of the tragic acceptance of life itself."

B219. Jeffers, Una. "How Carmel Won Hearts of the Jeffers Family," *Pine Cone* (Carmel, Cal.), April 19, 1940, p. 9.

Biographical material dealing with the Jeffers family's early years in Carmel.

B220. Jones, Howard Mumford. "Reply to Carpenter," *American Literature*, XII (March, 1940), 108.

Prominent critic complains of Carpenter's quoting of Jones' opinion of Jeffers as "Dull Naughtiness." Jones points out this was a headline for his Chicago *News* review of *The Women at Point Sur* (see A93) and was not written by Jones. He also suggests that one review should not be assumed to represent an overall opinion of a writer's work.

B221. Meyer, Sylvia. "Poetry Corner," *Scholastic* (High School Teachers' Edition), XXXVI (February 19, 1940), 25.

Minor recognition in school publication. Recommends, with cautions, that high school students read Jeffers, even though he sees man "as a rat." However, "don't let your will be paralyzed. It is one thing to read such a philosophy, quite another to accept it."

B222. Miller, Benjamin. "The Demands of the Religious Consciousness," *Review of Religion*, IV (May, 1940), 401-415.

"In his poem 'Hope Is Not For the Wise,' Robinson Jeffers has expressed much of the temper of our 'aesthetic naturalism.'" His humanistic introversion represents recognition of man's egocentricity as a hindrance to moral ascent. "This is a harsh and severe view of life and could never become a popular interpretation. Yet, its pessimistic realism does not present an unexciting prospect to the religious consciousness."

B223. Stelter, Benjamin F. "Alumnus Powell on Alumnus Jeffers," *Occidental Alumnus*, XXIII (November, 1940), 5, 13.

Review of Powell book. See C65. Description of student Powell's enthusiasm for Jeffers by Powell's former English instructor. Jeffers is "constantly, though slowly gaining and holding his audience . . . nonplussing those who insist he has no creed." One might wish, however, that Jeffers had more of the "spirit-cleansing attribute of human laughter" in his work.

B224. White, William. "On Some Unnoticed Jeffers Poems," *Papers of the Bibliographical Society of America*, XXXIV (December, 1940), 362-363.
Bibliography of newly discovered poems.

B225. Worden, Perry. "Robinson Jeffers: A Poet's Culturing," *Star News* (Pasadena, Cal.), May 4, 1940, p. 8.
Of possible biographical interest. Anecdotes of Jeffers' stay in Pasadena. Emphasis on "how, with a deeply-implanted love for nature and a better understanding of the physical world about him, all these science studies and outdoor explorations contributed so to the master-expression of the Carmel poet once a Pasadenan." Includes review of Powell's book. See C65.

1941

B226. Short, R. W. "The Tower Beyond Tragedy," *Southern Review*, VII (Summer, 1941), 132-144.
Unfavorable discussion. Jeffers' philosophy is bogus, his artistic sense weak. He is inconsistent. His characters are flat, narrow puppets. Each generation has its own kind of sensationalism which fades with the next. "Byronism waned into the Yellow Period; Eugene O'Neill and D. H. Lawrence give way to Faulkner, Caldwell, and Jeffers."

B227. Watts, Harold H. "Multivalence in Robinson Jeffers," *College English*, III (November, 1941), 109-120.
In Jeffers' poetry, unlike the Greeks, multivalence, or the clash of values on three levels of existence, human, passively non-human, and actively non-human, account for the drama. His poetry "is curious, it casts strange lights into the spirit of the poet himself, but it presents no drama which can intelligence our spirits. For we are bound by the ambiguities of an imperfect existence."

B228._____. "Robinson Jeffers and Eating the Serpent," *Sewanee Review*, XLIX (January-March, 1941), 39-55.

Discussion of Jeffers as a mystic, who, because he is a rationalist, rejects Christianity's techniques. "Having rejected the Christian God, he does not bend the knee weakly at the altar of humanity or nature or evolution or the cosmic system. He presses on to the bitter end that awaits alienated man. He fuses the isolated self with the isolated god;" and since he finds man hateful, "Jeffers assigns to his god and to himself the cosmic tortures recorded in his narratives—the draining of the bitter poison of the serpent." His philosophy might be termed "masochistic pantheism."

1942

B229. Gates, G. G. "The Bread That Every Man Must Eat Alone," *College English*, IV (December, 1942), 170-174.

Jeffers is neither fascist, nihilist, nor romantic. He attempts to discover how "an inconsistency and an incompatibility of the individual with his social milieu," can be resolved. "His point of view, regardless of any question of its validity, is now being voiced wittingly or unwittingly by some who sense deep worldly wrong."

B230. White, William. "Uncollected Poems of Robinson Jeffers," *American Notes and Queries*, I (January, 1942), 149-151.

Of bibliographical interest. Reprint of three previously uncollected poems that appeared in the University of Southern California's *University Courier* in 1905-1906. "These poems which have been dug out of their tomb are not reprinted for their intrinsic merit, but for the benefit of any student . . . who should care to trace the development of a pale lad," who became the author of "Tamar."

1943

B231. Arms, George W. "Jeffers' *Fire on the Hills*," *Explicator*, I (May, 1943), item 59.

Study of this poem, in which Jeffers secures "the reader's acceptance of his own violent reaction to what he has seen," through anticipation, and careful handling of images and metrical pattern. "That our interpretation attributes more conscious craftsmanship to Jeffers than usual, we acknowledge."

B232. Johnson, William Savage. "The 'Savior' in the Poetry of Robinson Jeffers," *American Literature*, XV (May, 1943), 159-168.

Discussion of Jeffers' concept of "Savior." Three distinct types are described: the mythic savior (Jesus); fictional (Barkley, Margrave); historical (Wilson, Hitler). "In Jeffers the good life is dominated by a more negative ideal than in either Eliot or Yeats. For Mankind as a whole he finds little hope. For the individual the good life is still possible, but only by withdrawal."

B233. Seubert, Eugene E. "Robinson Jeffers: Poet of an Age of Violence," *Studies of the Northwest State Teachers College*, VII (June 1, 1943), 3-28.

Biography, plot and theme of all the narratives. Philosophy, particularly the influence on it of the Carmel coast and Spengler. "Jeffers' evaluation of life was made before Dunkerque, before our own entry into the war, and before Stalingrad. It is entirely possible that critics of a later time will find that Jeffers has been too closely in the grip of the emotional forces rampant in his lifetime; that his imagination has been overwhelmed by the events of his day even as we lose our breath in the cyclonic sweep of his poetry; and that at the very moment when debacle seemed most imminent, the forces of reconstruction and idealism were gathering for a new victory."

1944

B234. Benét, William Rose. "Poetry's Last Twenty Years," *Saturday Review of Literature*, XXVII (August 5, 1944), 100-104.

Portrait, page 102. Brief mention in paragraph listing American poets, including Frost, Sandburg and Benét. "Our most disillusioned poet, of a love for bloody tragedy that goes back to the original Greek, has been Robinson Jeffers."

B235. Coffin, Robert Peter Tristram. "Poetry Today and Tomorrow," *Journal of Aesthetics and Art Criticism*, III (1944), 59-67.

"In spite of what some of our most intellectual critics say today, doubt has never yet produced a major poetry." The prominent poet and critic finds that "Robinson Jeffers is an eloquent example. With an imagery and a sense for detail richer than any other poet this side of the Elizabethans, with a line that is as sonorous at times as some parts of the *Book of Job*, Jeffers, because he believes only in death, has written a dead poetry."

B236. DeVoto, Bernard. "They Turned Their Backs on America," *Saturday Review of Literature*, XXVII (April 8, 1944), 5-8.

A part of DeVoto's 1944 attack on those critics who look to "decadent" Europe instead of vital America. "Neither Mr. Hemingway nor Mr. Brooks nor Mr. Jeffers has been granted the jurisdiction over the American spirit freely exercised by Emerson with the consent of his readers."

B237. Wells, Henry W. "A Philosophy of War: The Outlook of Robinson Jeffers," *College English*, VI (November, 1944), 81-88.

A blatantly propagandistic critique in which Jeffers is found to support the war effort through his emphasis on stoicism, and to be "unAmerican" in his Germanic celebration of violence. "Jeffers is a giant with a Janus head. One face looks menacingly toward the night, the other heroically toward the day. The broadly epic and heroic Jeffers we must admire; the narrowly Teutonic and cynical Jeffers we may seriously deplore."

1945

B238. Cook, Reginald L. "A Meditative Sentinel," *Arizona Quarterly*, I (Summer, 1945), 43-45.

Discussion of Jeffers' nature poetry. "He rejects the Christian God for the nature God, but he is not therefore either a negativist or a despairing man. The tragedy which he sees in life is the result of man's introversion." He is often excessively stoic, and his short poems are sometimes "simply reasoned commentaries, editorialized verse. They do not embody . . . they explain. . . . Yet in no other poet in American literature are we so aware of nature as the elemental matrix. . . ."

B239. Steward, Randall. "American Literature Between the Wars," *South Atlantic Quarterly*, XLIV (October, 1945), 371-383.

The new physics gave many moderns the impression that the universe was somehow doomed. This view "found its most forceful literary expression in the poetry of Robinson Jeffers. . . . Inspired by the new physics, Jeffers regarded life as a blemish and extinction as the greatest good. . . . No author has ever shown a greater avidity for life than Wolfe. In this respect he stands at the opposite pole from Jeffers."

1946

B240. Anonymous. "To Become American Arts and Letters Academy Members," *Times* (New York), May 17, 1946, p. 19.

Biographical interest. Jeffers included in list of those to become members.

B241. Cunningham, Cornelius Carman. "The Rhythm of Robinson Jeffers' Poetry as Revealed by Oral Reading," *Quarterly Journal of Speech*," XXXII (October, 1946), 351-357.

Cunningham and his graduate speech classes at the University of Virginia have been reading Jeffers' poetry for two years and have discovered that "the beat to which Jeffers' poetic rhythm tends is the beat of iambic-anapestic duple meter. . . . Like every great artist who becomes the voice of an age, the spokesman for its *Zeitgeist*, Jeffers has caught its rhythm, too. That spirit and rhythm are not in the tradition of Whitman and the King James Bible, but in the tradition of Swinburne, the master of of rimed duple meter, and the Ancient Greek dramatists, Aeschylus, Sophocles, Euripides. . . . Jeffers can be numbered with them when his art is correctly sensed."

B242. Fitts, Dudley. "Hellenism of Robinson Jeffers," *Kenyon Review*, VIII (Autumn, 1946), 678-683. Reprinted in: Ransom (ed.). *Kenyon Critics*. New York: World Publishers, 1951, pp. 307-312.

Discussion by eminent classical scholar. Compares him unfavorably to Euripides, who exercised restraint. "Although Mr. Jeffers can be effective, even memorably effective, at a low pitch, and can occasionally rise above himself to a genuinely eloquent pathos, he is . . . incapable of tragic force. He lacks insight and control. His characters to him are speaking puppets, not fleshy men and women. He does not penetrate, he cannot sympathize."

B243. Hackman, Martha. "Whitman, Jeffers, and Freedom," *Prairie Schooner*, XX (Fall, 1946), 182-184.

Discusses Jeffers who is not a fascist or a misanthrope. "Jeffers' philosophy at the moment is contrary to the current of popular thought, in which security and material comfort have come to be confused with the idea of freedom. His insight into this confusion and his protest against it may continue to be ignored. He deserves recognition, however, as a poet, not, like Whitman, of democracy, whatever that absurd term may be found to mean, but of individual human freedom."

B244. O'Conner, William Van. "Nature and the Anti-Poetic in Modern Poetry," *Journal of Aesthetics and Art Criticism*, V (September, 1946), 35-44.

A New Critic mentions Jeffers as one who sets man beneath nature. Thus, "His tragedy becomes a pathetic gesture. The only positive teaching of Jeffers, apparently, is the need to escape into nirvana. For all his concern with nature, Jeffers, preoccupied with perversion, fails to consider man as natural. Like Lawrence, but without his espousal of life, he is seeking a solution to man's long dissociation from the natural."

1947

B245. Anonymous. "Acting Mayor J. B. Hynes of Boston Bans 'Dear Judas,' Play Based on Jeffers Poem," *Times* (New York), August 14, 1947, p. 25.

The play ran one week in Ogunquit, Maine, under protest from Catholic attorney Francis W. Sullivan, who felt it "offensive, dangerous and should not be performed as it would surely damage the faith of the people who viewed the play." The Boston city censor "explained that the showing of the play here would violate the beliefs of many Bostonians in God and might even create trouble by stirring up religious feeling."

B246._____. "Dances in Dear Judas," *Times* (New York), October 19, 1947, section 2, p. 6.

Description of musical additions to *Dear Judas*. "Mr. Jeffers has written his poem not for the theatre but to be read. It is a kind of Noh Drama, peopled by ghosts revisiting the scene of their living passions and dwelling thus in two conflicting mental moods. The mere speaking of his lines could never give the pulse of true theatrical substance as the use of movement and music does."

B247._____. "Shine Republic," *Occidental Alumnus*, XXIX (June, 1947), 11.

Reprint of a holograph of the Jeffers poem, "Shine Republic," which has been presented to the Occidental College Library. Jeffers identified as "the great American poet, and one of Occidental's distinguished alumni."

B248. Cail, Harold C. "Dear Judas Bows at Maine Theatre," *Times* (New York), August 5, 1947, p. 26.

Review of *Dear Judas'* opening in Ogunquit, Maine. The play is not "particularly offensive," but it is controversial. Reference to Jeffers: "Meyerberg has followed the Jeffers poem closely, eliminating only one particular passage that was included in the charge that the poem was revolting to a Christian."

B249. Fitzell, Lincoln. "Western Letters," *Sewanee Review*, LV (Summer, 1947), 530-535.

'Mention in discussion of Easterners who came west: "There is also the brilliant stranger who has come to stay (as a stranger) like Robinson Jeffers, the poet of Carmel who distrusts mankind but loves the cold sea rocks below Monterey, California. . . . The poet's verse turns out to be as wild in contour as its frame of smitten rocks and hag blown trees, but in humanity just a bit off-key."

B250. Fowler, William T. "On 'Medea,' " *Times* (New York), November 30, 1947, section 2, p. 2.

Witty letter to Drama Editor taking issue with Jeffers' division of "Medea" into two acts. The intermission "constitutes a disservice to the play in that it breaks the mood established during the first half of the evening and leaves an audience's interest sagging when the second begins."

B251. Glicksberg, Charles I. "The Poetry of Doom and Despair," *Humanist*, VII (Autumn, 1947), 69-72.

Auden is contrasted with Jeffers, who "is the most talented poet of modern pessimism." Jeffers was no metaphysician as was Schopenhauer. "No modern poet has reflected more strikingly than Jeffers the iconoclastic influence of the scientific enlightenment. . . . To set Nature above and apart from man is to fall into the old romantic concept that Nature . . . is superior." Jeffers' absolute pessimism "is an expression of what might be called psychic suicide."

B252. Matthiessen, F. O. "American Poetry, 1920-1940," *Sewanee Review*, LV (Winter, 1947), 24-55. Reprinted in: Spiller, Robert E., *et al. Literary History of the United States*. New York: Macmillan Co., 1948, pp. 593-595.

Short discussion of his long poems as being of an unrelieved violence. "Some of his shorter poems are far more moving, since he has a broad descriptive mastery . . . and his other interest in the exact processes of science has enabled him to give almost clinical accounts of moments of death."

B253. Nichols, Lewis. "The Fates and Furies," *Times* (New York), October 19, 1947, section II, pp. 1, 3.

Interview with Judith Anderson. Jeffers adapted Medea at her request.

B254. Nims, J. F. "Greater Grandeur," *Poetry: A Critical Supplement* (October, 1947), 5-6.

An explication of poems that appeared in the October 1947 issue of *Poetry*.

B255. Sensenderfer, R. E. P. "Living Theater—Judith Anderson is Triumphant as 'Medea' in Euripides' Tragedy at the Locust," *Bulletin* (Philadelphia, Pa.), October 7, 1947, p. 46.

Review of the pre-Broadway try-outs of *Medea*. "Robinson Jeffers tells this in free but singularly rhythmic verse. He calls it a free adaptation but it follows Euripides closely. He catches the clarity and simplicity of the original in stately but pellucid English. The only liberty he takes is reducing the cumbersome Greek 'chorus.' "

B256. Walcutt, Charles Child. "Fear Motifs in the Literature Between Wars," *South Atlantic Quarterly*, XLVI (April, 1947), 227-238.
Brief mention in section dealing with poetry of the 20's. The initial reaction to World War One was "let-down, despair, and—inevitably—guilt. . . . Robinson Jeffers, for example, cries out against civilization."

B257. Zolotow, Sam. " 'Dear Judas' Trial Opposed in Maine," *Times* (New York), July 11, 1947, p. 10.
News article. Francis Sullivan asks that the trial run of *Dear Judas* be cancelled because "I don't think it's right to have the play presented. My objection to it, I have reason to believe, is that it does not portray Christ and the Blessed Mother as they should be portrayed. And I have reason to believe that it makes the character of Judas a victim of determinism." Meyerberg, the producer-adaptor, says his production will not be stopped.

1948

B258. Anonymous. Critique of *Medea*, *New Statesman and Nation*, XXXVI (October 9, 1948), 303.
London production. Criticizes fever pitch at which play begins and continues, "I found the verse of Mr. Robinson Jeffers quite pleasant to listen to."

B259._____. " 'Media' Opens in S. F. with Judith Anderson," *Fortnight*, V (September 24, 1948), 7.

Critique of San Francisco production of *Medea*. "The poetic lines are easily comprehensible to anyone who occasionally shifts gears to Shakespeare."

B260._____. "Medea to Halt Run," *Times* (New York), March 26, 1948, p. 26.
Jeffers mentioned as the author of "an instant success."

B261._____. "People Who Read and Write," *New York Times Book Review*, October 3, 1948, p. 8.
Discusses the critical reception of *The Double Axe*. "According to a coast to coast file of reviews, the overwhelming majority or critics, though clearly out of sympathy with Mr. Jeffers' opinions, in *The Double Axe and Other Poems*, were favorably disposed—or, to put it another way, all but a handful were willing to swallow the politics for the sake of the poetry."

B262. Foote, Robert O. "Footlights," *Star News* (Pasadena, Cal.), September 12, 1948, p. 7.
Mention as author of *Medea*. Jeffers has been "turning out some of the finest poetry that has been written in the English language in this generation."

B263. H., J. "Robinson Jeffers Writes a New Preface to His Tale of Fury, Tragedy and Medea," *Chronicle* (San Francisco, Cal.), September 5, 1948, drama section, pp. 9, 11.
Reprints Jeffers' account of how he came to adapt *Medea*. Introduction labels Jeffers "America's foremost living poet."

B264. Hobart, John. "A Great Actress and a Great Role: 'Medea' Triumphs at the Geary," *Chronicle* (San Francisco, Cal.), September 8, 1948, p. 11.

Review of San Francisco production of *Medea*. It is a "monumental horror play." Jeffers "has preserved the outline of Euripides' tragedy, but he has recast it in his own language—into words that sting and writhe like vipers."

B265. Kupferman, Lawrence. "Mail Order Verse," *Times* (New York), February 8, 1948, section 6, p. 5.

Letter in reply to Jeffers' article, "Poetry, Gongorism, and a Thousand Years" (New York *Times*, January 18, 1948, section 6, p. 16). Quotes Jeffers as saying poets should "write poetry like Keats! No doubt they will oblige him by return mail. Jeffers writes longingly of the glories that were Greece; but he forgets one important thing—that any creative artist is the creature of his age and gives expression to it."

B266. Miles, Josephine. "Pacific Coast Poetry, 1947," *Pacific Spectator*, II (Spring, 1948), 134-150.

Reviews year's activities. Compares quatrain of Yvor Winters, "To the Holy Spirit," with Jeffers' "Natural Music," both published in 1947 by the Book Club of California. "How much more neatly solved such a mode sounds than that of Robinson Jeffers. . . . Both have many followers, but perhaps still in mass the neat quatrain is strongest."

B267. Schallert, Edwin. "Judith Anderson Wins Great 'Medea' Triumph," *Times* (Los Angeles, Cal.), September 28, 1948, part 2, p. 2.

Favorable review of Los Angeles production of *Medea*. The action "is wrapped up in the poetic words of the Greek dramatist as translated by Jeffers—one of the finest lyricists of today."

B268. Scheuer, Philip K. "Judith Anderson Puts Her All into Amazing 'Medea' Portrayal," *Times* (Los Angeles, Cal.), September 26, 1948, part 4, pp. 1, 3.

Interview with Judith Anderson after opening of *Medea*. She states that "Jeffers has taken Greek tragedy and made it not only tolerable but, finally, exciting."

B269. Waite, Elmont. "Carmel, California," *Saturday Evening Post*, CCXX (May 15, 1948), 139.
Brief mention in travel article. Jeffers is one of many Carmel artists. "His adaptation, *Medea* . . . has drawn wild applause. . . . For many years, too, his long, violently dramatic narrative poems have made his a great name in college classes everywhere."

1949

B270. Anonymous. "Exiles and Others," *Saturday Review of Literature*, XXXII (August 6, 1949), 109.
Picture-article dealing with various authors of the Twenties who chose to live in exile. Caption with Jeffers' photograph: "Robinson Jeffers found refuge on California's windy coast, poetized gloomily on man's fate."

B271. Benét, William Rose. "Remembering the Poets: A Reviewer's Vista," *Saturday Review of Literature*, XXXII (August 6, 1949), 46-52.
Mention in article by leading critic. Tells how Sterling introduced him to Jeffers' work and told him of the building of Jeffers' stone house. There Jeffers "still lives, and he has since written many other poems of terror and tragedy, becoming, to my own regret, our great and savage misanthrope of American poetry. But neither he nor the eupeptic Amy Lowell were half-hearted in their art."

B272. Demarest, Michael. "Californians: The Dark Glory," *Script*, XXXV (February, 1949), 19-24.

Minor. Primarily biographical material. Jeffers is "classed now with such masterminds of the morose as Thomas Hardy, Sophocles, and the prophet Jeremiah."

B273. Flewelling, Ralph. "Tragedy: Greece to California," *Personalist*, XXX (July, 1949), 229-245.
In part a discussion of the influence of the Greeks on Jeffers. "It has been allotted to one modern poet, a Californian, to plumb the depths of modern moral darkness. . . . However much we writhe to find ourselves under this lash of a modern Cassandra, we find here not only the spirit of ancient tragedy, but are given food for thought."

B274. Roddy, Joseph. "View From a Granite Tower," *Theatre Arts*, XXXIII (June, 1949), 32-36.
Enthusiastic review of Jeffers' career, ideas, in a prominent theatre publication. Jeffers "is famous as a dramatist—and has far more merit as a poet. . . . As a prophet, he offers only despair and destruction. His unusual and unsavory approach to eminence has for the most part been unsuccessful. But it has made him an outstanding phenomenon in poetry."

B275. Van Doren, Mark. "The Poetry of Our Day Expresses Our Doubt and the Times' Confusion," *New York Herald Tribune Weekly Book Review*, XXVI (September 25, 1949), 9.
Early admirer's enthusiasm palls. Mention of Jeffers, who, "having long ago given up mankind as a hideous job, continues to find sermons in the stones about Carmel. They are sermons, however, for hawks and redwoods, for tides and burning stars, and so they must be indifferent to what men think of them."

1950

B276. Deutsch, Babette. "Poetry at the Mid-Century," *Virginia Quarterly Review*, XXVI (Winter, 1950), 67-75.

One of the earliest admirers remembers, briefly. In discussing Whitman's influence on post-World War One poets: Whitman's "free strophes, his discovery upon the peaks of the Rockies of the law of his own poems were later to be echoed in the more savage attestations to cosmic consciousness of Robinson Jeffers."

B277. Glicksberg, Charles I. "Modern Literature and the Sense of Doom," *Arizona Quarterly*, VI (Autumn, 1950), 208-217.

In an article discussing the historical background of the pessimism and decadence of modern literature in which Kafka, Dylan Thomas and Dali are mentioned, Jeffers is cited as an example of the lost generation's premonitions of disaster. Jeffers' "furious sadism" is an expression of our age and although "Jeffers' philosophy is one of stoical detachment from the pathological self-love of humanity, his blast of misanthropic denunciation represent the frustrated passion of inverted love. . . . Jeffers, the Cassandra of our generation, declares that faith, whether Christian or Communist, is preposterous."

B278. O'Neal, Charles. Letter on *Tower Beyond Tragedy*, *Times* (New York), December 24, 1950, section 2, p. 4.

Complains that Jeffers, in an article on *Tower Beyond Tragedy* (New York *Times*, November 26, 1950), referred to the Carmel Forest Theatre production as "being 'largely amateur.' " O'Neal says all performers were Equity members and the Greek soldiers were professional soldiers from Fort Ord, Cal. Jeffers replies beneath the letter that "it was a long time ago and I spoke carelessly. One of my sons carried a spear in the play, but not as an amateur. He did it as a filial duty."

B279. Powell, Lawrence Clark. "Robinson Jeffers," *Montevallo Review*, I (Summer, 1950), 46-52.

Originally a lecture delivered at the University of Southern California by a foremost Jeffers critic. Discusses "Give Your Heart to the Hawks," "Cawdor," and "Thurso's Landing" as works which "incorporate the elements of great and lasting poetry."

B280. Wecter, Dixon. "Literary Lodestone: 100 Years of California Writing," *Saturday Review of Literature*, XXXIII (September 16, 1950), 9-10, 37-41.

Barest mention. The flowering of California was "nourished through the years by a cultural humus that has grown steadily richer down to the current crop of Robinson Jeffers, John Steinbeck, William Saroyan, and hosts of others."

1951

B281. Anonymous. "Six Win Poetry Awards," *Times* (New York), November 1, 1951, p. 26.

Poetry's six annual awards including $100 to Robinson Jeffers for "Six Poems." "The awards, made 'with reference to each poet's general achievement or promise,' were selected from the October 1950-September 1951 issues."

1952

B282. Blackmur. R. P. "Lord Tennyson's Scissors: 1912-1950," *Kenyon Review*, XIV (Winter, 1952), 1-20.

Brief mention by prominent New Critic. In discussing the "faulty relation between language and sensibility, between metre and rhythm" of some poets: "But all of them are better than the flannel-mouthed inflation in the metric of Robinson Jeffers with his rugged rock-garden violence."

B283. Schallert, Edwin. "Anderson Reading Effective," *Times* (Los Angeles), June 2, 1952, part 3, p. 9.

Review of an evening of readings from *Tower Beyond Tragedy* and *Medea* presented as part of the Ojai (Cal.) Festival. "It was hard to tell whether Mr. Jeffers had fully provided them with the material that should go with the program, as the narration that introduces the scene fell short of complete effectiveness, and there were other signs of cloudiness in the presentation."

1954

B284. Folk, Barbara Nauer. "Robinson Jeffers Taken to Task," *Catholic World*, CLXXIX (July 1954), 270-273.
Christian viewpoint of his poetry, which fails because it has been made subservient to his "pantheistic notions." Jeffers "could have been great. Careful consideration of some of his poetry, especially his shorter poems would bear this out." This makes his failure "even more lamentable."

B285. Hogan, Beecher. "The Robinson Jeffers Manuscripts at Yale," *Yale University Library Gazette*, XXIX (October, 1954), 81-84.
Of bibliographic interest. Description of Yale's complete collection of 1925-1933 Jeffers manuscripts.

B286. Tory, Alan. "Robinson Jeffers: 'Untamed Lion' of a Poet," *Fortnight*, XVII (October 20, 1954), 15-16.
Trivial, favorable biographical data about the author of the forthcoming play, *The Cretan Woman*. "Fundamental in Robinson Jeffers, as in all poets of stature, is the love of beauty, and a most uncanny power to catch it. Where he revolts against man, it is because he is appalled at what man can do to man."

B287. Untermeyer, Louis. "Poets Without Readers," *Americas*, VI (September, 1954), 4.

Brief mention. "Robinson Jeffers may have little of Frost's quaint allure but he goes beyond him in sheer power of language. Instead of subtlety and grace there is knotted strength and a kind of black grandeur; instead of hopeful assurance there is uncompromising bitterness."

1955

B288. Anonymous. "Poetry Society of America Award to Robinson Jeffers," *Times* (New York), January 21, 1955, p. 17.

"A special $1,250 Borestone Mountain Poetry Award was given to sixty-eight-year-old Robinson Jeffers of Carmel, California, for his 'Hungerfield and Other Poems,' published last year by Random House. Mr. Jeffers reportedly had declined the award a year ago, saying it should go to a younger man."

B289. Bracher, Frederick. "California's Literary Regionalism," *American Quarterly*, VII (Fall, 1955), 275-284.

Critic considers Jeffers a California writer because his identification is both real and emotional. "Robinson Jeffers found the stupendously rugged coastline south of Monterey, and the isolated, half-primitive people who lived there, ideal poetic material for the expression of his misanthropic philosophy. Jeffers regards man as a festering, but happily temporary, excrescence on a clear landscape."

B290. McTaggart, Arthur. "The Function of Greek Myth in the Poetry of Robinson Jeffers," *Phoenix* (Seoul, Korea), I (Summer, 1955), 1-5.

Jeffers "has written some of our most stirring dramatic poetry," using pre-classical Greek myths as the basis for his action. However, "he has returned the myths to their old pitilessness, and has dragged us along with his characters to a renewed awareness of the depth and meaning in these antique fables." Article appears in a journal intended for Korean students of English.

1956

B291. Anonymous. "Robinson Jeffers, Calif. Poet Laureate, Lauded in Analysis of Work," *San Quentin News* (San Quentin, Cal.), August 30, 1956, p. 2.

Interesting minor review, written by a prisoner, of Powell's book (see C65), recently added to the prison library. "The examples of the poet's work which appear in this volume indicate a man who is all Truth. There does not seem to be the slightest hint of a man who would adulterate his principles for audience acclaim, or popular appeal."

B292. Fitts, Dudley. "The Poet Appraised," *New York Times Book Review*, December 9, 1956, p. 12.

Review of Squires' book (see C101) by a leading classical scholar, used as an opportunity to reevaluate Jeffers. "Why is it that Jeffers can be so effective in occasional short poems, free lyrics, and so preposterously and sprawlingly bad when he lets himself go? For he is demonstrably bad, as Mr. Squires notes again and again, and never worse than in his great set pieces, those Cambyses-ridden declamations of textbook sin. The truth, if one may hazard a guess, is that we have here a poet of limited force in a minor tragic vein, a rhetorician who can be compelling in brief flashes of insight—a small-scale Seneca, say."

B293. Powell, Lawrence Clark. "The Double Marriage of Robinson Jeffers," *Southwestern Review*, XLI (Summer, 1956), 278-282. Reprinted in his: *Books, West Southwest*. Los Angeles: Ward Ritchie Press, 1957, pp. 110-120.

Discussion, by leading Jeffers critic, of "the two things that changed Jeffers from a young bohemian to a major poet." They were "his wife and his move to Carmel." Commends the shorter poems as "among his happiest work, often overlooked in the excitement created by his tragic narratives and Greek adaptations, and yet they contain many elements of his genius: feeling for history and the passage of time, precise observation . . . and a vivid and fluent vocabulary and a sense of form. There is a simple nobility which distinguishes his best work."

1957

B294. Badosa, Enrique. "Robinson Jeffers," *Atlantico* (Madrid) VIII (1957), 75-84.

Spanish review of Jeffers' career. "Pero es tan vasto el ámbito del poema jeffersoniano, que en él, por mas que el hombre lo presida, se advierte una enorme soledad. . . . muchos de sus poemas, hermosos, profundos, tienen, a veces, esa inmensa y poco acogedora resonancia de las casas deshabitadas largo tiempo."

B295. Carpenter, Frederic Ives. Review of Squires' *The Loyalties of Robinson Jeffers, American Literature*, XXIX (May, 1957), 225-226.

See C101. Mixed review by Jeffers expert. "Jeffers' poetry, as Mr. Squires points out, is very uneven, and perhaps it is natural that any book criticizing it should also be uneven. At its best, the challenge and excitement which characterize the poetry also characterize the book of criticism. . . . If at his worst he falls victim to the partial enthusiasms and the occasional philosophical inconsistencies of his poet, we may the more easily forgive him."

B296. Carroll, Paul. "Prophet Without Honor," *Poetry*, XC (July, 1957), 254-256.

See C101. Review of Squires' book used as an opportunity to reevaluate, unfavorably, Jeffers' work. The shorter poems are good and "Roan Stallion" is less bad than the other long narratives. "The fact is that Jeffers has written too much too poorly. If the job of poetry is to transfigure our raw experiences—and this includes the experience of ideas—then Jeffers has, for the most part, bungled. . . . If, like Yeats, Jeffers had only buried his notions and dogmas in a book of prose, or had, like Eliot, the patience and humility to conserve and refine his great intuition, then we might have had the rare privilege of listening to a poet whose intellect truly danced among words."

B297. Exner, Richard. "Der Dichter Robinson Jeffers," *Neue Deutsche Hefte*, XXXVI (July, 1957), 345-347.

German recognition of Jeffers. "Ob seine Worte einmal von vielen gehört werden, weiss neimand. Unbeliebtheit und Verschollen-sein zu Lebzeiten sind durchaus keine Garanten eines unsterblichen Ruhmes. In seinem Gedicht . . . man musse Nacht im eigenen Liebe haben . . . um im Sturme treu zu sein. Diese Haltung ist Robinson Jeffers wichtiger als der literarishe Ruhm, dem er nicht entsagen will, auf den zu warten er sich aber leisten kann wie selten ein Dichter."

B298. Miller, James E. Review of Squires' *The Loyalties of Robinson Jeffers, Prairie Schooner*, XXXI (Spring, 1957), 3-5.

See C101. Squires devotes too much space to an attack on the New Criticism although "It is no doubt true that the New Criticism has done Robinson Jeffers less than justice." However, Squires adds little positive. On Jeffers: "The awesome attitude, which permeates all of Jeffers' poetry, while in small sips seems only a bit cool, in a full gulp becomes absolutely chilling."

B299. Rexroth, Kenneth. "In Defense of Jeffers," *Saturday Review of Literature*, XL (August 10, 1957), 30.

See C101. The most violent attack on Jeffers since Winters in the thirties. "In my opinion Jeffers' verse is shoddy and pretentious and the philosophizing is nothing but posturing. His reworkings of Greek tragic plots make me shudder at their vulgarity. . . . His lyrics and reveries of the Californian landscape seem to me to suffer in every line from the most childish laboring of the pathetic fallacy. . . . His philosophy I find a mass of contradictions—high-flown statements indulged in for their melodrama alone, and often essentially meaningless. . . . As for Mr. Squires' examples of Jeffers' poetic gems, the less said the better. To me they sound like the rhetoric of a Southern state representative."

B300. Sullivan, A. M. Review of Squires' *The Loyalties of Robinson Jeffers, Catholic World*, CLXXXIV (March, 1957), 478-479.

Review of C101. Squires "skirts the moral values and responsibilities of the poet." Of Jeffers: "Jeffers is a poet of stature and power; and a deadly infection of mood that lingers with the reader, influences the sick beauty and sodden air of his themes. His obsession with sadism and incest circumscribes his dramatic genius. He writes in the tradition of the Greeks, but his characters are pursued by a spirit more evil than the spite of the deities of Olympus."

1958

B301. Anonymous. "People," *Time*, LXXII (October 20, 1958), 41.

Brief news article. A prize of $5,000 from the Academy of American Poets was awarded to Jeffers, "a grave, chilly-eyed solitary who hews out his tragic, relentlessly surging lines. . . . ."

B302._____. "Robinson Jeffers Wins Poetry Award of $5,000," *Times* (New York), October 15, 1958, p. 19.

News article. Jeffers receives fellowship of the Academy of American Poets, for "distinguished poetic achievement." The award "is believed to be the most financially valuable honor an American poet can receive."

B303. Benamau, Michel. Review of Squires' *The Loyalties of Robinson Jeffers, Études Anglaises,* XI (April-June, 1958), 185-186.

See C101. Squires reviewed favorably in France. Of Squires' book: "une étude courageuse et lucide." Of Jeffers' poetry: "Meme si l'on préfère Frost et Stevens, il faut reconnaître la maturité et la dignité du message de Robinson Jeffers."

B304. Drew, Fraser Bragg. "The Gentleness of Robinson Jeffers," *Western Humanities Review*, XII (Autumn, 1958), 379-381.

A thoughtful defense of Jeffers as a "poet who is as memorable for his gentleness and love as for the terrible holocaust of 'Tamar.' . . . Here is a gentleness and a tenderness which can lighten the burden and linger after the nightmare is forgotten." Offers "The Loving Shepherdess" and "For Una" as examples.

B305. Frost, Robert. "A Poet Speaks of Poets," *Times* (Los Angeles), May 22, 1958, part 3, p. 5.

Brief mention in an interview conducted by Carter Barber. Frost said, "I am an admirer of Robinson Jeffers. He has kept California as a base. He hasn't run out to New York."

B306. Fuller, Dorothy V. Review of Squires' *The Loyalties of Robinson Jeffers, Arizona Quarterly*, XIV (Spring, 1958), 70-71.

See C101. Review of Squires becomes a reevaluation of Jeffers' work. Dislikes Squires' concentration on the long narratives. "But the shorter poems, taken as a body, present the Inhumanist position without the exaggeration of the long narratives. . . . In the matter of form, too, the best of the short poems represent a restraint and a skill not found in the long narratives except in isolated passages."

1959

B307. Anonymous. "Rugged, Romantic World Apart," *Life*, XLVII (July 6, 1959), 56-63.

Brief description of Jeffers as "Big Sur's Laureate." Portrait.

B308. Drew, Fraser Bragg. "Librarian and Teacher—Allies for Poetry," *Library Journal*, LXXXIV (May 15, 1959), 156-162.

Brief mention by Jeffers critic and librarian. One of the ways librarians encourage interest in poetry is through exhibits such as the one held in Butler Library, University of Buffalo, entitled "Three Modern Poets: Robinson Jeffers, T. S. Eliot, Hart Crane." Photograph of the Jeffers exhibit.

B309. _____. "The Loving Shepherdess of Jeffers and Scott," *Trace*, XXXI (April-May, 1959), 13-16.

A study of the relationship of Jeffers' Clare Walker and Sir Walter Scott's Madge Wildfire to their prototype, Feckless Fannie. In "The Loving Shepherdess," Jeffers, "the poet of violence and terror," tells "one of the tenderest stories in modern literature without sentimentality and achieving as fine a tragedy as he had ever created from Greek or Californian legend. Clare Walker is as memorable as his earlier heroines."

B310. Ferguson, Joe M., Jr. Review of Squires' *The Loyalties of Robinson Jeffers*, New Mexico Quarterly, XXIX (Spring, 1959), 125-127.

See C101. "This book is one of few recent tributes to an American poet whose reputation has been declining since 1935." Blames the decline, not on technique but on "the trend of his thought." Perhaps his philosophy of Inhumanism is "of greater dimensions than we suspect, for it is precisely of human self-consciousness that Jeffers would have us rid ourselves. Once we do, life and the universe offer us new esthetic possibilities, as does Jeffers' own poetry."

B311. Foster, George H. "Literature in the Twenties," *Shenandoah*, X (Spring, 1959), 11-14.

Brief mention. On the twenties as a time of reappraisal: "It was true that for Lewis, Mencken, Dreiser, Jeffers, the battle was all but lost and the religious element in democracy derided. Well, they were cleaning house, some of them eager to set fire to it."

B312. Kunitz, Stanley. "American Poetry's Silver Age," *Harper's Magazine*, CCXIX (October, 1959), 173-179.

Brief. Prominent critic-poet describes a droll dialogue between a poet and a youth aspiring to be a poet. The older poet speaks: "What a generation of poets that was! Each name suggests so many others. I think among the survivors, of Robinson Jeffers, who gave his heart to the hawks—a gesture temporarily out of favor."

B313. Moss, Sidney P. "Robinson Jeffers: A Defense," *American Book Collector*, X (September, 1959), 9-14.

Traces Jeffers' critical reputation. His decline is traced to his attitude toward humanity, especially as seen in "Be Angry at the Sun" and "Mara." "What these critics of Jeffers have failed to note is that such a view, by its very uniqueness and Jeffers' power in rendering it, is enormously impressive, aside from the fact that there is enough strange sanity and bitter truth in the vision to commend it."

B314. Seidlin, Oskar. "The Oresteia Today: A Myth Dehumanized," *Thought*, XXXIV (Autumn, 1959), 434-452.

Compares the Oresteia of Goethe, Hauptmann, Sartre and Jeffers. Of Jeffers' "Tower Beyond Tragedy": "Jeffers' answer is clearly inhuman, a violent abdication of man as man, the reduction of existence to nothingness. His horribly blissful vision is the end of all conscious life, the tower beyond tragedy, that stage of numb aloofness and immobility where nothing will touch us any more, where we are, indeed, beyond the tragedy and time, because we are no longer man. I know in all literature hardly a more frightening embracement of deranged nihilism than Cassandra's prayer."

B315. Waggoner, Hyatt H. Review of Monjian's *Robinson Jeffers: A Study in Inhumanism, American Literature*, XXXI (March, 1959), 99.

See C105. Extensive quotation from Miss Monjian, who "carefully reviews existing criticism and scholarship on Jeffers."

B316. Woodbridge, H. C. "A Bibliographical Note on Jeffers." *American Book Collector*, X (September, 1959), 15-18.

A reasonably thorough checklist of major post-Alberts criticism.

1960

B317. Anonymous. "Poetic Possibilities," *Times Literary Supplement* (London), July 1, 1960, p. 420.

Review of Lutyens' book. See C110. Brief Jeffers mention. Lutyens introduces Jeffers effectively although "A large, rhetorical, untidy poet like Mr. Robinson Jeffers does not lend himself to close textual examination."

B318. Honig, Edwin. "American Poetry and the Rationalist Critic," *Virginia Quarterly Review*, XXXVI (Summer, 1960), 416-427.

Mention of Jeffers as an anti-rationalist. "When, in 'Hurt Hawks' Robinson Jeffers writes, 'I'd sooner except the penalties, kill a man than a hawk,' he appears to be opposed to the humanism of poets like Whitman and Stevens. But if one reads the whole poem, and then reads his other poems in which the same indignant cry of the 'inhumanist' persists, one sees that the poet's outraged denunciations of mankind are another means of propounding the principles of the good life in a physical world that has been devastated by the prime instruments of modern rationalism—industrialization and war."

B319. Reynolds, Tim. "The Stone-Mason," *Poetry*, XCVII (November, 1960), 81-82. Reprinted in: *Critic*, XX (June-July 1962), 16.

Tribute by recognized poet:
"Too, I have seen him, who quarried out and
    worked this raw existence,
the stone-mason: seen him walking by day
    in the shade of the big trees
framing the tower of boulders he hung against
    the sky, back broad
and hard-headed—but bent, but slow after
    a spent life of building
something more lucid than any visible light,
    lighter than fog. . . . "

1961

B320. Anonymous. "Robinson Jeffers Gets Poetry Prize," *Times* (New York), January 20, 1961, p. 33.

News article. "Robinson Jeffers, a poet of craggy meter and bleak imagination, received the 1960 Shelley Memorial Award for poetry last night. . . . Mr. Jeffers was cited for his more than a dozen volumes of poetry and verse drama."

B321. Harmsen, Tyrus G. "Jeffers Collection–Occidental College," *Book Club of California Quarterly News Letter*, XXVII (Winter, 1961), 3-9.
A description of the Jeffers collection by the head librarian. Basically the same as the Occidental bibliography (1955). See C97.

B322. Middlebrook, Samuel. "A Free Warrior's Opinions," *New York Times Book Review*, September 10, 1961, p. 46.
Review of Gregory's book. See C98. The Jeffers essay is "rather excessively titled. . . . Mr. Gregory's gusto in appraising this great Californian, however, makes his suggestion of the supposed neglect of Jeffers understandable."

1962

B232. Anonymous. Obituary, *Time*, LXXIX (February 2, 1962), 62.
"Died. Robinson Jeffers, 75, solitary poet of gloom, whose half-century of tragic, ironic verse won the 1960 Shelley Memorial Award. . . . Best known for his vividly free adaptation of Euripides' *Medea*."

B324._____. Obituary, *Newsweek*, LIX (February 5, 1962), 57.
"John Robinson Jeffers, 75, misanthropic poet . . . whose works included a heralded translation of 'Medea' . . . . "

B325._____. "A Poet Dies," *Chronicle* (San Francisco, Cal.) January 22, 1962, pp. 1, 9.

Portrait, list of works. Special mention of *Medea*, "Recognized as one of his major works."

B326._____. "Rare Moment of Peace for Robinson Jeffers," *Life*, LII (February 2, 1962), 38.
Photographs of Jeffers and grandson in Hawk Tower. Comment on his life. "His rolling verse evoked the sounds of the sea, and over forty years he produced a dozen great poems ('Roan Stallion,' 'Tamar,' etc.) and such memorable plays as *Medea*. His poetry bore the stamp of his dark and troubled credo: that man is only a passing evil defiling the eternal beauty of nature."

B327._____. "Robinson Jeffers," *Herald Tribune* (New York), January 22, 1962, p. 8.
"He wrote with a cadence and in terms of contempt for humankind and civilization."

B328._____. "Robinson Jeffers," *Chronicle* (San Francisco, Cal.), January 23, 1962, p. 34.
Editorial. Jeffers "began to open the eyes of the world to the beauty and power of the Pacific at Carmel." He wrote much poetry, "But a good argument might be made, we think, for the view that the greatest thing Jeffers did for American poetry was to learn Greek ... His version of the 'Medea' ... is a truly great work of translation."

B329._____. "Robinson Jeffers," *Illustrated London News*, CCXL (February 3, 1962), 189.
"Mr. Robinson Jeffers, one of the most accomplished American poets of the generation of T. S. Eliot and Ezra Pound. ... He is one of the most interesting of American poets and will be remembered."

B330._____. "Robinson Jeffers Dead at 75," *Times* (New York), January 22, 1962, p. 23.

"He was perhaps best known for his free adaptation of 'Medea.' "
Brief excerpts from poetry, listing of play productions. "Mr. Jeffers
thought more of nature than of man."

B331._____. *Robinson   Jeffers   Newsletter,* I   (November 19,
1962), 1-2.
First of a series to be issued by the "Robinson Jeffers Committee,"
with the purpose of informing members of activities in the study of
Jeffers.

B332._____. "Robinson Jeffers, Poet, Dies at 75," *World-Telegram
and Sun* (New York), January 22, 1962, p. 19.
Special mention of "Medea." Major poems listed. Jeffers rediscovered
"the Pacific in stark, powerful words."

B333. Antoninus, Brother (William Oliver Everson). "A Tribute to
Robinson Jeffers," *Critic,* XX (June-July, 1962), 14-15.
Attack on Rexroth's opinion of Jeffers (See B299). Account of his
own debt to Jeffers by a competent poet of a later generation. Jeffers,
like Frost, "hewed out a kind of epochal place for himself in the
literature of his time. Among contemporary poets, English or American, Jeffers is unique in that he has been the only one to project a truly
cosmic vision of man, induct a whole cosmology, as Homer and Dante
did before him. I am speaking here in terms of conception, what is
called vision, rather than presuming to anticipate the judgement of
history as to the aesthetic achievement. Though I, myself, do not doubt
that achievement, and suspect that the 'excesses' of his early enthusiasts
are very near the truth, his latter day friends have mostly learned to be
more cautious."

B334. Caughey, J. W. "Robinson Jeffers," *Pacific Historical Review,*
XXXI (February, 1962), 105-106.

Tribute in a social sciences journal, to a Californian who "symbolized the rugged individualism of the frontier spirit. . . . His descriptions of the Big Sur coast and the back-country will endure after the population explosion has taken its toll of their unspoiled beauty. . . . His verse rings out in candor, caustic and uncompromising. . . . More than most of our poets, Jeffers addressed himself to cosmic themes. Part of the genius of the poet, nevertheless, is his sharper perception of intimate details and entities."

B335. Caughey, La Ree. "For Robinson Jeffers, 1887-1962," *Literary Frontier*, XIII (March, 1962), 17. Reprinted in: *Occidental Alumnus*, XLIV (May, 1962), 8-9.
    Minor memorial tribute. "The lengths Jeffers went to expound the thesis of inhumanism brought heavy criticism and lost him readers." However, "He looked squarely at the universe and wrote in complete freedom and with candor. . . . Among California's many poets, not just the moderns but those of all times, he stands out in heroic stature."

B336. Czermak, Herbeth. "Robinson Jeffers: A Brief Survey of His Work in Subsequent Defense," *Die Moderne Sprachen*, VI (October, 1962), 22-27.
    Favorable discussion in a language journal published in Germany. Discusses Jeffers' career and attempts to answer the charges leveled against his philosophy. "Jeffers has been called—the very opposite of Whitman—dangerous to the United States. The reason is his preoccupation with Nature and his conviction that man is relatively insignificant. Many other writers of our age shared his fate: D. H. Lawrence, for instance, has been labeled a fascist because he, too, realizes man's ultimate insignificance in a cruel and (at best) indifferent universe."

B337. Hogan, William. "Robinson Jeffers' Vision of Doom," *Chronicle* (San Francisco, Cal.), January 24, 1962, p. 31.
    Tempered approval in a memorial tribute. The shorter works are "to my mind more effective," than the long narratives. "Jeffers saw the world in his own peculiar light; he lived as he wished, and wrote as he felt he must. If his thoughts were often too dark or negative for comfort, he stated them magnificently."

B338. Jorgensen, Virginia E. "Hearing the Night-Herons: A Lesson on Jeffers' 'Hurt Hawks,' " *English Journal*, LI (September, 1962), 440-442.

An analysis of the pessimistic philosophical content of "Hurt Hawks." "The imprint of a major American poet is evident."

B339. Levy, William Turner. "Soundings," *Churchman* (St. Petersburg, Fla.), March, 1962, p. 12.

Memorial in an Episcopal monthly newspaper. In Jeffers' death "America lost a major poet," and although "it is doubtful that Jeffers' proper rank will be accorded him for at least a decade," he "will ultimately be numbered among the four or five greatest American poets."

B340.———. "Speaking of Books," *New York Times Book Review*, June 3, 1962, p. 2.

A tribute to Jeffers by an Episcopal clergyman, friend, and English professor. "Oh, Lovely Rock," and "Evening Ebb" are singled out for special praise. "It will not be a short volume which places Jeffers in the company of Whitman and Frost; it will be one which will enable us, by the leading of his eye and voice, to reach conclusions that may well be far different from his own." Jeffers is an artist "whose mortal examinations of darkness serve to temper alike our hopes and despairs, helping us reclaim an age he had feared lost."

B341. Lilienthal, Theodore M. "In Memoriam—Robinson Jeffers, 1887-1962," *Book Club of California Quarterly News Letter*, XXVII (Spring, 1962), 42.

West coast admirer blames unpopularity on "his psychological and involved method of writing." Jeffers' "tremendous capacity for expressing his disdain for man, and his magnificent word paintings of nature in all her elements, give one the comparison to a physician using his scalpel with expert touch, in baring the core of man's deterioration. . . . In his many short poems, his tenderness and loving attitude toward everything in nature show another side of a great poet."

B342. Littlejohn, David. "Cassandra Grown Tired," *Commonweal*, LXXIX (December 7, 1962), 276-278.
Unfavorable examination of Jeffers' career. His lack of success was due to his inhuman subject matter and not his style. "Jeffers could only say the same things over and over, from one generation to another; not only do the subjects lose their force, but so does he. After forty years of screeching, Cassandra grows tired."

B343. Stiehl, Harry. "Achievement in American Catholic Poetry," *Ramparts*, I (November, 1962), 26-38.
Speaking of Brother Antoninus (William Oliver Everson), brief mention is made of Jeffers. The young Antoninus "was a disciple of Lawrence and Jeffers and the exponent of a kind of pastoral pantheism. . . . You must read him *en masse*, as you read Whitman or Jeffers or Claudel. . . . ."

B344. Van Doren, Mark. "Robinson Jeffers, 1887-1962," *Proceedings of the American Academy of Arts and Letters Annual Meeting of the Academy*, December 5, 1962, 293-297.
Tribute by leading critic and early admirer. "If Jeffers was wrong, he will be wrong forever, and he would be the first to admit this. Right or wrong, however, his poems have power. And this power, at a guess, will last into other centuries than this one which he thought so pitifully mistaken."

B345. Weston, Edward, and Brett Weston (photographers). "A Robinson Jeffers Memorial," *Ramparts*, I (September, 1962), 65-72.
Excerpts from Jeffers' poetry illustrated with photographs of the Pacific coast, Jeffers, and a hurt hawk.

B346. Waters, Edward. "Music," *Library of Congress Quarterly Journal of Current Acquisitions*, XX (December, 1962), 62-63.
The Library of Congress received tapes of the "Robinson Jeffers Memorial Program" held at the Theatre of the Golden Bough in Carmel,

California. Accompanying this was a description of the occasion by Mrs. Charles E. Simpson of Monterey saying that this tribute "for a fine man and a good neighbor who just also happened to be a major American poet," was well attended.

1963

B347. Angoff, Charles. "Three Towering Figures: Reflections Upon the Passing of Robert Frost, Robinson Jeffers, William Carlos Williams," *Literary Review*, VI (Summer, 1963), 423-429.

Jeffers included in a tribute in which he is considered at least an equal of Frost and Williams. "The death of Robinson Jeffers caught the American reading public by surprise. Many of them had thought he had died a long time before. And in their surprise they suddenly realized what a giant had passed from the scene. . . . Jeffers said all" he had to say "in mounting thunderations. He was the closest America has yet produced to that other great Nay-Sayer, Jonathan Swift. But like Swift he hated profoundly because he loved profoundly."

B348. Bennett, Melba Berry. *Robinson Jeffers Newsletter*, II (November, 1963), 1-3.

Jeffers activities including mention of the errors in *The Beginning and the End*, and translations into Italian, Czech and German.

B349._____. *Robinson Jeffers Newsletter*, III (December, 1963), 1-2.

Report of recent recordings and works in progress.

B350. Dudek, Louis. "Art, Entertainment and Religion," *Queens Quarterly*, LXX (Autumn, 1963), 413-430.

Brief mention in Canadian journal. Jeffers, Blake, Whitman, Nietzsche, Shaw, Ibsen, Cummings, Pound, Lawrence, Gide, Camus are of a group of "radical revisionists," who point to "some individual radical secular approach to life."

B351. Jarrell, Randall. "Fifty Years of American Poetry," *Prairie Schooner*, XXXVII (Spring, 1963), 1-27. Reprinted in: *National Poetry Festival Held in the Library of Congress, October 22-24, 1962: Proceedings.* Washington: Library of Congress, 1964, pp. 113-138.

Leading poet and critic whose own intricate, tortuous, ironic poetry is antipodal to Jeffers' unrestrained, powerful lines, mentions unfavorably the looseness of Jeffers' style. Jeffers "despises the bonds and qualifications of existence." This is why "his poems do not have the exactness and concision of the best poetry; his style and temperament, his whole world-view, are to a surprising extent a matter of simple exaggeration."

B352. Kiley, Bertram. Review of *Robinson Jeffers* by Frederic I. Carpenter, *American Literature*, XXXV (November, 1963), 389-390.

Favorable review of C117. Disputes the possibility of satisfactorily synthesizing Jeffers' complex philosophy. The book's weaknesses stem from weaknesses in Jeffers.

B353. Lilienthal, Theodore M. "The Robinson Jeffers Committee," *Book Club of California Quarterly News Letter*, XXVIII (Fall, 1963), 81.

Announces formation of group to promote the works of Jeffers.

B354. White, William. "Robinson Jeffers' Space," *Personalist*, XLIV (April, 1963), 175-179.

A comparison of Whitman and Jeffers. "Jeffers consistently maintains a cosmic viewpoint. This is especially true of the short lyrics. Jeffers soars into space, not to affirm but to *deny* and reject humanity. While Jeffers 'borrows' Whitman's technique and builds phrase upon phrase, his cosmic view is completely at odds with his literary forefather's".

1964

B355. Bennett, Melba Berry. *Robinson Jeffers Newsletter*, IV (February, 1964), 1-3.

Jeffers activities. H. Arthur Klein, in a letter says, "It is truly extraordinary how many of the major insights of modern physics, cosmology, physiology, and biochemistry are comprehended in Jeffers' works." Robert Brophy, is quoted describing his experiences with Jeffers' collections at various libraries visited while working on his doctoral dissertation.

B356._____. *Robinson Jeffers Newsletter*, V (March, 1964), 1-2.

Jeffers activities to include publication of a new Czech edition of poems.

B357._____. *Robinson Jeffers Newsletter*, VI (May, 1964), 1-2.

Jeffers activities.

B358._____. *Robinson Jeffers Newsletter*, VII (June, 1964), 1-2.

Jeffers activities.

B359._____. *Robinson Jeffers Newsletter*, VIII (September, 1964), 1-2.

Jeffers activities.

B360. Gustafson, Richard. "The Other Side of Robinson Jeffers," *Iowa English Yearbook*, IX (1964), 75-80.

Thoughtful discussion of Jeffers' philosophy as an alternative for the frantic materialism of today. " . . . now that the antagonisms of wartime are over, it is time to see Jeffers not as a ranting Fascist, but as a poet who consistently sought for humanity a deliverance from chaos and senseless passion."

B361. Powell, Lawrence Clark. "The Lure of California," *Book Club of California Quarterly News Letter*, XXIX (Fall, 1964), 75-78.

Mention in a travel article. "As Dana is the prose master of the coast, so is Jeffers the poet laureate. In him the Lord gave us a poet to match our coast. In the power and beauty of his vision, and in the noble clarity of his language, Robinson Jeffers is our supreme poetic spokesman."

B362. Ramsey, Warren. "The Oresteia Since Hofmannsthal: Images and Emphasis," *Revue de Littérature Comparée* XXXVIII (July-September, 1964), 359-375.

Article in Paris journal treats "Tower Beyond Tragedy" as one version of the *Oresteia*. "No tragic *agon* can be expected from Jeffers' characters, no wrestling with angelic decision. . . . There is, on the other hand, conflict between isolated individual and massed forces of society. . . . Attitudes of negation are also expressed. . . . There are taut, powerful passages. . . . But the poem also offers long stretches of loose-jointed, careless verse. Jeffers is saved by knowledge of the myth honestly acquired. Fully assimilated fragments, pathetic rather than tragic, fall naturally into a *style indirect libre* as narrative as it is dramatic. The poet is capable of fine casualness."

B363. Scriba, Jay. "View From the Eagle's Nest," *Journal* (Milwaukee, Wis.), May 7, 1964, part 1, p. 22.

Reevaluation in literary column. "A generation ago . . . Jeffers was often ranked with T. S. Eliot as our greatest poet, and with Eugene O'Neill as our greatest writer of tragedy," and although "only a few years later new critics sneered at Jeffers," today, "two years after Jeffers' death, it appears that . . . [he] may endure longer than his detractors predicted." There are "signs of renewed interest in his work."

B364. Strickhausen, Harry. "Recent Criticism," *Poetry*, CIV (July, 1964), 264-265.

Review of Squires on the occasion of his 1956 *The Loyalties of Robinson Jeffers* being reissued as a paperback. Orestes' meditations in "Tower Beyond Tragedy" prove Jeffers fatalistic, not nihilistic. "Yet confusion about Jeffers' ideas has led to an obscuring of his best poetry and to condemnation of it on very strange grounds. Thus, this study is extremely useful."

B365. Swallow, Alan. "Poetry of the West," *South Dakota Review*, II (Autumn, 1964), 77-87.

Prominent left-wing critic views him favorably and finds Jeffers' inspiration not in the West, but in Whitman and the Greeks. "Surely one cannot take Jeffers too seriously in the perspective of English poetry; he is a failure, although quite a magnificent one; and snatches of his narratives and a few shorter poems, such as the absurdly defective, yet somehow moving and powerful 'Night,' will keep his memory warm."

1965

B366. Bennett, Melba Berry. *Robinson Jeffers Newsletter*, IX (February, 1965), 1-2.

Jeffers activities. Works in progress.

B367. _____. *Robinson Jeffers Newsletter*, X (April, 1965), 1.

Jeffers activities.

B368. _____. *Robinson Jeffers Newsletter*, XI (August, 1965), 1.

Jeffers activities.

B369. _____. *Robinson Jeffers Newsletter*, XII (November, 1965), 1, 2.

Jeffers activities. Publication notice of Vintage Books' *Robinson Jeffers: Selected Poems*. Listing of various readings, recordings.

B370. Carpenter, Frederic Ives. "Robinson Jeffers and 'Humanity'—Some Anecdotes," *Robinson Jeffers Newsletter*, X (April, 1965), 2. Reprinted in same periodical: XV (September, 1966), 1, 2.

Biographical material. "He scorned humanity in the abstract . . . rather than humanity as individuals."

B371. Champlin, Charles. "Judith Anderson's 'Medea' New Dimension in Theater," *Times* (Los Angeles, Cal.), October 14, 1965, part 5, p. 19.

Minor review of a Los Angeles revival of *Medea*. "The supporting performances are not uniformly good, though now and again I think part of the fault lies with Jeffers' words."

B372. Kirsch, Robert R. "Volume Speaks Eloquently of Poet Robinson Jeffers," *Times* (Los Angeles, Cal.), October 8, 1965, section 5, p. 4.

Favorable reevaluation in a review of *Robinson Jeffers: Selected Poems*. Vintage Books, 1965. "He speaks in a language tortured into beauty, brought from the deeps of a sensitive, intuitive and independent spirit. . . . His songs sounded against the chorus of the obvious; his was a strong single voice, unpredictable, heedless of popularity, that disease of American writing."

B373. Klein, H. Arthur. "The Poet Who Spoke of It . . . ," *Robinson Jeffers Newsletter*, XI (August, 1965), 2-6.

Demonstration of Jeffers' penetrating understanding of science and his "fears of a world beset by the Bombs."

B374. Miller, Jim. "Jeffers: Oxy's Alienated Alum," *Occidental* (Pasadena, Cal.), November 5, 1965, p. 6.

Minor reevaluation. Biography. "Although critical estimates are almost always based on his long narratives, it is on his lyrics that his reputation will rest. . . . Along with Ezra Pound, he is one of the most controversial literary figures of the Twentieth Century."

B375. Ridgeway, Ann N. "The Letters of Robinson Jeffers—A Progress Report," *Robinson Jeffers Newsletter*, XII (November, 1965), 2-5.

A report presented to the Jeffers Colloquium at Occidental College on June 29, 1965. Emphasis on his prose style and on his personal integrity. "In a different way from his poems, which as works of art must, necessarily, take on lives unique to themselves, Mr. Jeffers' letters have the restorative force of continuing his presence among us."

B376. White, William. "Robinson Jeffers: Poet of Black Despair," *English Language and Literature*, XVII (November, 1965), 91-101.

Introduction to Jeffers in a journal published in Seoul, Korea. Discusses Jeffers' career with extensive quotations. Detailed comparison with Whitman. "If he did not receive the prominence he deserves during his lifetime, we can nevertheless be certain that Jeffers will be read by the discerning few long after many versifiers now being acclaimed are dead and well forgotten."

1966

B377. Anonymous. Review of Melba Bennett's *Stone Mason of Tor House*, *New York Times Book Review*, December 25, 1966, p. 20.

Unfavorable review of Bennett's book condemning her overenthusiastic praise and her lack of objectivity. "Nowadays we find his prophetlike declamations overblown and his language forced. He is one of those serious voices of the near past who have become somewhat embarrassing in the present. For these reasons, Jeffers has not been critically worked over by the professors and graduate students. We do need, then, a sensible evaluation. . . . The present book doesn't help." See C127.

B378. Bednar, Kamil. "Robinson Jeffers in Czechoslovakia," *Robinson Jeffers Newsletter*, XIII (February, 1966), 2-3.

Description of Czechoslovakia's "enthusiastic reception" of the author's translation of Jeffers. "I have great faith in Jeffers' lasting position in the field of poetry. Because he has based his poetry on the imperishable realities of the sea and the earth there is more hope that his poetry, too, will endure."

B379. Bennett, Melba Berry. *Robinson Jeffers Newsletter*, XIII (February, 1966), 1.
Jeffers activities.

B380._____. *Robinson Jeffers Newsletter*, XIV (June, 1966), 1-3.
Jeffers activities. Quotation from a letter by Eva Hesse on the problems of translating Jeffers into German and notes on Jeffers and science.

B381._____. *Robinson Jeffers Newsletter*, XV (September, 1966), 1.
Jeffers activities.

B382._____. *Robinson Jeffers Newsletter*, XVI (December, 1966), 1-2.
Jeffers activities.

B383. Brophy, Robert J., S. J. "A Textual Note on Robinson Jeffers' *The Beginning and the End*," *Papers of the Bibliographical Society of America*, LX (July-September, 1966), 344-348.
Brophy, a new generation's Jeffers admirer, discusses the regrettable textual errors in *The Beginning and the End*, which "offers the last and fullest expression of Jeffers' concept of cosmic history, the nature of God, and the potential dignity of man."

B384. Chatfield, Hale. "Robinson Jeffers: His Philosophy and His Major Themes," *Laurel Review*, VI (Fall, 1966), 56-71.

Review of Jeffers' critical reputation. Most dislike is based on misinterpretation. Jeffers and modern religious thought tend to agree in a hatred of man's anthropocentrism. Jeffers does not contradict himself. His readers "fail to understand that humanity can be insignificant in a true cosmic context and vitally important in human terms at the same time."

B385. Nolte, William H. "Jeffers' 'Fog' and the Gulls in It." *Robinson Jeffers Newsletter*, XVI (December, 1966), 2-5.

Explication of the poem, "Fog," which expresses "A leading element of Jeffers' Weltanschauung."

B386._____. "Robinson Jeffers as Didactic Poet," *Virginia Quarterly Review*, XLII (Spring, 1966), 257-271.

Comparison of Eliot and Jeffers, determines that Jeffers is the superior poet. "Eliot's pessimism, once thought so black, was never as deeply felt nor half so moving as that of Jeffers." While Eliot's "philosophy rings hollow when you realize that his view of man extends backward only to the birth of Christ," Jeffers looks and finds "eternal flow." This is because Jeffers, who "possessed a learning in both the sciences and the classics which makes Eliot's narrow scholastic training seem paltry by comparison, saw the Christian era as little more than a moment in man's descent from the primordial past." Jeffers' stoicism "will always befriend us in the dark days when they come."

B387. White, William. "Robinson Jeffers: A Checklist 1959-1965," *Serif*, III (June, 1966), 36-39.

Designed to supplement the September, 1959 *American Book Collector* checklist. See B316. "The ... good studies of Jeffers' poetry ... are hardly a critical outpouring; yet it does indicate that he has not been entirely neglected." However, the neglect is striking when compared with Frost, Hemingway and Faulkner.

1967

B388. Bennett, Melba Berry. *Robinson Jeffers Newsletter*, XVII (April, 1967), 1-2, 6.
Jeffers activities. Mention of the good sale of Miss Bennett's *The Stone Mason of Tor House*.

B389._____. *Robinson Jeffers Newsletter*, XVIII (June, 1967), 1-2.
Jeffers activities, including listing of several reading programs.

B390._____. *Robinson Jeffers Newsletter*, XIX (November, 1967), 1-4.
Jeffers activities. Bibliography of Jeffers' works in translation, compiled by Bennett and Tyrus Harmson, Occidental College Librarian.

B391. Lyon, Horace. "Jeffers As a Subject for Horace Lyon's Camera," *Robinson Jeffers Newsletter*, XVIII (June, 1967), 2-5.
Biographical material by friend and photographer of Jeffers.

B392. Rorty, James. "The Ecology of Robinson Jeffers," *Book Club of California Quarterly News Letter*, XXXII (Spring, 1967), 32-36.
One of the first admirers offers a favorable review of Melba Bennett's *The Stone Mason of Tor House*. See C127. Jeffers' work has established him, "after Yeats, as perhaps the most important poet writing in English in this century. . . . In addition to being one of the greatest poets and playwrights of his generation, Jeffers was a great patriot, a great religionist, and a great person."

B393. Steward, George. Review of *The Seacoast of Bohemia* by Franklin Walker, *American Literature*, XXXIX (May, 1967), 254-255.
See C129. Brief mention. The Carmel artists' colony "petered out. Robinson Jeffers came to live there, but he was ostentatiously never of a colony."

1968

B394. Bennett, Melba Berry. *Robinson Jeffers Newsletter*, XX (January, 1968), 1-2.
Jeffers activities including report on Jeffers' fame in Japan.

B395. _____. *Robinson Jeffers Newsletter*, XXI (April, 1968), 1.
Jeffers activities.

B396. _____. *Robinson Jeffers Newsletter*, XXII (August, 1968), 1.
Jeffers activities including progress reports on Czech translation. The final edition of the *Newsletter* edited by Miss Bennett before her death.

B397. Drew, Fraser B. "Carmel and Cushendun: The Irish Influence on Robinson Jeffers," *Eire-Ireland*, III (Summer, 1968), 72-82.
Traces the Irish monuments and the Irish history that influenced *Descent to the Dead* and especially the following short poems: "An Irish Headlands," "Second Best," "Northern Heather," "Now Returned Home," "Patronymic." "From *Descent to the Dead*, and the handful of other Irish poems, and from that five percent of Una Jeffers' travel journals which makes up *Visits to Ireland*, it becomes clear that Ireland, after modern California and ancient Greece, is the third most important locale for Robinson Jeffers' work."

B398. Hart, James D. "Robinson Jeffers: A Poet's Poet," *Book Club of California Quarterly News Letter*, XXXIII (Spring, 1968), 36-38.
Review of Brother Antoninus' book. See C136. In this book, we have "an important text on a great California poet who far transcends the regional setting he chose."

B399. Powell, Lawrence Clark. "California Classics Reread: Give Your Heart to the Hawks," *Westways*, LX (November, 1968), 18-21, 58.

Biography, critical analysis. Chooses *Give Your Heart to the Hawks* as Jeffers' best because of the title poem and especially the Irish poems. "No other bard of his time, other than Yeats, approached the power and the glory, the strength and the tenderness, or the prophetic vision of Jeffers."

B400. Steuding, Robert F. "Intensification of Meaning in 'Shine, Perishing Republic': A Linguistic Analysis," *Robinson Jeffers Newsletter*, XXI (April, 1968), 2-4.
Explication of Jeffers' poem. It, "with its perfect correlation of phonological, supra-segmental, semantic and syntactical features in the creation and intensification of meaning, is a work of supreme craftsmanship and singular greatness."

B401. White, William. "Some Notes on Jeffers," *Robinson Jeffers Newsletter*, XX (January, 1968), 2-3.
Bibliographical notes, including list of errors in Vintage Books' *Robinson Jeffers: Selected Poems* (1963).

1969

B402. Anonymous. "A Sunday Afternoon with Robinson Jeffers," *Official Bulletin of the Poetry Society of America*, February, 1969, pp. 25-31.
Describes February 16, 1969 Jeffers program in New York. Mark Van Doren, an early admirer, said: "Jeffers was never wiser than when he insisted that the proper function of poetry was not to express but to present. . . . these are the only messages that Homer and Shakespeare have for us."

B403. Boyers, Robert. "A Sovereign Voice: The Poetry of Robinson Jeffers," *Sewanee Review*, LXXVII (Summer, 1969), 487-507. Reprinted in: Mazzaro, Jerome (ed.), *Modern American Poetry: Essays in Criticism.* New York: David McKay Company, 1970, pp. 183-203.

Cites unfairness of some critics who over-reacted to earlier praise. The long poems are bad, though *Roan Stallion* is not as bad as it has been called. Prefers Jeffers' short poems, "many of them rather lengthy by standard of the conventional lyric." They would make a large and impressive volume, "for at his best Jeffers could blend passion and restraint, image and statement, contempt and admiration, as few poets of any time have been able to, and often with a music so ripe and easy that it is able to impress itself upon our senses without our ever remarking its grace and majesty, its sureness of touch. . . . If he was not among our supreme poets, they have been few who were his equals."

B404. Brophy, Robert J. "From the Editor," *Robinson Jeffers Newsletter*, XXIII (April, 1969), 2.

Written on becoming editor after the death of Melba Bennett. Notes Jeffers' contemporaneity. "It has been my continuous experience in the classroom and in public readings and lectures that the poet inevitably 'turns on' audiences, especially youthful ones."

B405._____. "Jeffers Research: Dissertations: A Summary and Reflection," *Robinson Jeffers Newsletter*, XXIV (September, 1969), 4-9.

Annotated bibliography of the "thirteen doctoral dissertations done between 1932 and 1967 on the poetry of Robinson Jeffers."

B406._____. Review of *Robinson Jeffers: Fragments of an Older Fury* by Brother Antoninus, *Robinson Jeffers Newsletter*, XXIII (April, 1969), 3-4.

Favorable review of Antoninus' book. See C136. "Some will find Antoninus as a critic overly polemic in scoring Jeffers' detractors and somewhat too involved personally in the critical effort." However, the book provides a valuable "in-depth analysis of the psychological mechanisms within Jeffers' works."

B407._____. Review of *The Selected Letters of Robinson Jeffers, 1897-1962* edited by Ann N. Ridgeway, *Robinson Jeffers Newsletter*, XXIII (April, 1969), 3.

Favorable review of Ridgeway's work. See C139. "The resources here are equal to any researcher's appetite." They help "clarify and elucidate the poet's life work."

B408._____. "The Tor House Library: Jeffers' Books," *Robinson Jeffers Newsletter*, XXIII (April, 1969), 4-11.

Analysis of Jeffers' 2000 volume library.

B409. Bush, George E., and Jeanne K. Welcher. "A Checklist of Modern Plays Based on Classical Mythic Themes," *Bulletin of the New York Public Library*, LXXIII (October, 1969), 525-530.

Included in the checklist are *The Cretan Woman*, *Medea* and *Tower Beyond Tragedy*.

B410. Hart, James B. Review of *The Selected Letters of Robinson Jeffers, 1897-1962* edited by Ann N. Ridgeway, *American Literature*, XLI (May, 1969), 302-303.

See C139. Favorable review. The letters offer insights into Jeffers' personality. He had great dignity.

B411. Jeffers, Donnan. "Robinson Jeffers in Foreign Translation," *Robinson Jeffers Newsletter*, XXIV (September, 1969), 3-4.

Supplement to November 1967 list (see B390).

B412. McHaney, Thomas L. "Robinson Jeffers' 'Tamar' and 'The Sound and the Fury,'" *Mississippi Quarterly*, XXII (Summer, 1969), 261-263.

A study of the similarities in character, plot and symbolism in the Jeffers poem and the Faulkner novel.

1970

B413. Bednar, Kamil. "Jeffers in Czechoslovakia," *Robinson Jeffers Newsletter*, XXVII (November, 1970), 8-9.
Progress report and appreciation by the Czech poet and Jeffers translator. Sees Jeffers' popularity in that country as a result of his "spiritual power." Jeffers "has the courage to stand face to face to every truth accessible to man."

B414. Brophy, Robert. "Jeffers Research: Masters' Theses: Occidental College Library," *Robinson Jeffers Newsletter*, XXV (February, 1970), 4-8.
Annotated bibliography of Jeffers Masters' theses in the Clapp Library of Occidental College.

B415._____, and William White. Review of *Not Man Apart: Lines from Robinson Jeffers* edited by David Ross Brower, *Robinson Jeffers Newsletter*, XXV (February, 1970), 3-4.
Although the volume had originally been intended to illustrate Jeffers' poetry and later became primarily concerned with conservation, "the Jeffers enthusiast . . . cannot but be grateful the book was done at all." See C124.

B416._____. *Robinson Jeffers Newsletter*, XXVI (July, 1970), 1-8.
Listing of publications and recordings in print. Current Jeffers activities. Discussion of the future of the *Robinson Jeffers Newsletter*.

B417._____. *Robinson Jeffers Newsletter*, XXVII (November, 1970), 1-3.
Report on Robinson Jeffers Festival. Recent publications.

B418._____. " 'Tamar,' 'The Cenci,' and Incest," *American Literature*, XLII (May, 1970), 241-244.

The editor of the *Newsletter* compares, with specific illustrations, the theme of incest in Shelley's "The Cenci" and in Jeffers' "Tamar." Incest, in both works, serves not a prurient function but rather works as a "structure shattering symbol." Shelley and Jeffers, both, question the "most cherished values of civilization: authority, law, and divine providence."

B419. Champlin, Charles. "A Rare Look at the Art of Fine Printing," *Times* (Los Angeles, Calif.), April 13, 1970, part 4, p. 1.
Briefest mention. The Book Club of California published "a lot of Robinson Jeffers, early and late."

B420. Eberhart, Richard. "Three Memoirs of Robinson Jeffers," *Robinson Jeffers Newsletter*, XXVII (November, 1970), 5.
Brief biographical reminiscence.

B421._____. "A Tribute and Appreciation," *Robinson Jeffers Newsletter*, XXVII (November, 1970), 6-7.
An appreciation by the prominent poet, reprinted from the cover of the 1970 Caedmon recording of *The Poetry of Robinson Jeffers* (Caedmon TC1299). Sees Jeffers' power in his "stark recognition of our limitations" and his "impersonality."

B422. Mauthe, Andrew K. "Jeffers' Inhumanism and Its Poetic Significance," *Robinson Jeffers Newsletter*, XXVI (July, 1970), 8-10.
Useful discussion of the cyclical nature of the universe in Jeffers' poetry. Reference especially to "Margrave."

B423._____. "The Significance of Point Lobos in 'Tamar,' " *Robinson Jeffers Newsletter*, XXV (February, 1970), 8-10.
Point Lobos, in "Tamar," functions not only as setting, but as an active influence on the action and as symbol both of the unchanging and the continually regenerating aspects of nature.

B424. Rorty, James. "Three Memoirs of Robinson Jeffers," *Robinson Jeffers Newsletter*, XXVII (November, 1970), 4-5.

Praise from one of the earliest admirers for "the profundity of Jeffers' vision." Of biographical interest.

B425. Scott, Robert Ian. Review of *Not Man Apart: Lines from Robinson Jeffers* edited by David Ross Brower, *West Coast Review*, IV (January, 1970), 49-50.

Quibbles over the manner in which Jeffers' poems have been fragmented; "to make the poems label the photographs, too many of the poems have been dismembered and most of their meaning lost." Nevertheless, as a sampler and an introduction to Jeffers' poetry, the book "has no rivals" and is "not to be ignored." See C124.

B426. Shapiro, Karl. "The Poetry Wreck," *Library Journal*, XCV (February 15, 1970), 632-635. Reprinted as: "The New Poetry—A Literary Breakdown," *Times* (Los Angeles, Calif.), April 19, 1970, section E, p. 1.

Brief mention of Jeffers as a poet published by the same company that now publishes the deplorable writings of a fictitious Dylan MacGoon.

B427. Van Doren, Mark. "Three Memoirs of Robinson Jeffers," *Robinson Jeffers Newsletter*, XXVII (November, 1970), 3-4.

High praise and discussion of Van Doren's correspondence with Jeffers. Of biographical interest.

1971

B428. Hughes, John W. "Humanism and the Orphic Voice," *Saturday Review*, LIV (May 22, 1971), 31-33.

A review of Coffin's *Robinson Jeffers: Poet of Inhumanism* (See C145). Harsh attack reminiscent of the forties. Couples Jeffers and Lawrence as "puny bourgeois neurotics." Jeffers, a monomaniacal proto-fascist, misunderstands Nietzsche and insanely misinterprets Greek tragedy.

B429. Scott, Robert Ian. Review of *Cawdor and Medea* by Robinson Jeffers, *West Coast Review*, V (January, 1971), 60-61.
Review of a new edition published by New Directions Books in 1970. Praises its appearance. "Jeffers is a poet of powers not equalled since Lucretius; in his tragedies, he seems a new Euripides." Notes similarities with Buddhism.

B430. Vardamis, Alex A. "Orphic Voice," *Saturday Review* LIV (June 12, 1971), 25.
Letter to the editor. Defense of Jeffers against Hughes' charge of fascism. See B428.

C

BOOKS ABOUT ROBINSON JEFFERS

1916

C1. Braithwaite, William Stanley. *Anthology of Magazine Verse for 1916 and Yearbook of American Poetry*. New York: L. J. Gomme, 1916, p. 238.
See A5. Annual anthology by American negro poet. The anthology usually favored chaste, romantic poetry.

1924

C2. Braithwaite, William Stanley. *Anthology of Magazine Verse for 1924 and Yearbook of American Poetry*. Boston: B. J. Brimmer Co., 1924, p. 124.
Listing of *Tamar and Other Poems* in section titled: "Volumes of Poems Published during 1923-1924."

1925

C3. Braithwaite, William Stanley. *Anthology of Magazine Verse for 1925 and Yearbook of American Poetry*. Boston: B. J. Brimmer Co., 1925, pp. xvii, 146, 161.

Listing of two reviews of *Tamar*. In introduction: His poetry "is full of immense power, and has aroused enthusiastic praise. For intensity of passion he has been compared to Keats, with much of the latter's Greek temper. He has the welter and surge of oceanic forces in his lines which often concern themselves . . . with homely details of character and event."

1926

C4. Braithwaite, William Stanley. *Anthology of Magazine Verse for 1926 and Yearbook of American Poetry.* Boston: B. J. Brimmer Co., 1926, pp. 91-93, 49-50, 108-110, 113-116, 120.

Various listings of poems and reviews published. Estimate by George Sterling (pp. 91-93). "If modern poetry were sustained by such work . . . it would be classical in the highest sense."

C5. Sterling, George. *Robinson Jeffers: The Man and the Artist.* New York: Boni and Liveright, 1926.

First book-length study of Jeffers by his first admirer, fellow poet, and friend. Published shortly before Sterling's suicide. Brief biography, physical description of Jeffers, short review of criticism. Extremely laudatory. On "Tower Beyond Tragedy," "There is no line in this drama that is not alive and alert with an immense and conscious power, that does not shake with a foreboding passion of doom, while permeating all is a sheer and vital beauty. The poem is one of the glories of English literature." Jeffers is our "western genius." His "lines glow or blaze with a thousand manifestations of beauty . . . no facile nor superficial beauty, but one soaring far and high in imagination." "Tamar," "stands among the unforgettable dreams of art."

REVIEWS

a. Anonymous. "One Poet Writes of Another in Sterling's Tribute to Jeffers," *Pine Cone* (Carmel, Cal.), October 22, 1926, p. 1. B13.

b. _____ . "Our Thinking Work," *Chicago Schools Journal*, IX (April, 1927), 317-318. B33.

c. _____ . Review of *Robinson Jeffers: the Man and the Artist, American Mercury*, X (April, 1927), xvi. B35.

d. _____ . "Sterling's Essay on Jeffers," *Argonaut*, CI (February 19, 1927), 8. B36.

e. B., F. B. "Robinson Jeffers: A Study of the Work of An American Poet," *Transcript* (Boston, Mass.), February 19, 1927, book section, p. 3. B37.

f. Bjorkman, Edwin. "An American Poet," *Times* (Asheville, N. C.), July 13, 1927, p. 13a. B38.

g. Broun, Heywood. Review of *Robinson Jeffers: the Man and the Artist, Carmel Cymbal*, III (February 23, 1927), 16. B40.

h. Farrar, John. "This Stream of Poets," *Bookman*, LXV (March, 1927), 80-81. B46.

1927

C6. Auslander, Joseph and Frank E. Hill. *The Winged Horse*. Garden City, N. Y.: Doubleday, Page and Co., 1927, p. 411.
Very brief mention in history of poetry intended for young readers. Included in list of those writing today.

C7. Braithwaite, William Stanley. *Anthology of Magazine Verse for 1927 and Yearbook of American Poetry.* Boston: B. H. Brimmer Co., 1927, p. xiv.

Brief mention. "Mr. Robinson Jefer's [sic] new volume 'The Women at Sur Point,' has not created the stir made by his previous book, but it increases the impression that here is a poet, the counterpart in American literature to James Branch Cabell, who will slowly arrive at full recognition, but such a recognition as will place him high and permanently."

C8. Markham, Edwin (ed.). *The Book of Poetry.* New York: William H. Wise and Company, 1927, vol. I, p. 705.

Very brief note by a California poet of an older generation. "This is the author, . . . the strange new poet whom George Sterling hailed as a genius, clasping hands with the great Greeks across the centuries."

1928

C9. Ellis, Havelock. *An Artist.* Austin: John S. Mayfield, 1928.

A letter privately printed as tribute to Jeffers by the crusader for sexual freedom. Singles out *Roan Stallion, Tamar and Other Poems* for special praise. "I can only say that I have a great regard and admiration for Jeffers. So far as I know, he is the strongest poet to come out of America in recent times."

C10. Graham, Bessie. *The Bookman's Manual.* New York: R. R. Bowker Co., 1928, p. 186.

Brief mention. Estimate of the poetry as "tragic folk tales of Northern California in epical verse" by the poet of cruelty and horror.

C11. Jolas, Eugene. *Anthologie de la Nouvelle Poésie Américane.* Paris: Simon Kra, 1928, p. 112.

Brief biographical and critical comment preceding a translation of "Roan Stallion," the publication of which, "a été considéré par les meilleurs critiques des États-Unis comme un véritable évènement dans l'Historie de la littérature américaine."

C12. Lehmann, B. H. Foreword to *Poems*. San Francisco: Grabhorn Press, 1928. pp. v-xi.

Stress on the superiority of Jeffers' lyrics. "This is poetry, every line of it, poetry, authentic and powerful, brooded in a mind informed with the neutral universe, heard by an ear sensitive to rhythms current in the world, vocal on a tongue that uses the speech of living men."

C13. Untermeyer, Louis (ed.). *Modern American and British Poetry*. Rev. Ed. New York: Harcourt, Brace and Company, 1928, pp. 221-222.

First appearance in an Untermeyer anthology. Biographical note. Compares Jeffers to Sophocles and Whitman. "This was masculine poetry, stark, even terrible in its intensities. Whatever defects this verse has—and it must be confessed that Jeffers piles on his catastrophes with little humor and less restraint—there is no denying its elemental power."

1929

C14. Adamic, Louis. *Robinson Jeffers, A Portrait*. Seattle: University of Washington Bookstore, 1929.

Extremely laudatory to the point of worship, by a consistent admirer. This is "strange verse of excessive intensity and terribleness in terms of a mad philosophy that is the result of his profound introversion and great knowledge of facts and theories pertaining to the universe of men. . . . I prefer . . . the shorter pieces to the more ambitious poems."

C15. Braithwaite, William Stanley. *Anthology of Magazine Verse for 1929 and Yearbook of American Poetry*. New York: G. Sully and Co., 1929, pp. xxxviii, 620, 626, 627, 634, 636, 644.

Various listings of poems and reviews that appeared during the year. *Cawdor* is a volume of "exceptional significance."

C16. DeCasseres, Benjamin. *The Superman in America.* Seattle: University of Washington Bookstore, 1929, pp. 22-25, 27.

A prominent essayist and Nietzschean gives the highest praise Jeffers, or almost any author, has ever received. "I find in him the tragic terror of Aeschylus, the supreme artistic aloofness and impersonality of Shakespeare, the divine melancholy and remote spiritual pathos of Chopin, the imaginative insanity of Blake, the lurid grandeur of Coleridge, the hallucinant chiaroscuro of De Quincy, the satanic joy in the hideous of Baudelaire, the psycho-analytical topsy turvyism of Dostoievsky, the beautiful morbidity of D'Annunzio, the horror-love of Dante, the eeriness and incestuous motives of Wagner, and above all, and beyond all, the defiant and aurealed wickedness of Nietzsche's Antichrist and Superman."

C17. Drinkwater, John, William Rose Benét, and Henry Seidel Canby (eds.). *Twentieth Century Poetry*. Boston: Houghton Mifflin Co., 1929, p. 379.

Anthology contains brief biography and a highly laudatory critique including mention of mature nature of subjects. "This poet is probably the one of greatest stature that the far west of our country can claim, and he seems in our own day to overshadow most of the other writers of his time." Prefers the shorter poems.

C18. Ficke, Arthur Davison. "A Note on the Poetry of Sex." In Calverton, Victor Francis, and Samuel D. Schmalhausen (eds.). *Sex in Civilization*. New York: Macaulay Co., 1929, pp. 666-667.

Freudian criticism by a poet, in a discussion of the use of sex in modern poetry. "As to Robinson Jeffers' nightmare sex designs—these will of course repel the generality of human beings all the more because of their extraordinary eloquence and their unquestioned genius. His aim is to blast the human universe apart."

C19. Kreymborg, Alfred. *Our Singing Strength.* New York: Coward McCann, 1929, pp. 173, 264, 284, 295, 624-630.

Prominent poet-critic offers various brief mentions and discussion of Jeffers as the philosophical antithesis of Whitman.

REVIEWS.
a. Conklin, G. Review of *Our Singing Strength, Bookman*, LXX (February, 1930), 685-686. B120.

b. Snow, Francis. Review of *Our Singing Strength, Current History*, XXXI (January, 1930), 632. B130.

c. Tate, Allen. Review of *Our Singing Strength, New Republic*, LXII (February 26, 1930), 51-52. B131.

C20. Manly, J. M. and E. Rickert. *Contemporary American Literature.* New York: Harcourt, Brace and Co., 1929, pp. 204-205.

Brief bibliography, biography. Complete critical judgment: "Mr. Jeffers has been hailed as the most powerful of the recent poets. Study the range of his subject matter and its limitations."

C21. Schmalhausen, Samuel Daniel. "Our Disillusioned Poets." In his: *Our Changing Human Nature.* New York: Macauley Co., 1929, pp. 165-168.

High praise as one who expressed the disillusionment of our country. Jeffers neither rejected nor accepted America, but faced it. He "is the most audacious and creative of modern poets. The burning intelligence of the man witnesses to a quite perfect detachment from the life-distracting activities of the silly contemporary world."

1930

C22. McWilliams, Carey. *The New Regionalism in American Literature.* Seattle: University of Washington Book Store, 1930, pp. 20, 27.

Journalist-social commentator makes brief, passing mention. Jeffers is not a true regional writer because he lacks antiquarianism, locality of place, a detached viewpoint, and "commonality of folk."

1931

C23. Blankenship, Russell. *American Literature as an Expression of the National Mind.* New York: Henry Holt and Co., 1931, pp. 627-632.

Biography. Discusses Jeffers as a primitive. In comparison to Hardy, Jeffers is found to lack his compassion for suffering. "In the judgement of many, Robinson Jeffers will develop into the most powerful poet in American literature. So sweeping a verdict may be premature, for the poet is young, and his first distinctive volume was published only a few years ago. Praises the breathtaking vocabulary that makes him "a poet of amazing performance." He is typical of the twenties.

C24. Calverton, Victor Francis. *American Literature at the Crossroads.* Seattle: University of Washington Book Store, 1931, p. 21.

Brief, passing mention by Marxist critic. "Poets such as Amy Lowell, Robert Frost, Carl Sandburg, Vachel Lindsay, Robinson Jeffers and Edgar Lee Masters are typical of " advocates of free verse. "Almost all the earlier leaders were indirectly influenced by the poetry of Whitman. . . . They are unequivocally American."

C25. Dilly Tante (Pseud. Stanley J. Kunitz). *Living Authors.* New York: H. W. Wilson, Co., 1931, pp. 196-197.

Biography. "He earned the title of the poet of tragic terror."

C26. Lanz, Henry. *The Physical Basis of Rime: An Essay on the Aesthetics of Sound.* Stanford, Cal.: Stanford University Press, 1931, p. 351.

Analysis of a "photographic record" of Jeffers' phrase "Humanity is needless." "Rhythmically it is interesting to see the effect of unusual consonated environment, consisting largely of m, n, and l, upon the unaccented vowel."

C27. Lewis, Sinclair. *The American Fear of Literature.* New York: Harcourt, Brace and Co., 1931, p. 15.

Brief mention in Lewis' controversial Nobel Prize speech. Complains that although the American Academy of Arts and Letters does contain E. A. Robinson and Robert Frost, it does not contain the "really original and vital poets, Edna St. Vincent Millay and Carl Sandburg, Robinson Jeffers and Vachel Lindsay and Edgar Lee Masters."

C28. Markham, Edwin (ed.). *Songs and Stories.* Los Angeles: Powell Publishing Co., 1931, p. 395.

Poet's anthology contains brief critical statement and biography. "Jeffers, a poet of elemental imagination and strange psychological insights, often strikes out a superb line, a high emotional passage. . . . Yet we are forced to say that at times a film of obscurity blurs his noble thought."

REVIEW
Walton, Eda Lou. "California's Place in the Literary Firmament," *New York Times Book Review,* August 9, 1931, p. 10. B150.

C29. Untermeyer, Louis. "Contemporary Poetry." In: Macy, John (ed.). *American Writers on American Literature.* New York: Horace Liveright, 1931, pp. 514-515.

Brief mention by a usually favorable critic. Jeffers sings an "endless *Dies Irae.* Superficially Jeffers' pessimism seems to possess" an "enduring strength" and his "aim is of the highest. But although *Roan Stallion and Tamar, The Women at Point Sur, Cawdor* and *Dear Judas* are indubitably poetic, they miss the deepest element of major poetry. They have force but they lack final power; they have force in lieu of a faith."

1932

C30. Austin, Mary. *Earth Horizon.* Boston: Houghton Mifflin Co., 1932, p. 354.

Brief mention of possible biographical interest. In speaking of a visit to Taos and the Luhan estate, she mentions Jeffers among those one is likely to meet.

C31. Calverton, Victor Francis. *The Liberation of American Literature.* New York: Charles Scribner's Sons, 1932, pp. 472-474.

Marxist discussion of Jeffers and O'Neill as examples of writers who turned from hope to despair.

C32. Johnson, Merle. *American First Editions.* New York: R. R. Bowker Co., 1932, p. 203.

Bibliographical entry.

C33. Knight, Grant C. *American Literature and Culture.* New York: Long and Smith, 1932, pp. 464, 465, 476-477.

Evaluation of Jeffers' reputation which may be deflated with the perspective of time. Mention of "Thurso's Landing" which is a "carnival of madness" but which has a quality almost Shakespearean. Jeffers is "the most powerful" of all our poets.

C34. Lewisohn, Ludwig. *Expression in America.* New York: Harper and Brothers, 1932, p. 583.

Brief mention. Jeffers has "real power."

C35. Luhan, Mabel Dodge. *Lorenzo in Taos.* New York: Alfred A. Knopf, 1932.

Addressed to Jeffers, this book relates Mabel's madcap efforts to "seduce" Lawrence. After his death, she turns to the next best prospect, Jeffers. An attempt to explain to him why Lawrence failed to fulfill her wish to recreate in literature, "the invisible but powerful spirit that hovered over the Taos Valley." Jeffers, she felt, was the only artist worthy to be Lawrence's successor, a new poet-laureate of Taos. Jeffers, accompanied by Una, visited Taos.

C36. Monroe, Harriet, and Alice Corbin Henderson. *The New Poetry*, New Edition. New York: Macmillan Company, 1932, 719-720.

Anthology includes: "Night," "Joy," "Hurt Hawks," "Shine, Perishing Republic." Prefatory comments praise his "unabashed sincerity," and his long lines which have "a deep pulsing rhythm which suggests the majesty of classic hexameters." In his works, he carries his theme to the "extreme of horror—the bottomless pit is opened."

C37. Powell, Lawrence Clark. *An Introduction to Robinson Jeffers*. Dijon: Imprimerie Bernigaud and Privat, 1932.

Full-length study, the earliest version of the best general introduction to Jeffers and his poetry. It will be updated in the 1934 and 1940 editions. Consideration of his narratives, lyrics, style, philosophy. His best narrative poems are the "tragic folk-tales of the Carmel Region." His lyrics are "apt to be more artistic, for they are more restrained and balanced, and do not suffer from excess of violence, as do the worst of the narratives." In a quoted letter, p. 211, Powell received from T. S. Eliot, Eliot calls Jeffers "a first-rate poet."

C38. Smith, Chard Powers. *Pattern and Variation in Poetry.* New York: Charles Scribner's Sons, 1932, pp. 118, 146, 147-148, 154, 235-237, 316, 366, 380, 383, 387-390.

Highly technical discussion of Jeffers' accents, long and short cadences, and pseudolines (lines of arbitrary length). Jeffers doesn't write free verse, but "a new kind of conventional verse." Sees Sandburg and Jeffers as "pioneers of a new movement" because of their technique. Jeffers' early imagination "steams with hips, thighs, breasts, blood and sexual excesses." Nevertheless, he is a "great poet." Compares him to Hart Crane.

C39. Ward, A. C. *American Literature 1880-1930.* London: Methuen and Co., 1932, pp. 201-202.

Favorable criticism from an English source. Jeffers is probably "the most exciting among the more recent American poets. . . . " His narratives "give that immediate delighting shock of surprise which is the perpetually recurrent miracle of poetry." In his poetry "there is both majesty and immensity, as well as depths of sweet renewing love and pity; again and again the genuine voice of poetry speaks."

1933

C40. Alberts, Sidney Seymour. *A Bibliography of the Works of Robinson Jeffers.* New York: Burt Franklin, 1933.

Primary and secondary standard bibliography. Almost complete to 1933. Includes a preface by Jeffers, a few previously unpublished framents, and many early uncollected poems. This bibliography has never been superseded.

C41. Benét, William Rose (ed.). *Fifty Poets.* New York: Duffield and Green, 1933, pp. 87-89.

Anthology of a poem chosen by each of fifty poets. In the introduction to Jeffers' choice, "The Stone-Cutters," Benet observes, "the form is loose and elastic. Power is always apparent."

C42. Hicks, Granville. "Trumpet Call." In his *The Great Tradition: An Interpretation of American Literature Since the Civil War.* New York: Macmillan Company, 1933, pp. 263-265.

Marxist. In a discussion of pessimism among modern writers: Jeffers "sees that his world not only will perish but deserves to; but he is too moved by his vision of destruction to see that another world may take its place. Blindly he reaches out for symbols to express his sense of doom, and violent horror will serve his purpose. But in piling horror upon horror . . . he moves farther from ordinary experience."

C43. Nelson, J. H. *Contemporary Trends Since 1914.* New York: Macmillan Company, 1933, p. 490.

Brief discussion of Jeffers' mood as an emanation from the despair following the failure of religion and philosophy in the modern world. "He is a poet of deep and elemental human passions, as well as a reverent worshipper of beauty, aware of the terrible irony in the fact that the loveliness of the world is at once so enduring and, from the point of view of the individual, so fleeting."

1934

C44. Kreymborg, Alfred. *A History of American Poetry.* New York: Tudor Publishing Co., 1934, pp. 624-630.

Contrasts Jeffers' "hatred" of humanity with Whitman's "love" of humanity. "Jeffers has it in him to become a dramatic poet of a high order. His achievement falls short of his major intention."

C45. Linn, Robert. "Robinson Jeffers and William Faulkner." In: Nathan, George Jean (ed.). *American Spectator Year Book.* New York: Frederick A. Stokes Co., 1934, pp. 304-307.

Interesting comparison of Jeffers' and Faulkner's connections with "harlotry" and Yellow Journalism. Partly, they both appeal to the intelligensia's purient and macabre interests. "Jeffers writes the great American musical-comedy, in which the chorus is made up of dead men, and the daughter of Christ commits incest with God's grandson, while the audience of an ocean painted in patented colors laughs harshly with salt and sea-lions in its throat."

C46. Powell, Lawrence Clark. *Robinson Jeffers: The Man and His Work.* Los Angeles: Primavera Press, 1934.

Updated version of his *An Introduction to Robinson Jeffers.* See C37.

REVIEW

Hutchinson, Percy. "The Poetry of Robinson Jeffers: A Sound and Careful Study of the California Poet's Work and of the Life and Personality Behind It," *Times* (New York), September 2, 1934, section 5, p. 2. B180.

1935

C47. Brooks, Charles Stephen. *A Western Wind.* New York: Harcourt, Brace and Co., 1935, pp. 33-34.

Chapter titled "The People of Carmel." Describes Jeffers' life style and his tower. "Its narrow windows look three ways upon the sea and there is a lyric at each casement."

C48. Deutsch, Babette. *This Modern Poetry*, New York: W. W. Norton and Co., Inc., 1935, pp. 193-199.

Discusses Jeffers' themes of incest, love, peace, in a chapter also dealing with Lawrence and Yeats. "Tower Beyond Tragedy" is especially dignified. His best work appears in his short poems. Jeffers "is restrained by his greater learning from Lawrence's brash pronunciamentos," but "his extravagant imaginations lead him toward the pitfall of rhetoric," and "his bitter earnestness sometimes traps him into sententious utterance."

C49. Powell, Lawrence Clark.*Robinson Jeffers 1905-1935* [catalogue] of; *An Exhibition Commemorating the Thirtieth Anniversay of His Graduation from Occidental College.* Los Angeles: Ward Ritchie Press, 1935.

Superseded by 1955 catalogue.

1936

C50. Atkins, Elizabeth. *Edna St. Vincent Millay and Her Times.* Chicago: University of Chicago Press, 1936, pp. 245-246.

In discussing poets of the period who have philosophical significance, "There is Robinson Jeffers, who in a few very short lyrics, though never in his terrible long poems, it seems to me ... almost reaches cosmic expression." If not T. S. Eliot, "then Jeffers or Macleish or Millay seems destined to be the great philosophic poet of our time."

C51. Beach, J. W. *The Concept of Nature in Nineteenth Century English Poetry.* Macmillan Company, 1936, pp. 542-546.

In some generalizations on the modern poet's use of earlier concepts of Nature (beauty, purpose, reason, benevolence), he finds that nature in Jeffers comes back in "all her romantic splendor and sublimity," but accompanied by a "ruthless nihilism." In Jeffers, "Nature is an excellent and beautiful" spectacle, without any requirement for "futile and mean" man.

C52. Bennett, Melba Berry. *Robinson Jeffers and the Sea.* San Francisco: Gelber, Lilienthal, Inc., 1936.

Biography. Includes collection of sea passages from Jeffers and some personal reminiscences. Minor. "I have tried to restrain my enthusiasm in this thesis; to make a fair and sane survey of some very great poetry, but here in discussing his truly marvelous skill in the use of words, it is impossible to be temperate."

C53. Gilbert, Rudolph. *Shine, Perishing Republic: Robinson Jeffers and the Tragic Sense in Modern Poetry.* Boston: Bruce Humphries, Inc., 1936.

Hyperbolic praise and miscellaneous comments. Unintentionally comic, often pathetic. Only possible equal of Jeffers is E. Merrill Root. Defends Jeffers against the "Communists" and Philistines. He "must be the most significant poet of America since Walt Whitman." Jeffers is "our Sophocles," and one must make a "daring leap into the midst of the foaming, resounding storm-waves of his titanic poems. . . . The force of his creative imagination disrupts the reader like an electric drill boring into a rock. . . ."

1937

C54. Bush, Douglas. "American Poets." In his: *Mythology and the Romantic Tradition in English Poetry* (Harvard Studies in English, Vol. 18). Cambridge, Mass: Harvard University Press, 1937, pp. 518-525.

In tracing the influence of classical mythology on several modern poets, finds Latin and Greek cannot make Jeffers, a decadent romantic, into a classical artist. Explains that "most Greeks would have considered him an unbalanced barbarian," but, at least, "there is no question of Mr. Jeffers' tremendous sincerity, though there may be of his philosophic depth and poetic art."

C55. Loggins, Vernon. "Questioning Despair." In his: *I Hear America.* New York: Thomas Y. Crowell Co., 1937, pp. 60-70, 74, 229, 309, 319, 351, 354.

Discusses Jeffers' symbols (rocks, hawks), influences (sociology, science), and his life in some detail. His works are individually analyzed (plot, symbol, theme). Critical reputation. "Jeffers is the supreme modern poet of despair. He has said the last word on pessimism as the twentieth century feels it. . . . Jeffers is a titan as well as a tower beyond tragedy."

C56. Winters, Yvor. "The Experimental School in American Poetry." In his: *Primitivism and Decadence.* New York: Arrow Editions, 1937, pp. 15-63. Reprinted in his: *In Defense of Reason.* Denver: Alan Swallow, 1947, pp. 30-74.

Vindictive attack which runs to bitter sarcasm. Example: " . . . his writing, line by line, is pretentious trash. There are a few good phrases, but they are very few, and none is first-rate."

1938

C57. Millay, Edna St. Vincent. Letter. In: Macdougall, Allan Ross (ed.). *Letters of Edna St. Vincent Millay.* New York: Harpers and Brothers Publishers, 1952, p. 295.

In a letter dated May 25, 1938, to Arthur Davison Ficke, Miss Millay speculates about why she and some other poets have never received the Pulitzer Prize. She decides it is because of the political and moral narrowness of the judges. "Then I thought of Robinson Jeffers. Why had he never received it? This is easy. In his case, it is the subject matter of his poetry. Rape, incest, homosexuality. . . ."

C58. Power, Sister Mary James. "Robinson Jeffers Takes God to Task." In her: *Poets at Prayer.* New York: Sheed and Ward, 1938, pp. 63-68.

Confused, trite discussion of Jeffers' pantheism and his anger with God "for not bettering the affairs of mankind." Because "Jeffers believes that man is the sport of a pitiless God," he fires "rebukes at Omnipotence."

C59. Quinn, Arthur Hobson, *et al.* (eds.) *The Literature of America*, Vol. II. New York: Charles Scribner's Sons, 1938, p. N64.

Anthology. Brief biography. "He professes a cynical disbelief in civilization. . . . He rejoices in nature without man and reacts most strongly to frustration and failure."

C60. Rodman, Selden (ed.). *A New Anthology of Modern Poetry.* New York: Random House, 1938, pp. 44, 425.

Anthology. Brief introduction. "The sweep of Whitman is in his majestic verse, but the love has turned to hate, at best to pity and disgust. 'Roan Stallion' was one of the first, and remains the best of that succession of long poems."

1939

C61. Greenan, Edith. *Of Una Jeffers.* Los Angeles: Ward Ritchie Press, 1939.
Biography of Mrs. Jeffers, written by Una's first husband's second wife; a vivid, personal glimpse of Una and her early years with Robin.

1940

C62. DeVoto, Bernard. "Lycanthropy." In his: *Minority Report.* Boston: Little, Brown and Co., 1940, pp. 257-264.
Discusses Hemingway and Jeffers, both of whom treat their characters as animals. Jeffers, however, goes farther in preferring plants and stones to animals. Includes the article "Rats, Lice and Poetry" (see B193).

C63. Luccock, Halford E. *American Mirror.* New York: Macmillan Co., 1940, pp. 35, 48, 109, 266-269.
Various brief mentions. Decides Jeffers is fascist and anti-Christian, for he "acclaims the superman, rejects the Christian God, the Christian and humanitarian scale of values. . . . But when one asks to what Jeffers' glorification of violence leads, the familiar outlines of fascism appear, including faith in a strong man, a 'Fuehrer' inhibited by no weakening ethical superstitions."

C64. Millett, Fred B. *Contemporary American Authors.* New York Harcourt, Brace and Company, 1940, pp. 149-150, 406-407.
Bibliography, biography and critical comment. "Jeffers' technical powers are impressive. No other American poet of our time is his equal

in imaginative magnitude or emotional violence. But most of the time Jeffers' poetry is overviolent, the coloring is barbaric. . . . Nor can Jeffers' reading of life go unchallenged."

C65. Powell, Lawrence Clark. *Robinson Jeffers, the Man and His Work.* Pasadena: San Pasqual Press, 1940.

Updated version of 1934 edition (see C46) to include brief mention of Jeffers' works from 1934 to 1940. This remains the latest version of the best available biography and general introduction to Jeffers.

REVIEWS
a. Stelter, Benjamin F. "Alumnus Powell on Alumnus Jeffers," *Occidental Alumnus*, XXIII (November, 1940), 5, 13. B223.

b. Worden, Perry. "Robinson Jeffers: A Poet's Culturing," *Star News* (Pasadena, Cal.), May 4, 1940, p. 8. B225.

C66. Wells, Henry W. *New Poets from Old: A Study in Literary Genetics.* New York: Columbia University Press, 1940, pp. 214-230 and *passim.*

A pedantic discussion of literary influences on Jeffers. "Jeffers is a great and original artist . . . but he is in no sense the voice of an unlettered man crying in the wilderness." The major influences on Jeffers are Shakespeare and Elizabethans. "More than any other non-dramatic poet, he shows the power of Elizabethan drama to mold contemporary poetry."

C67. Wilder, Amos N. "Nihilism of Mr. Robinson Jeffers." In his: *Spiritual Aspects of the New Poetry.* New York: Harper and Brothers, 1940, pp. 141-152.

Balanced reply to Winters' attacks, by a theologian. Discussion of Jeffers' mysticism. Finds some comparison with oriental religions. "Jeffers offers an escape into a nihilist Nirvana—a return through the original fountain."

1941

C68. Cargill, Oscar. *Intellectual America, Ideas on the March.* New York: Macmillan Company, 1941, pp. 741-761.

Shows Jeffers' affinity to Shelley, summarizes long narratives. Decides Jeffers is an indicator of America's sickness. "At his best Jeffers enriches our thought by demonstrating the glory and beauty of an imperious will. . . . At his worst, Jeffers is still symptomatic of the moral confusion of his time, its mirror and mouthpiece. If the future chooses to judge us by Jeffers' most abortive work, the future will not go far wrong."

C69. Matthiessen, F. O. *American Renaissance.* London: Oxford University Press, 1941, pp. 339n, 592-593.

Brief mention of Whitman's influence on Jeffers. "Jeffers has voiced the negation to Whitman's triumphant optimism, in free verse which, superficially like that in the *Leaves*, actually is built much more deliberately into grave metrical patterns. . . ."

C70. Ransom, John Crowe. *The New Criticism.* Norfolk, Conn.: New Direction, 1941, pp. 216, 236-237.

Discusses Winters' criticism of Jeffers. Winters attacks Jeffers' theology as much as his style. Wonders if Jeffers is only a writer of trash, why discuss him at all.

1942

C71. Gregory, Horace, and Marya Zaturenska. "Robinson Jeffers and the Birth of Tragedy." In their: *History of American Poetry 1900-1940.* New York: Harcourt, Brace and Company, 1942, pp. 298-412.

Covers career, poetry, Winters controversy. His verse resembles Melville, Whitman; his philosophy, Nietzsche. Particular discussion of the "Roan Stallion" as an excellent example of the classical rule of unity. His fame will rest not with his philosophy, but with his ability to depict nature.

1943

C72. Wells, Henry W. "Grander Canyons." In his: *The American Way of Poetry*. New York: Columbia University Press, 1943, pp. 148-160.

Discusses the aspects of the California landscape (sculptural, vast, harsh, un-European) that have influenced Jeffers. He "ranks among the most searching and brilliant of native poets, whether his interpretations are naive, dramatic, philosophical, mystical or scientific. His philosophical naturalism is distinctly more profound, for example, than that of D. H. Lawrence."

1944

C73. Gilbert, Rudolph. "Robinson Jeffers: The Philosophic Tragedist." In his: *Four Living Poets.*Santa Barbara, Cal.: Unicorn Press, 1944, pp. 23-41.

Unrestrained praise. Discusses Jeffers' mysticism. "We know of no living English or American poet who may be compared with Jeffers, either in creative power, philosophic, psychological insight or lyric utterance. We sense in him a unity of thought with some of the greatest poets of the past. . . ."

1945

C74. Cestre, Charles. *La Littérature Américaine.* Paris: Librairie Armand Colin, 1945, p. 205.

Mention of Jeffers' place in American literature. "Robinson est, parmi les whitmaniens, celui qui, le plus nettement, transforme la vitalité exubérante du chef de l'école en fougue barbare. . . . Il peint des caracteres parfois admirables de stoicisme et de force de volonté. Mais sa maniére perverse de s'élancer aux extrêmes et de s'appesantir sur les aspects violents de l'âme humaine rend difficile, malgré la virtuosité avec laquelle il évite les termes brutaux de le suivre sur la voie rigueuse où il entraîne la poésie."

C75. Tate, Allen. *Sixty America Poets 1894-1944.* Washington: Library of Congress, 1945, pp. 55-59.

Thorough primary bibliography compiled by Francis Cheney and revised in 1954. Tate, in introductory comments, finds much to praise in Jeffers. "He has been attacked by Yvor Winters as a decadent romantic and there is some truth in the charge." Yet, he is "a poet of great power; and his short poems . . . achieve a fine restraint and modulation of tone."

C76. Wish, Harvey. *Contemporary America: The National Scene Since 1900.* New York and London: Harper and Brothers, Publishers, 1945, pp. 331, 516.

Brief mention. His *Tamar* is "exotic, violent, and colorful. In its expression of spiritual decay, sex frustration, and introspection, his poetry impressed his followers as powerful in content and interpretative in quality."

1947

C77. Bentley, Eric. *The Cult of the Superman.* London: Robert Hale Limited, 1947, pp. 117, 227.

Brief mention. Jeffers is one of the "Heroic Vitalists" akin to fascists. They have followed Nietzsche in a "quest for a new immortality."

1948

C78. Breton, Maurice. *Anthologie de la Poésie Américane Contemporaine.* Paris: Les Editions Denoel, 1948, pp. 48-49, 234-235.

Like Sherwood Anderson and Faulkner, Jeffers is a neoromantic states the introduction to this anthology. "Malgré ses outrances, cependant, il est des parties de son oeuvre qui ne sont pas sans grandeur, celles, notamment, où son imagination transpose sur le plan moderne des motifs eschyléens dans une langue forte et imagée comme celle de la poésie grecque et où le paysage Californien, âpre et tourmenté, merveille de lumière et de coloris, fournit aux sombres drames de Jeffers un décor idéal."

1949

C79. Powell, Lawrence Clark. *Robinson Jeffers, A Lecture to Professor James L. Wortham's Class in Narrative Poetry Given on May 22, 1949.* Los Angeles: The Press of Los Angeles City College, 1951.

Powell recalls his twenty years of admiration for Jeffers' poetry. Evaluates narratives ("Give Your Heart ...," "Cawdor," "Thurso's Landing" are "great and lasting poetry"), reviews Jeffers' critical reputation, and predicts that one day Jeffers will be recognized for his greatness. "Jeffers is not presently in fashion. The bright young men of the quarterly reviews, who worship the seven types of ambiguity, have no use for him because he does not fit into their pre-conceived pattern of what modern poetry should be. Confronted by the bulk of Jeffers, they are like the blind man describing the elephant."

1950

C80. Arms, George, and Joseph Kunitz. *Poetry Explication.* New York: Alan Swallow, 1950, p. 93. Revised edition by Kunitz, Joseph. 1962, pp. 153-154.
　　Checklist of major explications of Jeffers' poems.

C81. Commager, Henry Steele. "Cult of the Irrational." In his: *The American Mind.* New Haven: Yale University Press, 1950, pp. 128-132.
　　Places Jeffers in the romantic tradition of Wordsworth, Shelley "whom he imitates" and Arnold "whom he recalls." Jeffers philosophy ends in nihilism, however.

C82. Matthiessen, F. O. (ed.). *The Oxford Book of American Verse.* New York: Oxford University Press, 1950, p. xxv.
　　Brief introduction. Comments point to the vast differences between Eliot and Jeffers. "Jeffers and Eliot, born only a year apart, are separated by something even wider than that between the California and the England to which they have been drawn. They are as far apart as Spengler and St. John of the Cross, and find a meeting point only in their equally somber convictions of modern decay."

C83. Southworth, James G. "Robinson Jeffers (1887-　　)." In his: *Some Modern Poets.* New York: Macmillan Company, 1950, pp. 107-121.
　　Lengthy negative criticism to counterbalance indiscriminate rage for "*Medea*'s author." Discusses Jeffers' emphasis on violence, oversimplified characters, prosy style, repetition, lack of form. Finds short poems dull. The heightened metaphors "create an emotional mood that intensifies the general impact of his long narratives. It is only when the reader has finished and returns to examine the means by which Mr. Jeffers has created his effect that he feels that the means are, or verge on, the meretricious. . . . The pleasure derived from his work is that of immediate excitement like that of a thriller."

C84. Waggoner, Hyatt H. "Robinson Jeffers: Here Is Reality." In his: *Heel of Elohim.* Norman, Okla.: University of Oklahoma, 1950, pp. 105-132.

Clearly reasoned negative criticism from a first-rate critic. Attacks Jeffers' acceptance of a mechanistic, purposeless universe. "He is the only modern poet whose work is widely held to be important who has accepted without qualification the view of life and man explicitly offered or implicitly suggested by the traditional scientific texts. This at once accounts for his great popularity . . . and for his larger failures as a poet."

1951

C85. Bogan, Louise. *Achievement in American Poetry, 1900-1950.* Chicago: Henry Regnery Co., 1951, p. 77.

Brief mention in discussion of poetic groups that sprang up after World War I that were outside the main literary stream. "Later, the isolated Robinson Jeffers was to begin to construct a peculiar misanthropic world through a series of dramatic poems acted out against a wild background of California coastline."

C86. Miles, Josephine. "The Primary Language of Poetry in the 1940's." In her: *The Continuity of Poetic Language.* Berkeley, Cal.: University of California Press, 1951, pp. 383-458.

Counts the most frequently used terms in representative texts by representative poets. Word counts of Jeffers' poems appear on pp. 394-402. For example, Jeffers uses more than most poets the words "old," "man," "look," and "big." Much of his writing "is more active, more storytelling, than any other poetry in the decade, and therein lies his singularity, his special virtue which he has not shared."

C87. Straumann, Heinrich. *American Literature in the Twentieth Century*. London: Hutchinson House, 1951, pp. 144-147.

Briefly discusses Jeffers' "radical conception of human nature," and Jeffers' "consciousness of the beauty of nature and of the evil that has come into existence with the creation of the mind of man. . . . There appears to be no limit to the cruelty, perversions, destruction and crime in the behavior of his characters, and yet there is also in his poetry an intense awareness of the beauty of this world, which contrasts strangely with the infinite power of evil in man's existence."

C88. Whicher, George F. "The Twentieth Century." In: Quinn, Arthur Hobson (ed.). *The Literature of the American People*. New York: Appleton-Century-Crofts, Inc., 1951, pp. 878-879.

Generally favorable review of Jeffers' philosophy. "Not since Swift has there appeared in English a writer capable of such tonic misanthropy." He is "the undisputed master of contemporary baroque writing."

1952

C89. Deutsch, Babette. "A Look at the Worst." In her: *Poetry in Our Time*. New York: Henry Holt and Co., 1952, pp. 1-27.

Comparison of Hardy with Jeffers. Deutsch, an early admirer of Jeffers, now qualifies her praise. She finds him often grandiloquent and pompous. Jeffers' ideas "are not always sufficiently wrought into the body of the poetry. His performance is a warning against allowing ideas to stalk too pompously on the poetic stage." Yet, his poetry contains "a serenity founded on tragic awareness of the human condition and of the grandeur of the nonhuman universe."

C90. Wilder, Amos Niven. *Modern Poetry and the Christian Tradition.*
New York: Charles Scribner's Sons, 1952, pp., 63, 110, 183, 184, 244.
   A theologian traces Christian influences in Jeffers' poetry. Special
attention for "To His Father." "Secularized writers as different as
Dreiser, Gide, Pound and Jeffers evidence the influence of their
Protestant lineage in healthy ways and sometimes pay their homage to
it."

C91. Wilson, Edmund. *The Shores of Light: A Literary Chronicle of the
Twenties and Thirties.* New York: Farrar, Straus and Young Inc., 1952,
pp. 678, 685-686.
   Brief mention from a famous critic. Emphasizes the prose-like
character of Jeffers' poetry.

1953

C92. Brooks, Van Wyck. *The Writer in America.* New York: E. P.
Dutton and Company, Inc., 1953, pp. 40, 117.
   Robinson Jeffers mentioned along with Millay and O'Neill as
examples of the fickleness of the American literary world.

C93. Highet, Gilbert. "An American Poet." In his: *People, Places and
Books.* New York: Oxford University Press, 1953, pp. 22-28. Reprinted
in his: *Powers of Poetry.* New York: Oxford University Press, 1960, pp.
129-134.
   High praise. General comments designed to arouse interest in Jeffers.
Summarizes major themes. "His poetry is not meant to be liked. It is
meant, I think, to do people good. But it is very remarkable poetry, and
he is a very distinguished man. America has produced . . . in nearly two
centuries—very few great poets. Robinson Jeffers may prove to be one
of those great poets."

C94. May, Rollo. *Man's Search for Himself.* New York: W. W. Norton an; Company, Inc., 1953, pp. 126-129.
Psychological discussion of "The Tower Beyond Tragedy." Jeffers' drama is a reflection of the dependency of the son on the mother.

1954

C95. Jeffers, Una. *Visits to Ireland, Travel Diaries of Una Jeffers.* Los Angeles: Ward Ritchie Press, 1954.
Jeffers made the selections from his wife's journals and writes a foreword for the book, which includes entries written by the poet and the twin sons, as well as the more frequent entries of Una. Jeffers states that he has restricted his selections to the diary of the 1929 trip.

1955

C96. Bowden, Harry. *Robinson Jeffers.* San Francisco: Bern Porter, 1955.
Minor. A six-page pamphlet. Biography and thematic discussion.

C97. Gay, Alice. *Robinson Jeffers at Occidental College; a Check List of the Jeffers Collection in the Library, Published on the Fiftieth Anniversary of His Graduation, June 1955.* Los Angeles: Ward Ritchie Press, 1955.
Supersedes 1935 Catalogue. See C49.

C98. Gregory, Horace. "Poet Without Critics: A Note on Robinson Jeffers." In: *New World Writing: Seventh Mentor Selection.* New York:

New World Writing, 1955, pp. 40-52. Reprinted in: Beaver, Harold Lowther (ed.). *American Critical Essays: Twentieth Century.* New York: Oxford University Press, 1959, pp. 70-88. Reprinted in: Gregory, Horace. *The Dying Gladiators and Other Essays.* New York: Grove Press, 1961, pp. 3-20.

Excellent appreciative criticism from a major critic. Praises Jeffers' narrative style ("Tamar" is one of the "major accomplishments in twentieth-century poetry"), his aristocratic attitude (not unlike that of Faulkner and Yeats). Urges the rereading of Jeffers. He has flaws, but they are the flaws of a major poet. "Jeffers has re-established the position of the poet as one of singular dignity and courage. He is neither voiceless nor without his readers; and he is not without wisdom in seeming to await the verdict of posterity."

C99. Sievers, W. David. *Freud on Broadway.* New York: Hermitage House, 1955, pp. 123-124.

Adverse comments on the Broadway production of *The Tower Beyond Tragedy.* Its prime asset was its "musical language," but it "proved to be lifeless and dull."

C100. Spiller, Robert Ernest. *The Cycle of American Literature.* New York: Macmillan Company, 1955, p. 234.

Brief mention. In a discussion of *Poetry*: "It . . . helped to bring into being a vigorous naturalistic movement in the poetry of Vachel Lindsay, Robert Frost, Edgar Lee Masters, Carl Sandburg, and finally Robinson Jeffers."

1956

C101. Squires, James Radcliffe. *The Loyalties of Robinson Jeffers.* Ann Arbor: University of Michigan Press, 1956.

Excellent book-length critical discussion of Jeffers' poetry with emphasis on the philosophy in the narrative poems. Includes biography; history of Jeffers' critical reputation; Jeffers' philosophy in terms of Schopenhauer and Spengler; his psychology in terms of Jung; his poetic art in terms of Lawrence, Whitman, and especially Lucretius. *The Double Axe* "achieves the greatest success." Concludes: "America has produced three great poets in the century which has seen her rise to greatness—Eliot, Frost, and Jeffers."

REVIEWS

a. Benamau, Michel. Review of *The Loyalties of Robinson Jeffers*, *Études Anglaises*, XI (April-June, 1958), 185-186. B303.

b. Carpenter, Frederic Ives. Review of *The Loyalties of Robinson Jeffers*, *American Literature*, XXIX (May, 1957), 225-226. B295.

c. Carroll, Paul. "Prophet Without Honor," *Poetry*, XC (July, 1957), 254-256. B296.

d. Ferguson, Joe M., Jr. Review of Squires' *The Loyalties of Robinson Jeffers*, *New Mexico Quarterly*, XXIX (Spring, 1959), 125-127. B310.

e. Fuller, Dorothy V. Review of Squires' *The Loyalties of Robinson Jeffers*, *Arizona Quarterly*, XIV (Spring, 1958), 70-71. B306.

f. Miller, James E. Review of Squires' *The Loyalties of Robinson Jeffers*, *Prairie Schooner*, XXXI (Spring, 1957), 3-5. B298.

g. Rexroth, Kenneth. "In Defense of Jeffers," *Saturday Review of Literature*, XL (August 10, 1957), 30. B299.

h. Sullivan, A. M. Review of Squires' *The Loyalties of Robinson Jeffers*, *Catholic World*, CLXXXIV (March, 1957), 478-479. B300.

1957

C102. Anzilotti, Rolando. "Robinson Jeffers, Tragico Solitario." In his: *Tre Saggi Americani*. Pistoia: Tipograpfia Pistoiese, 1957, pp. 71-97.

Discusses Jeffers' career, works, and critical reputation. Bibliography includes works translated into Italian.

C103. Frohock, Wilbur Merrill. *The Novel of Violence in America.* Dallas, Texas: Southern Methodist University Press, 1957, p. 6.

Briefest mention. Jeffers' poems used as a passing example of bloody violence.

1958

C104. Magill, Frank N. "Robinson Jeffers." In his: *Masterplots Cyclopedia of World Authors.* New York: Salem Press, 1958, pp. 565-566.

Biography. Favorable evaluation. Interesting because it is an indication that Jeffers, the vatic poet, is again finding favor. "He has never been accorded the prominence he deserves. This age of literary movements and splinter groups has been baffled by this lonely figure of despair. The horrors of future atomic warfare may prove him a major prophet."

C105. Monjian, Mercedes Cunningham. *Robinson Jeffers, A Study in Inhumanism* (Critical Essays in English and American Literature, 3). Pittsburgh: University of Pittsburgh Press, 1958.

Published masters essay. Scholarly explanation of Jeffers' themes and philosophy. Dislikes the narratives, partially because the characters are flat, mere abstractions of passions. Prefers the short poems, which are "controlled, powerful, reverent." The short poems are "little dramatic structures that transcend" philosophy and doctrine. They are "artistic entities in themselves, not involvements in rhetoric and idea, only."

REVIEW
Waggoner, Hyatt H. Review of Monjian's *Robinson Jeffers: A Study in Inhumanism, American Literature*, XXXI (March, 1959), 99. B315.

C106. Wilder, Amos. *Theology and Modern Literature.* Cambridge, Mass.: Harvard University Press, 1958, pp. 95-110.
An entire chapter is devoted to a detailed discussion of the religious aspects of "Dear Judas." It is an example of the appeal of the crucifixion to man's hidden obsession with cruelty. Describes Jeffers as a rebel from Calvinism and as a follower of Spengler. Jeffers' philosophy is "an interesting option in our century for those who cannot accept the prevailing religious traditions but who are equally indisposed toward materialism and negation."

1959

C107. Jones, Howard Mumford. *Guide to American Literature and Its Backgrounds Since 1890.* Cambridge, Mass.: Harvard University Press, 1959, p. 169.
Bibliography. Jeffers' works included in section titled "The Cold War and the Moral Problem." Mentions that "Jeffers anticipated an important later attitude towards culture and civilization."

C108. Lilienthal, Theodore M. *Exhibition of Books and Manuscripts by Robinson Jeffers.* Los Angeles: Book Club of California, 1959.
Catalogue of Lilienthal's collection. Enlarged edition: Lilienthal, Frances and Theodore. *Robinson Jeffers Collection, In Memoriam 1887-1962.* 1964.

1960

C109. Hesse, Eva (ed.). *Dramen: Die Quelle; Medea; Die Frau aus Kreta.* Reinbek bei Hamburg: Rowohlt, 1960.

Translation of Jeffers' plays by Miss Hesse. Introduction discusses Jeffers' philosophy comparing him to Swift. Brief biography emphasizing his classical training and knowledge of Europe. Discusses each play separately, attempting to place themes within the trends of modern theatre. "Was Jeffers beschwert, ist nicht die Frage nach der formalen Fortdauer des Theaters—auf ihm lastet etwas ganz anderes, etwas, das er uns mit allen ihm zu Bewusstsein bringen will. Ob er so unrecht hat?"

C110. Lutyens, David Bulwer. "Robinson Jeffers: The Inhumanist at Grips with the Dilemma of Values." In his: *Creative Encounter.* London: Secker and Warburg, 1960, pp. 37-65.

Attempts to explain and justify Jeffers' philosophy of Inhumanism. Compares him to Yeats and Brecht. To accuse him of being a poet of despair is "to misunderstand the whole purpose and purport of his poetry. He contends that man must discover a design for living, and is convinced that this is the only way a solution can be found to the dilemma of modern man and the crisis of twentieth-century values."

C111. Nyren, Dorothy (ed.). "Robinson Jeffers." In her: *A Library of Literary Criticism.* New York: Ungar, 1960, pp. 257-261.

Brief ten to twelve line excerpts from various critics discussing (1.) his work in general, (2.) the Carmel narratives, and (3.) the adaptations of Greek tragedies.

C112. Rosenthal, M[acha] L[ouis]. "Rival Idioms: The Great Generation: Moore, Cummings, Sandburg, Jeffers." In his: *The Modern Poets.* New York: Oxford University Press, 1960, pp. 155-159.

Adverse comments from an NYU professor devoted to New Criticism. Finds Jeffers' didacticism and style objectionable. "Go through

Jeffers's most famous poems, and you will find this kind of blunted, hackneyed diction growing in scattered weed patches everywhere." Also, scattered in his works are "bland profundities."

C113. Rutman, Anita, and Luay Clark. *Robinson Jeffers: A Checklist of Ptd. & Ms. Works of Robinson Jeffers in the Library of the University of Virginia.* Charlottesville, Va.: University of Virginia Press, 1960.

The Virginia collection in Alderman Library. "Not a bibliography, though it will serve to supplement the works of S. S. Alberts since 1933."

C114. Shapiro, Karl (ed.). *American Poetry.* New York: Thomas Y. Crowell, Co., 1960, p. 7.

Anthology compiled by the famous American poet. Brief introductory comments. "And Robinson Jeffers following the intellectual fads of the early twentieth century (Freud and Spengler with their sexual and historical pessimism) condemns not only America but all the works of man. Jeffers dreams of a world in which man himself is no more—the not uncommon nihilistic image in so much popular writing of our day."

C115. Thorp, Willard. *American Writing in the Twentieth Century.* Cambridge, Mass.: Harvard University Press, 1960, pp. 220-221.

Favorable general comments. Discusses Jeffers' nihilism; violence; affinities with Nietzsche; his isolation from other poets, critics, schools.

1961

C116. Burtis, Mary Elizabeth, and Paul Spencer Wood. *Recent American Literature.* Paterson, N. J.: Littlefield, Adams, and Co., 1961, pp. 199-202.

Biography. Brief evaluation. "His poetry is often interesting, sometimes lyrically lovely, sometimes powerful, sonorous." Jeffers' treatment of the classics "is not especially memorable. His most enduring
work remains . . . passages of description."

1962

C117. Carpenter, Frederic I. *Robinson Jeffers.* New York: Twayne
Publishers, Inc., 1962.
Excellent book-length study of Jeffers' narratives and short poems,
his critical reputation and his philosophy. Separate sections are devoted
to each narrative poem. Concludes that Jeffers' greatest strength is his
power of pure expression. "All his best poems include striking passages
of poetic eloquence or imaginative beauty."

REVIEW
Kiley, Bertram. Review of *Robinson Jeffers, American Literature*,
XXXV (November, 1963), 389-390. B352.

1964

C118. Clough, Wilson O. *The Necessary Earth: Nature and Solitude in
American Literature.* Austin, Texas: University of Texas Press, 1964,
pp. 192-197.
Discussion of the function of nature for Jeffers. "On the last western
shore of the New World America, a western poet has framed beauty not
out of the conquest of a frontier but out of an austere denial of man's
fondest imaginings upon himself."

C119. Gross, Harvey. *Sound and Form in Modern Poetry.* Ann Arbor,
Mich.: University of Michigan Press, 1964, p. 88.

The dangers of use of Whitman's method in incompetent hands is illustrated by "Shine, Perishing Republic." "Meaning fights through the morass of the rhythms; syllable, stress, and syntax do not move but writhe, heave, grunt, and lie down again, gasping with the effort. The heavy stresses, impaled by alliteration, die on the page."

C120. Powell, Lawrence Clark. *The Little Package.* Cleveland: World Publishing Co., 1964, pp. 56, 133, 136, 264, 302.
Comment in various essays dealing with the pleasures of reading Jeffers and plans to honor his memory.

C121. Quasimodo, Salvatore. "Medea." In his: *The Poet and the Politician and Other Essays* (trans. Bergin, Thomas C., and Pacifici, Sergio). Carbondale, Ill.: Southern Illinois University Press, 1964, pp. 159-160.
Comparison of Jeffers and the Greeks with special reference to *Medea*. Favorable. "Jeffers does not correct the Greek spirit as other moderns do; he broadens it—and thus amplified this *Medea* comes out exactly matching the formal measure of Euripides. The sense of vendetta . . . explodes in this American tragedy with the violence of Jeffers' image."

1965

C122. Allen, Gay Wilson, Walter B. Rideout, and James K. Robinson. (eds.) *American Poetry.* New York: Harper and Row, Publishers, 1965, p. 791.
Briefest mention of Jeffers' critical reputation. "A few of his poems continue to have an audience, even though critical attention since the 1930's has diminished."

C123. Donoghue, Denis. *Connoisseurs of Chaos.* New York: Macmillan Co., 1965, p. 14.

Brief mention in a discussion of Poe's influence on American poetry. Poe leads to "Jeffers and Theodore Roethke."

C124. Eisely, Loren. In: Brower, David Ross (ed.). *Not Man Apart: Lines from Robinson Jeffers.* San Francisco: Sierra Club, 1965. New York: Ballantine Books, Inc., 1969.

Photographic essay of the Big Sur Coast. Introduction from Jeffers' *Selected Poems* and Jeffers' poetry as text for photographs. Eisely's introduction: "No one reading Jeffers can escape the impress of the untamed Pacific environment upon which he brooded. He was its most powerful embodiment."

REVIEWS

a. Brophy, Robert, and William White. Review of *Not Man Apart: Lines from Robinson Jeffers, Robinson Jeffers Newsletter,* XXV (February, 1970), 3-4, B415.

b. Scott, Robert Ian. Review of *Not Man Apart: Lines from Robinson Jeffers, West Coast Review,* IV (January, 1970), 49-50. B425.

C125. Untermeyer, Louis. *Bygones: The Recollections of Louis Untermeyer.* New York: Harcourt, Brace and World, 1965, p. 238.

Describes work on the Pulitizer Prize for Poetry Jury. "Twice my proposal that Robinson Jeffers receive an award was turned down by two senior members; they conceded the power of Jeffers's poetry, but they refused to honor an expression which they felt was anti-Christian, anti-American, and seemingly anti-human. I contended that even a nihilist deserved recognition if he were a good nihilist *and* a good poet."

C126. Welland, Dennis. "The Dark Voice of the Sea." In: Ehrenpreis, Irvin (ed.). *American Poetry.* Stratford-Upon-Avon Studies 7. New York: St. Martin's Press, 1965, pp. 197-219.

Discussion of how various authors view the sea. It is particularly important in Jeffers' poetry. He uses the sea to express his disdain for human nature. "Jeffers' vision of a desolate and hostile universe can become oppressive in its ultimate inhumanity, but the extent to which it convinces us depends very largely upon this use of the sea."

1966

C127. Bennett, Melba Berry. *Stone Mason of Tor House.* Los Angeles: Ward Ritchie Press, 1966.

One-sided and incomplete biography by a personal friend and admirer. Jeffers remains a quiet background figure and Una's viewpoint dominates the book. Liberal quotation from Jeffers' letters, essays, poems. The intellectual life of Jeffers is revealed but the book is unable to make Jeffers, the man, come to life. Includes brief analysis of each of his books.

REVIEWS

a. Anonymous. Reviews of Bennett's *Stone Mason of Tor House, New York Times Book Review*, December 25, 1966, p. 20. B377.

b. Rorty, James. "The Ecology of Robinson Jeffers," *Book Club of California Quarterly News Letter*, XXXII (Spring, 1967), 32-36. B392.

C128. Carpenter, Frederic I. "Robinson Jeffers and the Torches of Violence." In: Langford, Richard E., and William E. Taylor (eds.). *The Twenties.* Deland, Fla.: Everett Edwards Press, Inc., 1966, pp. 14-17.

Jeffers wrote, not tragedy, but prophecy. Favorable evaluation. Discussion of the impact of World War I and World War II on Jeffers and his rejection of historic idealism. The "torches of violence" in Jeffers' poetry have a purpose—not heat, but light. They illuminate the meaning of history. "The prophetic and historic importance of Jeffers' literary revolt is becoming increasingly apparent." His work seems to foreshadow the atomic age. "After his death we are only beginning to recognize the illumination which 'the torches of violence' may produce."

C129. Walker, Franklin. *The Seacoast of Bohemia: An Account of the Early Carmel.* San Francisco: Book Club of California, 1966, pp. 127-129.

Describes Jeffers' arrival at Carmel, and his decision to remain. "There Jeffers wrote beautiful and fearful poems about the country and its people. . . . The long sweeping lines in which the poems are written echo the crash of the surf."

REVIEW
Steward, George. Review of *The Seacoast of Bohemia, American Literature*, XXXIX (May, 1967), 254-255. B393.

1967

C130. Adelman, Irving and Rita Dworkin. *Modern Drama—A Checklist of Critical Literature.* Metuchen, N. J.: Scarecrow Press, Inc., 1967, pp. 172-173.

Checklist of reviews and articles especially for *Dear Judas* and *Tower Beyond Tragedy.*

C131. French, Warren (ed.). *The Thirties: Fiction, Poetry, Drama.* Deland, Fla.: Everett Edwards Press, Inc., 1967, p. 119.

Brief mention. Although Jeffers continued to write haunting poems in the thirties, he failed to enhance his earlier reputation.

C132. Hahn, Emily. *Romantic Rebels: An Informal History of Bohemianism in America*. Boston: Houghton Mifflin Co., 1967, pp. 220-221.
Mention of Jeffers as one of a group of artists who settled Carmel and vainly tried to keep it unspoiled.

C133. Koehring, Klaus Heinrich. *Die Formen Des "Long Poem" in der Modernen Amerikanischen Literatur*. (Beihefte zum Jahrbuch für Modernen Amerikanischen Literatur, 21). Heidelberg: Carl Winter Universitätsverlag, 1967, pp. 192-200.
Compares *Tamar* with E. A. Robinson's *Merlin* as epics treating modern problems. "Immerhin stellt Tamar einen eindrucksvollen Versuch dar, in der Gegenwart 'a modern myth about myth' zu realisieren." Notes the "Zietlosikeit seiner Thematik und der Echtheit seiner Figuren."

C134. Salzman, Jack (ed.). *Years of Protest: A Collection of American Writings of the 1930's*. New York: Pegasus, 1967, pp. 377, 387-388.
Comment on Jeffers' critical reputation in the 1930's. "Henry Miller, E. E. Cummings, and Robinson Jeffers were perhaps the three outstanding literary individualists of the period . . . Jeffers isolating himself in Carmel, California, awaiting the destruction of civilization."

C135. Stevenson, Elizabeth. *Babbitts and Bohemians. The American 1920's*. New York: Macmillan Company, 1967, p. 168.
Brief mention of *Roan Stallion* as one of several books of verse, the appearance of which helped make 1925 an important year in American publishing.

1968

C136. Antoninus, Brother (William Oliver Everson). *Robinson Jeffers: Fragments of an Older Fury*. Berkeley, Cal.: Oyez, 1968.

A long-standing disciple of Jeffers collects years of work on the poet into this book. Lengthy and careful explication, à la the New Critics, of "Post Mortem." Explains Jeffers' philosophy and defends him against the charge of fascism. Seven essays and an elegy. This book constitutes "all I can presently articulate about my old master, a man whom I knew deeply in spirit but never in life, one who was too near to me, too terrifying to me, and too necessary for me, back at the finding of the self which make the pivot of a life, ever to face in this flesh."

REVIEWS
   a. Hart, James D. "Robinson Jeffers: A Poet's Poet," *Book Club of California Quarterly News Letter*, XXXIII (Spring, 1968), 36-38. B398.

   b. Brophy, Robert J. Review of *Robinson Jeffers: Fragments of an Older Fury*, *Robinson Jeffers Newsletter*, XXIII (April, 1969), 3-4. B406.

C137. Gilbert, James Burkart. *Writers and Partisans.* New York: John Wiley and Sons, Inc., 1968, p. 169.

Brief mention in a discussion of *Miscellany* published by Dwight Macdonald: "A quality of dilettantism did characterize the early magazines at times, and Macdonald's remarks on T. S. Eliot in the middle of a long review on Jeffers provide a good example. Compared to Jeffers, he wrote, Eliot is a sophomore writing verses for the 'Lit.' "

C138. Powell, Lawrence Clark. *Fortune and Friendship: An Autobiography.* New York: R. R. Bowker Co., 1968, pp. 15, 27, 28, 30, 32-34, 41-43, 50, 59, 79, 163.

Includes numerous references to a friendship and admiration that began in Powell's undergraduate days at Occidental College.

C139. Ridgeway, Ann N. (ed.). *The Selected Letters of Robinson Jeffers 1897-1962.* Baltimore: Johns Hopkins Press, 1968.

Valuable collection for Jeffers scholars. Includes a foreword by Mark Van Doren and biographical data. Unfortunately excludes most of Jeffers' letters to Una, "because these may make a separate volume one day."

REVIEW
Hart, James B. Review of *Selected Letters, American Literature*, XLI
(May, 1969), 302-303. B410.

C140. Waggoner, Hyatt H. *American Poets, From the Puritans to the
Present.* Boston: Houghton Mifflin Co., 1968, pp. 469-477.
Scholarly comparison of the similarities of Emerson's and Jeffers'
philosophies. Both prefer universal beauty to the little triumphs of
man. Jeffers' best work is found in his short poems. "His verse very
seldom has the musical felicity that often charms us in Pound or
Stevens. It has none of the inevitability of phrase that makes Eliot's
lines stick in the memory." But it has power.

1970

C141. Durant, Will, and Ariel Durant. *Interpretations of Life: A Survey
of Contemporary Literature.* New York: Simon and Schuster, 1970, pp.
65-67.
The popular historian praises Jeffers' poetry "despite his morbid
emphasis upon deviltry, decay, and death." In a highly questionable
interpretation, finds Jeffers replacing religious faith with "socialistic
hopes."

C142. Everson, William (Brother Antoninus). "Introduction." In:
Jeffers, Robinson. *Cawdor and Medea.* New York: New Directions
Books, 1970, pp. vii-xxx.
In an introduction to a new edition of Jeffers' poems, the poet-critic
finds Jeffers "one of the most powerfully visionary poets that America
has produced." Compares him favorably to Emerson.

C143. Nolte, William. *The Merrill Checklist of Robinson Jeffers.*
Columbus, Ohio: Charles E. Merrill Publishing Co., 1970.
Brief 25 page checklist of primary and secondary sources.

C144._____. *The Merrill Guide to Robinson Jeffers.* Columbus, Ohio: Charles E. Merrill Publishing Co., 1970.

Favorable, intelligent criticism in this introductory essay on Jeffers, written by an English professor at the University of Southern California. Explains Jeffers' philosophy, discusses his rhythm and rhyme, and briefly compares him with Nietzche. Some biographical data. Includes explication of "Fog," previously published separately in *Robinson Jeffers Newsletter.* See B385.

1971

C145. Coffin, Arthur B. *Robinson Jeffers: Poet of Inhumanism.* Madison, Wis.: University of Wisconsin Press, 1971.

Detailed study of the philosophical framework of Jeffers' poetry with special reference to Nietzsche and Lucretius. Sees Jeffers as one who coped with the ideological needs of contemporary man.

REVIEW
Hughes, John W. "Humanism and the Orphic Voice," *Saturday Review,* LIV (May 22, 1971), 31-33. B428.

APPENDIX

Important Dates in Jeffers' Career

January 10, 1887 – Birth in Pittsburgh, Pennsylvania.

1899-1902 – Travel and education in Europe.

1905 – Graduation from Occidental College, Los Angeles, California.

1912 – *Flagons and Apples.*

1913 – Marriage to Una Call Kuster, August 2, Tacoma, Washington.

1914 – Move to Carmel, California. Death of father. Death of infant daughter.

1916 – *Californians.* Twin sons Garth and Donnan born.

1921 – Death of mother.

1924 – *Tamar and Other Poems.*

1925 – *Roan Stallion, Tamar and Other Poems.*

1927 – *The Women at Point Sur.*

1928 – *Cawdor and Other Poems.*

1929 – *Dear Judas and Other Poems.* Travel in Great Britain and Ireland.

1930 – First visit to New Mexico.

1931 – *Descent to the Dead.*

1932 – *Thurso's Landing and Other Poems.*

1933 – *Give Your Heart to the Hawks and Other Poems.*

1935 – *Solstice and Other Poems.*

1937 – *Such Counsels You Gave to Me and Other Poems.*

1938 – *The Selected Poetry of Robinson Jeffers.*

1941 – *Be Angry at the Sun.* Reads poetry at eastern universities.

1946 – Publication of *Medea.*

1947 – October 4 – *Dear Judas* opens in New York.
October 20 – *Medea* opens in New York.

1948 – *The Double Axe and Other Poems.*

1950 – September 1 – Death of Una Jeffers.
November 26 – *Tower Beyond Tragedy* opens in New York.

1954 – *Hungerfield and Other Poems.*
May 4 – *The Cretan Woman* opens in Washington, D.C.

January 21, 1962 – Death of Robinson Jeffers in Carmel, California.

1963 – *The Beginning and the End.*

Checklist of Major Publications

Flagons and Apples. Los Angeles: Grafton, 1912.
Californians. New York: Macmillan, 1916.
Tamar and Other Poems. New York: Peter G. Boyle, 1924.
Roan Stallion, Tamar and Other Poems. New York: Boni and Liveright, 1925. London: Hogarth Press, 1928. New York: Modern Library, 1935.
The Women at Point Sur. New York: Boni and Liveright, 1927.
Cawdor and Other Poems. New York: Liveright, 1928. London: Hogarth Press, 1929.
Dear Judas and Other Poems. New York: Liveright, 1929. London: Hogarth Press, 1930.
Descent to the Dead. New York: Random House, 1931. (Limited edition.)
Thurso's Landing and Other Poems. New York: Liveright, 1932.
Give Your Heart to the Hawks and Other Poems. New York: Random House, 1933. (Includes the poetry that originally appeared in *Descent to the Dead.*)
Solstice and Other Poems. New York: Random House, 1935.
Such Counsels You Gave to Me and Other Poems. New York: Random House, 1937.
The Selected Poetry of Robinson Jeffers. New York: Random House, 1938.
Be Angry at the Sun. New York: Random House, 1941.
Medea, Freely Adapted from the Medea of Euripides. New York: Random House, 1946.
"Poetry Gongorism and a Thousand Years," New York *Times*, Jan. 18, 1948, section VI, p. 16. Reprinted: *Poetry, Gongorism and a Thousand Years.* Los Angeles: Ward Ritchie, 1949. Reprint: Folcroft, Pa.: Folcroft Press, Inc.
The Double Axe and Other Poems. New York: Random House, 1948.
Hungerfield and Other Poems. New York: Random House, 1954.
The Beginning and the End and Other Poems. New York: Random House, 1963.

Robinson Jeffers, Selected Poems. New York: Vintage, Random House, 1965.

Not Man Apart. (David Brower, ed.). San Francisco, Calif.: Sierra Club, 1965. (See C124.) New York: Ballantine Books, Inc., 1969.

The Selected Letters of Robinson Jeffers, 1897-1962. (Ann N. Ridgeway, ed.). Baltimore, Md.: Johns Hopkins Press, 1968. (See C139.)

Cawdor and Medea. New York: New Directions Books, 1970. (See C142.)

INDEX